To Gillie and A[...]

So good to s[...]
that you saw a bit of
Remember that you will have a home (and a car)

Tall Grass

have to see more g

Stories of Suffering and this beautiful country

Peace in Northern Uganda whenever you want

Keep in touch,

David

Gillie & Allan.
It was lovely having you in the Pearl of Africa. Your lovely smiles and laughter will always linger on my mind. May you have great trips and may your love grow stronger.
Love you
Monica

Tall Grass
Stories of Suffering and Peace in Northern Uganda

Carlos Rodríguez Soto

FOUNTAIN PUBLISHERS
Kampala

Original title: *Hierba Alta. Historias de paz y sufrimiento en el Norte de Uganda (2008)*
Translation by the author

Fountain Publishers
P. O. Box 488
Kampala - Uganda
E-mail: sales@fountainpublishers.co.ug
         publishing@fountainpublishers.co.ug
Website: www.fountainpublishers.co.ug

Distributed in Europe and Commonwealth countries
outside Africa by:
African Books Collective Ltd,
P. O. Box 721,
Oxford OX1 9EN, UK.
Tel/Fax: +44(0) 1869 349110
E-mail: orders@africanbookscollective.com
Website: www.africanbookscollective.com

Distributed in North America by:
Michigan State University Press
1405 South Harrison Road
25 Manly Miles Building
East Lansing, MI 48823-5245
E-mail: msupress@msu.edu
Website: www.msupress.msu.edu

ISBN 978-9970-02-733-0

Cover photograph: Fr. Tarcisio Pazzaglia talking to rebel commander Moses
Okello in the bush near Pajule in 2001.

Contents

Foreword

I worked in Uganda from 1984 to 1987 and again from 1991 to the beginning of 2008. Except for two and a half years when I was in Kampala, I always worked in Acholiland, where in 1986 one of the most destructive and cruellest wars ever to take place in Africa broke out. This war has also been one of the most forgotten and invisible conflicts of our modern world.

From the year 2002 I started keeping a personal journal and a detailed chronology of everything I heard and saw, particularly concerning some peace initiatives in which I was involved. Little did I know then that the habit of writing daily was going to have a therapeutic effect on me; writing helped to prevent tragic situations that were beyond my control from overwhelming me. Although my journal was in English, I used much of that abundant material to write the first version of this book, in Spanish, which was published in 2008.

To pour all these recent events onto the computer keyboard has made me relive very painful situations which has taken an emotional toll on me. Ultimately, the reason why I decided to write this book (both in Spanish and in English) is because this experience may teach one or two things to other persons who live in other places of the world scourged by violence. Building peace in the midst of many frustrations, attacks, misunderstandings and risks is one of the noblest human tasks and is worth living for.

My Christian faith, which has inspired me and sustained me in the hardest moments, proclaims that those who work for peace shall be called "children of God". Their endeavours reflect God's true nature, which is to create harmony and happiness among human beings.

Weariness has been my constant lot, although I have always been aware that my fatigue shall never match that of the victims of the Northern Uganda conflict. But I have felt tired many times. Despite many plans to take a sabbatical year it never materialised. This is why the Spanish version of these pages were written at the office of *Leadership* magazine in Kampala, during the second half of 2007, when I took advantage of some free moments and the silent hours of the night. A few months later, I undertook the English translation, which I wrote in Madrid.

All the facts hereby narrated are strictly true. In some cases I have changed the names of some of the people I mention, to protect their personal security.

I owe a great debt of gratitude to many people in Uganda. If I mentioned all of them the list would be too long, but I feel especially obliged to mention the Archbishop of Gulu, John Baptist Odama, a pastor always close to his suffering people, who has been a beacon of hope in the struggle for peace and human rights. I am also extremely grateful to Adela Klassen for patiently reading through the text and making many useful corrections and remarks.

C.R.S

Madrid, Spain (December 2007)
Kampala, Uganda (February 2009)

1

The Killer of Women's Gang

There is nothing that can dazzle me and plunge me into confusion more than the tall grass of the African savannah. In October it may grow taller than two metres, forming walls along both sides of the footpaths that cut through the thick bush. The more we penetrate inland, the narrower the trail becomes in front of us. If we walk on foot the bending elephant grass, as it is called, will fall on our bodies and will cause us a most uncomfortable itching, making our journey anything but pleasant. If we go on trekking for several hours it will become extremely monotonous, since the grass will deprive us of any glimpse of a landscape worth its name that may cheer up our drooping spirits. Maybe we shall break some of the weak stems to overcome the boredom and to feel its fibres between our fingers. If we happen to be travelling by car, the walls of grass will make way for us, obeying our decisive treading of the land, but we had better go slowly and cautiously because we cannot know what may appear, it may be a rock or an anthill, hard as concrete, or even worse the sharp stump of a tree that has been cut by an axe or struck by lightning from top to bottom. Any of the three could make us overturn or cause considerable damage to our car tyres, leaving us stranded in the middle of the bush. Whenever such an incident happens in Africa, we can be consoled by the arrival of other human beings living in the hamlets scattered in the forest, who will come to our rescue and know how to put into practice the ancient law of solidarity with travellers in trouble. However, in the 20 kilometre stretch of winding road between Pajule and Lupul there was not a single person living there. It had been three years since all the inhabitants of that zone had left their homesteads and gathered in clustered settlements surrounding the few brick and iron roofed houses standing on either side of the Kitgum-Lira road, in the north of Uganda.

On this particular trip, my travelling companions were two Acholi traditional chiefs, Oywak and Lugai, both bearing the title of honour, *Rwot*. The Acholi of Northern Uganda have always been a society divided into small political units made up of groups of clans with a collaborative network among them. Their visible leaders are the persons who hold the title of *Rwot* (*rwodi* in plural). A *Rwot* is a king, although in Acholi society they are not separated from the rest of their kinsmen and they would also engage in farming or any other work like anybody else. Their role of coordination, mediation and arbitration of disputes is of paramount importance, for they exercise an activity of surveillance of their subjects' welfare.

On that day in October 2001, the three of us moved in an uneasy silence that no one dared to break. The day before, the two *rwodi* had been to the place where we were going and had returned late in the evening. When they came to see me at the Catholic mission I could read the discouragement in their eyes. Everything had started very early in the morning, when a young man - presumably a rebel collaborator brought a letter to Oywak, at his homestead in the Pajule trading centre. The handwritten note was signed by a rebel commander called Onekomon ki Koko ("He who kills women with cries"). He declared his intention to "negotiate peace", whatever that meant, and asked to meet with neutral mediators at a location deep in the bush.

Seven years had elapsed since the last of several serious attempts to negotiate a peaceful end to the war that had ravaged Northern Uganda since 1986. The initiative led by former minister Betty Bigombe, an Acholi from Lamogi (Gulu), failed at the beginning of February 1994.

Two years later, two Acholi elders called Okot Ogoni and Okot Lagony made another attempt at contacting the rebels in a peace mission, but they were killed under unclear circumstances as soon as they met them in the bush. In 1998, a new initiative sponsored by the Community of Sant'Egidio in Rome crashed as soon as it left the ground, and something very similar happened with a new attempt by the Carter Centre in 2001, soon after the signing of the peace agreement between the governments of Uganda and Sudan, which had supported the LRA since at least 1993.

The more attempts were made towards peace, the more cruel the war turned and the more the peace became but a distant dream in Acholiland. Despite the existence of a law that guaranteed a blanket amnesty to all the rebels, they were more elusive than ever and contacting them for any peace overture seemed next to impossible.

But in March 2001, the parish priest of Pajule, Fr. Tarcisio Pazzaglia, managed to meet with some of the rebels' junior commanders in the bush. The veteran Italian priest from the Comboni order was well known. His more than 40 years of service in the more neglected rural areas of Acholiland and his friendly character had gained him everybody's trust. For several months he discreetly exchanged several letters with a notorious rebel commander called Charles Tabuley, thanks to a contact person who still lived in his original homestead in the forest. Fr. Tarcisio and Rwot Oywak had a first meeting with rebel Captain Moses Okello, who assured the priest that his bosses were interested in serious peace negotiations. Nevertheless, things went amiss during a second meeting with the insurgents in the bush, this time with another commander called Topaco. As they were talking under a tree a Ugandan army mobile patrol stormed the venue and in the unexpected shootout Rwot Oywak was wounded in the leg. Tarcisio could not understand how things could end so badly after the military gave him all the necessary permission. Several days later, the military attributed the mishap to a "miscommunication incident", an explanation that for many was not convincing. Predictably, communication with the rebels broke down after that, but not for long. At the end of June that very year the chairman of the Gulu district local council, Walter Ochora, a former rebel himself, met with another rebel commander called Onen Kamdulu in the bush. For several weeks the Ugandan army (known as UPDF or Uganda People's Defence Forces) granted to the rebels a de-militarised area not far from Gulu town; but that initiative, which was widely publicised and immediately attracted funds for reintegration of former combatants, did not go very far.

This is why, when Rwot Oywak received that message from commander Onekomon, things looked a bit more promising and it seemed as if there was another chance for positive results. Oywak and Lugai did not think twice, took their bicycles and off they went to the bush.

When I saw them later that night wearing long faces I asked them how things were going. They answered with dismay.

"Once again, these soldiers want to spoil everything."

They told me that the main authorities from the newly formed district of Pader (under whose administration Pajule was) had been called for an urgent meeting, which was about to begin. They wanted me to attend the meeting.

It was around nine in the evening when we entered one of the simple houses of the trading centre that was dubbed a bar, motel and restaurant. Dim light from a kerosene hurricane lamp cast shivering shadows on the whitewashed brick walls. As soon as we entered the room we saw three military officers and four or five leaders from the local administration, all with serious faces. Jacob Komakech, the Local

Council (LC) 5 chairman of Pader, also a former rebel, was trying to chair the meeting.

Among the officers of the UPDF was a lieutenant-colonel who had arrived from Lira in the afternoon of that day. In a laconic fashion, he did not waste too many words to make himself understood. He said:

> "So, those criminals want to have meetings and want us to withdraw our soldiers from a wide area. We shall not give them that."

A tense silence followed the lieutenant-colonel's brash statement. Earlier the two cultural leaders, in their role as mediators, had communicated the rebels' demands to the group. However, the lieutenant-colonel went on with his instructions.

> "Tomorrow morning you can go to see them, as requested by you. Tell them that we are giving them up to midday to surrender unconditionally. Otherwise, we shall attack them."

Jacob Komakech spoke with more diplomacy.

> "Sir, we are very grateful for your kindness in giving us your time. I also agree with you that the rebels' demands are not realistic. At the same time I would like to add that I understand them very well, because I was a rebel some years ago, and I know very well that when one wants to lay down his arms the more difficult part is to take the first step and leave the bush. This is why they need help. I kindly request you to be patient and allow our two cultural leaders to have the whole day tomorrow to negotiate with them. If we give them an ultimatum it may be counter-productive."

Jacob's next comment pulled me out of my drowsiness, which was beginning to weigh heavily on my eyes at that time.

> "I would also like to propose that Fr. Carlos accompanies the cultural leaders. I think that a religious leader may give them even more trust. That is of course, if he agrees."

Feeling halfnumb, I raised my head and looked at all those pairs of eyes focused on me, waiting for my reply. I have never been a person who needs much time to think before making a decision. I did not take much time to think over my reply.

> "I will go, with much pleasure... that is of course, if the lieutenant-colonel gives us assurances that we shall not be attacked at midday. I would not like to go through the same experience as Fr. Tarcisio, you know..."

I noticed immediately that I had touched a very sensitive point. A cascade of promises, confirmations, pledges and guarantees followed quickly though, changing the gloomy mood. One of the leaders then concluded:

> "Thank you very much to all of you for your cooperation. We pray for the success of our brothers in their important mission tomorrow. I wish you all a very good night."

That night I could not sleep a single minute. A strange feeling, a mixture of joy and worry, invaded my soul. I had spent so many years in Acholi witnessing the effects of the LRA terror and I often felt as if I lived in a land of ghosts, a land where I had not yet met the ones causing so much death and havoc. Very early in the morning, after mass in the church, I slipped out discreetly to see Jacob Komakech, who was staying in one of the lodges at the trading centre. I thanked him for his intervention the evening before and I asked him whether it would not be a good idea to call the representatives of the Amnesty Commission in Kitgum.

All this I remembered as we drove to our meeting place with the rebels. I was trying to recollect my thoughts from the day before, when Lugai motioned me to stop the car.

We had reached a spot where the tall grass gave way to a forest of trees that offered a clearer view of the scenery ahead of us. I obeyed

Lugai and switched off the engine. The three of us came out of the pickup truck.

Lugai said

> "It is better to continue on foot for the rest of the journey. If they hear the noise of an engine they may think that it is an army vehicle and shoot us."

As a chief, who had been part of Betty Bigombe's team in 1993, Lugai had many years of experience as a peace mediator and his practical advice was to be heeded.

I carried with me a simple shoulder bag with a notebook, a pen and a plastic bottle containing water to drink. The blue wool bag, woven with geometric designs, was a gift from a Mexican nun a few years earlier. That day I did not know that it was to become my faithful companion in many other expeditions.

We did not advance many metres before coming across two adolescents, aged perhaps 16, in tattered combat fatigues and gumboots and wearing dreadlocks. Wielding their assault rifles, they made signs for us to continue ahead. I swallowed my saliva and mumbled a shaky "Good morning" in Acholi that they probably hardly heard. Neither of the two returned my greeting. I stretched out my shivering hand but I put it down after few seconds when neither gave me his and when one of them put his finger on the trigger of his Kalashnikov.

Never before had I seen a youth's face so deprived of any expression. I still find it hard to describe that visage which lacked the slightest sign of any human feeling. The boy's petrified eyes transmitted a coldness that would make anyone scared. I began to understand the coping mechanism that made the young LRA abductees camouflage their emotions in order to survive that hell. There was no choice but to suppress their feelings if they wanted to save their lives. And it was the same for me in that moment.

No sooner had we walked a few more metres than we arrived at an abandoned compound of grass-thatched mud and wattle huts. The place was surrounded by seven boys and two girls, all of whom were armed with guns. All the young lads, two of whom were not beyond 14 years of age, wore dirty and ragged military uniforms. I tried to compose myself and walked slowly and confidently greeting them one by one. It did not come as a surprise when I saw that, once again, none of them offered me his or her hand. On many occasions I had heard from young people who had escaped from the LRA how Joseph Kony, the LRA mysterious leader, had indoctrinated them with detailed regulations, one of which forbade them to shake hands with people outside their group, in the belief that if they did they would lose their spirit.

But when I approached the youngest boy, he did offer me his hand. When I took it I realised that it was crippled and bent at an angle as a result of a gunshot wound. He was 14 years old and it seemed to me that he was the one with the hardest expression in his eyes.

It was then that I took notice of Onekomon's presence. He was seated under a tree in a folding chair, with a confident look on his face. He did not bother to stand up when he greeted us and invited us to sit in front of him. His fingernails were outgrown and as he mumbled his words he looked at them. He reminded me of a big cat ready to attack his prey, pondering first the calibre of its claws.

Three years earlier I had had the chance of taking part in a course on conflict resolution, in South Africa. I remembered one of the tips we had been given in the lessons on mediation: "A face-to-face seating arrangement brings the idea of confrontation, whereas a side-to-side seating arrangement conveys more of the idea of joint problem-solving". I did not think twice about it and picked up my chair to sit next to Onekomon, who stopped his nail observation exercise and started telling us his ordeals. Predictably, his way of talking did not reveal much humility.

> "I am sure that nobody would ever be able to do what I have done. I have saved these boys and girls of mine and I have brought them here. It took us one week to walk from Kony's camp in Sudan, near Juba, until we entered Uganda through the bush near Palabek. We are now in our motherland and we shall remain here."

It was not a bad beginning. And he had told us a very important detail. These people had escaped from Kony's camp in Jebelein, a place located some 20 kilometres south of Juba, a city which at that time was under the control of the Sudanese Armed Forces of the Khartoum government. To reach Uganda they would have had to trek at least 150 kilometres passing through a vast area under the control of the SPLA rebels. The LRA, who received generous supplies from Khartoum, frequently engaged in battle with the SPLA; this is why an armed group passing through areas near the Ugandan border would certainly risk being attacked by the SPLA, a group commonly referred to by the LRA as "the Dinkas". Onekomon and his boys were deserters and as such Kony would consider them as traitors. If caught their punishment would be death. It was clear that they could not think of turning back, and this placed us in a position of advantage. Onekomon had boasted the day before of having come with 40 fighters, but I suspected that there would not be many more than the 12 of them that we had in our sight.

As Onekomon talked, Lugai interjected:

> "*Ladit*, we have spoken with the military authorities in Pajule about your demands. You want them to withdraw their forces from this zone, but…"

I did not think it was very prudent to begin with something that could trigger an unpredictable reaction, particularly when dealing with such a peculiar character. I was sorry for my bad manners, but I cut Lugai short. It was better not to mention anything that could in any way sound negative or confrontational. I said:

> "Dear friend, commander Onekomon, we are very happy to have come here to meet with you and we thank you for welcoming us. How can we help you?"

His answer took me by surprise.

> "I was abducted when I was very young, in 1987. All these young boys and girls that you see here with me have been kidnapped too. We want you to bring our parents here, to this place where we are, because we want to meet them."

So, that was the reason why Onekomon wanted a de-militarised area. I recalled what we had been taught during the course in South Africa, that in conflicts people usually begin exhibiting very hard and uncompromising positions in the form of demands, but behind the demands lie many undeclared interests, needs and fears that a skilled mediator must help in bringing out. The commander had just showed a very important interest: to meet the parents of all in this group. It dawned on me that, with patience, it would not be too difficult to explore such a request further in order to gain more understanding.

> "We shall be very happy to do everything possible to find your parents. But tell me: Do you think that they shall dare come to this bush where everybody fears to enter?"

I was surprised at the confident way in which I was approaching him. Then I proposed to him something I had been thinking about carefully since the day before.

> "Why don't you come with us to the mission? All will welcome you. And we shall bring your parents there."

For some moments, Onekomon changed the topic and the conversation went in a different direction. It was clear that he was not ready to give in so easily. Then, seemingly out of the blue, he made a sign to two of his escorts, who swiftly came in front of him and saluted him, ready to take orders.

> "I want these two soldiers of mine to go to the mission with one of you and survey the place to make sure that it is safe."

Rwot Oywak, an outgoing man who is also quick in making decisions, did not think twice about the request and asked me for the car keys. He then drove off with the two young rebels. Lugai and I remained behind with Onekomon. I was worried because I thought that anything might happen, an ambush by another loyal rebel group, a UPDF attack… but I was also convinced that we would never get anywhere without taking such risks.

At that moment, as a flashback, the warm memory of my friend Fr. Raffaele Di Bari passed through my mind. I first met him in Uganda in 1984, when I had just arrived for the first time. A typical Italian from the south, affectionate, friendly, witty and well-known for his loud jokes, he had spent many years in Acholi since coming to Uganda in 1958. He was an endlessly enthusiastic source of ideas for ways to help people develop and wherever he went he left in his place grinding mills, rice mills and sunflower oil machines.

Raffaele also worked in Pajule, together with Tarcisio. The missionaries, well into their seventies, were inseparable and they seemed to enjoy talking endlessly to each other all day long. Unfortunately, Raffaele was killed on 1st October 2000, a Sunday, when he was driving to celebrate mass in Acholibur, a chapel located 20 kilometres north of Pajule. On that day he had first gone to the military detach of Pajule to ask for information about the security situation and he had been told that the road was safe. He had taken the road north of Pajule, but five kilometres into the journey a barrage of gunshots rang out from the bush. He had fallen into a rebel ambush. A Ugandan nun and several boys quickly got out of the car and escaped. According to the sister, Raffaele was hit by several bullets and was crying in pain and bleeding. At once several adolescents in green fatigues emerged from the bush, heaped bundles of dry grass on the pickup and set it alight with the priest still inside. One of the youths who was travelling with him was abducted and his dead body was found a few days later somewhere in the forest nearby. The last minutes of Raffaele's life must have been extremely painful while his wounded body was consumed by flames. Later in the afternoon his charred remains were found and taken to Pajule, where he was buried the following day, next to the entrance to the parish church.

Perhaps an hour and a half had passed when we heard the rumble of the engine again. The car was returning. I sighed with relief when I saw Oywak, the two escorts and Bjoern, a German man who worked with us in the Justice and Peace Commission of Gulu, descend from the pickup with expressions of happiness. It was clear that the level of trust between the rebels and us was increasing. The two young rebels saluted Onekomon and he withdrew from us to listen to what they had to tell him.

"Can I take a picture?" Bjoern asked.

Onekomon gave his consent and he posed for the camera. It was the first time I had seen him smile in four hours. The environment was beginning to become more relaxed, but after a few minutes he quickly changed his mood and returned to his nail examination exercise and his talk about military affairs. Everything depended solely on his decision, and it was not very clear what and when he would decide.

I thought that he was trying to make it clear to us that he was the one in control and maybe he took some pleasure in making us feel lost.

Make the person in front of you feel confused, never show your true intentions explicitly, always take the long way round and play with delay. These were all tactics that the rebels knew how to use to perfection. In years to come I was going to be defeated again and again in my effort to understand that most peculiar psychology, and that defeat would cause me plenty of headaches.

Onekomon was truly a master of surprise. All of a sudden he gave an order and in a very few seconds all the young rebels gathered their belongings and climbed into our car.

Well, not all of them. One of them, the one wearing the more enigmatic face, who had remained standing under a nearby tree during our entire visit, did not move an inch. We all looked at each other not knowing what to do. I calmly went over to him and talked.

> "My friend, do not worry. Everyone is going to welcome you and you
> have nothing to fear. Come with us. You too shall meet your parents."

He did not bother to turn a hair, let alone look at me. He clenched his AK-47 assault rifle and looked tense. I began to fear that the boy could do something crazy thing that could cost us dearly. Onekomon came out of the car, walked slowly and motioned me to leave him. I withdrew and let the two of them sort it out.

That tense situation lasted a bit more than one hour. I remembered something that I have failed to learn, even the hard way, and which is particularly true in Africa. Almost every time that you see things going well and about to succeed something unexpected happens that can send all your efforts to hell or completely in the opposite direction. My stomach was telling me that such an African version of Murphy's Law could very well come true in this situation and that this could end in bloodshed. I discreetly studied the situation of the compound where we were, trying to figure out which route of escape would be the safest in case things took a turn for the worse.

We were lucky that there was no need for an escape route. After a long and tense period of waiting, Onekomon and his stubborn escort came to the car, opened the back door of the double cabin and got in. Nervous and concerned, I switched on the engine and engaged the first gear before accelerating smoothly, all the while only thinking of leaving that place as quickly as we could and reaching the mission without delay. I had hardly driven five kilometres when a puncture in one of the tyres forced me to stop. Never in my life have I changed a tyre in so few minutes. We continued our journey and after reaching the main road, drove towards Pajule.

As soon as we entered the Mission compound I slowed down. Many people came towards the car. Women were ululating. Many of them, jumping with joy, offered us branches of the *olwedo* tree, a shrub used for blessings in traditional ceremonies and considered a symbol of peace. When we stopped we saw some of the authorities of Pader and Kitgum districts, military officers and hundreds of people who had come to witness the joyful and rare event of the return of rebels who came to lay down their arms and surrender peacefully.

Among those who came to receive them were eight other young men who were part of Onekomon's rebels. They had separated from him two days earlier and surrendered to a military detach. One of Kony's most repeated statements to his young rebels when they were with the LRA, in order to discourage them from leaving, was that all who surrendered to the military were killed. The fact that the two groups saw each other alive and in good spirits increased their trust in us.

A few days later, as we slowly continued to gather the scattered pieces of this complicated jigsaw puzzle that was their story, we would learn that this group had broken off before and that it had been lead by a sergeant called 'Doctor Dog'. They had decided to abandon fighting earlier because of a dispute among themselves. It was not uncommon for rebels who had made up their minds to surrender to do a last-minute ambush in order to grab all the money they could before making the final step towards reintegration into civilian life. 'Doctor Dog' did not subscribe to such a practice and had left two days before. Maybe Onekomon had feared that his former comrade-in-arms would reveal this and other secrets to the UPDF and perhaps because of that he took the chance with us when he saw that he could have a safe and honourable route out if he left the rebels.

And so there we were seated under the verandah of the priests' residence in Pajule Mission. I have always wondered why Ugandans are so fond of speeches, which usually begin in a very similar fashion: "All protocol observed… at this juncture I do not have much to say…" Concerning these and other formalities, maybe they are the result of a combination of some cultural traditions laced with British politeness. Whatever the case, we spent the next few hours witnessing an exercise in oratory in which all took part: politicians, soldiers, civil servants, cultural leaders, religious leaders and every son or daughter of Adam with some small or big responsibility in Pader or in Kitgum. "We are all very happy to welcome you, our brothers who have decided to leave the ways of violence," some began, "because this war has lasted for too many years and it must end, and we greet the tireless efforts of the government… which we are supporting with our humble contribution…" etcetera, etcetera.

After a night without sleep and many tense hours in the bush I felt hungry and tired, but I also felt happy. I perceived that beyond the speeches there was no doubt that the willingness to move towards reconciliation and forgiveness, on the part of the people who were making the speeches or just listening, was sincere and it was worthy of admiration, especially when I considered how many stories of personal suffering lay behind the bewildered faces that looked at the boys.

The evening came and it found us in that improvised parliament with the young rebels still wearing their uniforms and still holding their arms. Among the many hundreds of people present, the one who seemed to be corroborating the statements with most enthusiasm was Latigo, the deaf and dumb mission cook who nevertheless could make you understand almost everything with a whole display of bodily signs.

I was beginning to be very worried. What would happen when the speeches were over? Everyone would walk away and we would remain alone with our guests. That dreaded moment finally arrived and when it did we were left in a tense and uneasy silence. One of the mission workers took me aside and whispered something that increased my fear.

> "Be very, very careful. These boys do not trust you. Just a few minutes ago I overheard two of them whispering that they are convinced you are going to poison them."

I called Fr. John Peter Olum, the mission priest, and shared my concerns with him. He then said that the most sensible thing we could do was to invite them to have supper with us at the same table. Following this suggestion, we called them all to the table once supper was ready. I had never thought before that one day we would sit around the same table to share food with some of the very people who for many years had made life hard for us. I grew more relaxed when I saw them take the food and eat. After the meal, we took the group to a dormitory where someone had prepared some mattresses, basins, jerrycans of water and soap for them to use. After wishing them good night we thought that it was high time we called it a day and we retired, leaving the rest to God's care.

The following day, we watched the group, still in their uniforms and holding their guns. We were still not sure what their intentions were. The military came at midday and told us that the division commander in Gulu wanted all of them to come to the headquarters without delay.

Onekomon gave an order and they all boarded the vehicles that took them there, where they remained for two weeks. After that time they asked us to take them back to Pajule, where Caritas Gulu organised everything needed for a two-month stay, including much needed psychological counselling. During that time the cultural leaders, led by Oywak and Lugai, did a traditional cleansing ceremony to welcome the former rebels back into the community.

The UPDF unit at Pajule also played their part. The unit was lead by Major Ssegawa. The first time I witnessed a football match between soldiers and the former rebels in the mission compound I was moved when I thought about how the people running behind the ball had, until very recently, been running after each other in order to shoot to kill instead of kicking a ball harmlessly in a casual game of football. Major Ssegawa died in June 2002 in a battle against the LRA in the mountains at the border region between Uganda and Sudan, when the rebels launched an all-out offensive.

The recently appointed Gulu Division Commander, Maj. Muheesi, visited the former rebels and after talking to them he asked them whether there was anything they needed. "A pair of decent shoes," answered Onekomon. Immediately the major took out his notebook and recorded the sizes of all the former rebels. The 13 pairs of shoes arrived two days later.

But not all interventions with this group were so positive. Some politicians promised the former rebels things like houses or large sums of money, promises that they clearly could not deliver. These empty promises would cost us dearly in the future, even though we had no part in making them.

But there was something we had promised each of them when we first met them in the bush, and we stuck to our word. Caritas brought each rebel's parents to visit. Each meeting was a moment of joy.

However, some of the rebels had been abducted several years earlier and we realised that the parents, too, needed some serious counselling. In many respects nothing could have prepared them to receive a son or daughter who had come back after undergoing such an experience. The young boy with rough manners, who was absent-minded and deeply traumatised was very different from the joyful and polite kid who had been snatched from them some years earlier.

One day, when they were about to leave Pajule and go back to their respective homes, two of them pointed at Fr. Raffaele's tomb. Slowly and smoothly the words came out. They had taken part in the lethal ambush that had taken the life of the old missionary one year earlier.

> "Our commander gave us orders to lay hidden by the side of the road, and to shoot at the first vehicle that would pass and burn it. When we saw a white man we were surprised".

A couple of months later, some relatives of Fr. Raffaele in Italy sent us money they collected to help former child rebels with their schooling. We did advertise it, but we had little doubt about using that money to pay for the education of the ones who shot him and burnt him to death on the lonesome road to Pajule.

2

Joseph Kony and the Spirit's War

"We are no ordinary soldiers like the ones of any other army," said Colonel Santo Alit in Acholi. "We are God's army and we are fighting for the Ten Commandments."

He was a short man well in to his fifties. I was rather uncomfortably seated on the ground next to a rock, taking notes as fast as I could, and at the same time interpreting in a low voice, in English, for two foreign diplomats who were seated next to me, the first secretary of the Embassy of Netherlands and a lady who held the same post in the Norwegian diplomatic mission.

"Joseph Kony is like Jesus Christ, who came to save us from our sins. Just as Judas Iscariot sold Jesus for thirty silver coins, many have tried to betray Kony, God's messenger, but they have failed because God always sends his angels to protect him."

With that firm conviction, Brig. Sam Kolo, the LRA's number three in command, explained their beliefs further. I scribbled in my notebook as I interpreted for the diplomats. The Dutch man seemed somehow bewildered when he asked:

"Excuse me, father, what are you saying about Jesus Christ?"

I felt like laughing out loudly, but the serious faces of the young armed rebels surrounding us instantly discouraged me from such behaviour.

"Excuse me, sir, I am just translating," I said to the Dutch man.

We were attending a meeting with seven rebel commanders in Paloda, a remote forest in the northern part of Kitgum district. It was 28ᵗʰ December 2004 and as far as I could remember it was my fifth time to meet with Kony's men. This time there were more than thirty people in our group including religious leaders, members of parliament, local political leaders and, for the first time, foreign diplomats and journalists.

The mediator who had made it possible to have this meeting, Betty Bigombe, had told us at the beginning that we would have no time to translate everything from Acholi to English and she had requested those who did not know the African language to sit next to someone who could interpret for them. This is how I came to play that role of impromptu interpreter of those strange, solemn sermons about the Ten Commandments, Jesus Christ the Saviour and his angels from heaven. Maybe the Dutch diplomat thought that I was taking advantage of the occasion to catechise him, but I made it clear that the words I was interpreting were not mine.

At the beginning of that meeting, the chief catechist and Kony's main religious advisor, Col. Jenaro Bongomin, had raised his hands to heaven, closed his eyes and with a mystical expression on his face started a long opening prayer that he lead as though he was in a trance. To the rest of the LRA he was known as "Pope Jenaro" and he was the one in charge of their religious affairs.

As I watched those men wearing combat fatigues and rosaries around their necks, and as I heard them talk about God and his angels, I could not help recalling one of the worst and most repugnant massacres perpetrated by the LRA in a village near Patongo, in Pader district, in November 2002. After murdering 20 people, the commander of the group gave an order to dismember two of the dead bodies, put the bloody parts in a big cooking pot and boil them in the presence of the terrified survivors. Such an act, an example of the horrible mutilations, child abductions and cruel massacres by the LRA, combined with the pseudo-religious prayers and biblical symbols, provoked in any normal person the most absolute rejection of the group and their beliefs. The endless accumulation of absurd, illogical, grotesque and macabre features could easily make anyone conclude that the LRA war in Northern Uganda was but one of many wild outbursts of meaningless violence which unfortunately matched the stereotypes of an African continent condemned to sink with such a succession of killings.

There have been rebel movements that have made some efforts at winning the sympathy of the people in the areas they controlled and publicising their cause abroad, but this has never been the case with the LRA. Instead, the LRA is structured according to a pattern of the "warlords" who seem to have converted the violence they inflict into a way of life that gives them power they are not ready to abandon, even if maintaining this violence means subjecting millions of people to the most miserable of livelihoods. Also, the LRA have never controlled any town or area in Northern Uganda. Their forces usually split into very small units, sometimes of groups as small as five or ten people that are highly mobile and unpredictable. They follow routes in the bush and leave behind them a trail of absolute terror among the population, killing in the most brutal ways, abducting children, maiming women and ambushing and burning vehicles and their passengers. The LRA's top commanders have been elusive. Kony has rarely made any public statements and they have not made the slightest effort to attract the sympathy of the people of Northern Uganda, let alone the international community. All this, combined with their religious rituals, confirms them as a dangerous and mysterious force that resembles more an armed cult than a rebel movement with political aims.

Even more than the LRA's capability to inflict violence, a greater source of much fear and mystery about the group stems from their religious beliefs and associations. Their ceremonies, rituals and beliefs melted into a cauldron of syncretism that staggers the imagination. They refer to the Bible, and in his sermons, which can last for several hours, Kony indoctrinates his followers, telling them that as God purified the sinful people of Israel with wars and calamities, so did he with the damned Acholi race who, by accepting Museveni, fell into a corrupt state. Kony sees himself as a new messiah chosen to create a new people, and he implements this task by eliminating all negative elements in his way and by begetting a new Acholi offspring, pure and uncontaminated, in the form of the children born inside the rebel movement. This objective – a new race – has justified the massive abduction of girls who have been forced to become sexual slaves. These girls are usually given to the different commanders as wives and mere chattels. It has been said that Kony himself has had over sixty wives, not much for him since he has been quick to point out that King Solomon had more than 600.

The LRA has also used elements of Islamic faith, most likely taken from the group's Sudanese patrons. The LRA has often threatened the population with harsh punishments should they break any of their regulations, which have included abstaining from work on Friday, from drinking alcohol and from rearing pigs. Also, there has been no doubt that Kony's peculiar creed includes a host of practices and beliefs from the Acholi traditional religion, particularly with respect to the belief in spirit possession. Kony considers himself to be the medium of the Holy Spirit and of various other spirits who advised him on his military actions. The more important of those ghosts or spirits is said to have the curious name of "Who are you". This spiritual character has been of great importance in holding his followers faithful to him.

The abducted children who have grown into adolescence under the shadow of his wings have lived an existence of total submission to him; he has controlled them with a dark combination of instilling feelings of terror and fascination. Abductees are convinced that Kony knows even their most inner thoughts and intentions and where they are every moment.

All this, could mislead people into thinking that Kony and his LRA rebels were just a manifestation of Africa's wild character, sunk in the mud of superstition and irrationality. Even the Ugandan government has been fond of presenting the LRA problem as a form of the "backwardness" they are on a mission to fight against. But all that is a part of a history much more complex and difficult to understand.

As is the case in many African countries, there are big cultural differences between the ethnic groups of the south and the ones of the north of Uganda. That said, if one studies the cultures in depth, one might find that the different traditional communities have more in common than one may think. But during colonial times the British used their "divide and rule" tactics to stress the differences between Northerners and Southerners, particularly by creating a model for the division of labour according to tribes. Ever since, different conflicts over ethnic, religious and political character have undermined time and again the project of building a single national entity.

The war in Northern Uganda, involving the LRA, started in 1986, although its roots can be traced to the times of the British protectorate, when the colonisers' indirect rule favoured the Baganda and some of the other Bantu ethnic groups from the south. These southern communities were given more opportunities for education and development, for example, than the people from the Nilotic ethnic groups of the north. The latter became a cheap and available reserve of manual labour and a source of recruitment into the army, the police and the prison service. The myth of the "martial races", developed by the British, provided the ideological base to support this policy, for which Ugandans were to pay a heavy price after gaining independence from Britain in 1962.

When the new Ugandan flag replaced the Union Jack, King Edward Mutesa II of the Baganda became Uganda's first president. Four years later, in 1966, his prime minister, Milton Obote, a Lango from the North, executed a coup d'état with the help of the army. "Kabaka" Mutesa fled into exile in Britain. Obote's coup started a pattern by which political power in Uganda is gained and maintained by the use of violence. In January 1971, while Obote attended a Commonwealth summit in Singapore, his army commander Idi Amin overthrew him and opened a bloody period in the country in which at least 300,000 people were assassinated. Amin, a Kakwa from Koboko in West Nile, purged the army of officers and soldiers whom he regarded as enemies, particularly those from the Acholi and Lango tribes. He did the same with politicians and intellectuals coming from these sub-regions, as well as from the south. One of the most prominent personalities murdered by Idi Amin was the chief justice, Benedict Kiwanuka, who refused to compromise the independence of the judiciary and bend to the dictator's power. The Church of Uganda archbishop, Janani Luwum, who had spoken out against Amin's atrocities, also became his victim.

Idi Amin was overthrown in April 1979, when Tanzanian soldiers supported by several thousand Ugandan insurgents, invaded the country by crossing the southern border into Uganda at the River Kagera. After a quick succession of three presidents, elections were held in December 1980 and won by former president Obote and his party, the Uganda People's Congress (UPC).

Yoweri Museveni, who had been a presidential candidate under a minority party known as Uganda Patriotic Movement (UPM), accused Obote of having rigged the elections. In February 1981, Museveni launched a bush guerrilla war against the government, a war that was to have a high death toll. Different human rights organisations have put the number of dead at 300,000, more or less the same as the number of the dead during Amin's dictatorship. Most of the victims during the war were civilians killed during the brutal repression launched by the UNLA (Uganda National Liberation Army), particularly in war zones like Luweero and in West Nile, where the army engaged in widespread revenge since it was Amin's home region. During the years of war between Museveni and Obote many of the army's troops were from Acholi (although most officers were Lango and Teso), which resulted in the Acholi being fairly or unfairly blamed for the killings and widespread atrocities committed in the infamous "Luweero Triangle" and other areas of Uganda.

In July 1985, Obote was overthrown by his own army, or more specifically by a group of disgruntled Acholi officers who were discontented and exhausted by a war that seemed to have reached an impasse and in which they were the ones dying. In addition to these concerns, the Acholi officers had complained for a long time of being sidelined every time promotions were given out in the UNLA. These promotions seemed to favour the Lango, Obote's tribe.

Although the main leader of the coup that overthrew Obote was Brig. Bazilio Okello, it was General Tito Okello (no relation to Bazilio), an Acholi from Namukora, in Kitgum district, who was sworn in as president. Some other groups who had fought Obote, FEDEMU and Andrew Kayiira's Uganda Freedom Movement in the south and Uganda National Rescue Front and Former Uganda National Army in West Nile, joined the new military junta. However, Yoweri Museveni's

National Resistence Army (NRA) was going to prove a much harder nut to crack. Under the mediation of Kenya's president, Daniel Arap Moi, peace talks (often dubbed as "peace jokes") between the NRA and the government of Uganda started in Nairobi. The negotiations continued until December 1985 when, under a lot of pressure, both sides signed a peace agreement.

But the accord between Okello's government and Museveni's NRA was not to last more than one month. Under the pretext that the army of the new regime was no different from Obote's as it allegedly continued to perpetrate serious human rights violations against the civilian population, Museveni (who during the talks had managed to cut off much of the south and west from the rest of the country) stormed Kampala. After three days of fighting the city fell to the NRA on 25th January 1986. Two months later the whole country came under NRA control and Okello's soldiers either surrendered or escaped to areas of South of Sudan. Many others simply hid their weapons and returned to their homes in the north, awaiting events.

After a six-month period of relative peace things took a turn for the worse. While searching for arms of former soldiers, some units of the new army, Museveni's NRA, started committing atrocities against villagers in the north. These acts only confirmed people's fears that the new soldiers from the south were coming to mete out revenge on the northerners for the atrocities allegedly committed by the Acholi soldiers in Luweero. Whatever the case, there is no doubt that those weeks of tension triggered the beginning of the rebellion. Some of Okello's former officers returned from Sudan, where they had re-grouped, and this is how the war of Northern Uganda started in August 1986. At that time a good part of the population supported the rebellion. As it so often happens, the discontent of groups that have nothing to lose and much to fear feed insurgencies. That first rebel group was called Uganda People's Democratic Army (UPDA), and was lead by former UNLA officers like Kilama, Odwar, Ojuku, Fearless Obwoya and Odong Latek. The rebellion quickly spread to other parts of the north, particularly to Lango and Teso, although it subsided in these sub-regions a few years later, partly because their leaders were sensible enough to ask their youth not to continue with an adventure that could only destroy their society while they gained nothing.

Towards the end of 1986, a young woman from Gulu called Alice Lakwena, who presented herself as a medium who could communicate with a variety of spirits, took control of most of the UPDA, which she transformed into the Holy Spirit Movement (HSM). Lakwena preached that the people of Acholi had been perverted and had turned away from God and they needed purification if they were to defeat Museveni. From then on, the rebellion in the north always had a religious dimension. The HSM had rules and beliefs as bizarre as the following: the prohibition to take cover during combat, the use of stones treated with oil in rituals, which were hurled at the army in the belief that the stones would turn into grenades and explode, and the use of blessings with water by senior rebel officers known as "controllers". One of their more curious rules went something like this: "thou shalt have two testicles, neither less nor more". All this would simply be cause for a laugh were it not for the fact that thousands of the youth who joined Lakwena's movement died like flies in front of the NRA. The new army was bewildered to see attacks being launched by bare-chested youth who advanced decisively singing religious hymns and carrying stones in their hands. Over one thousand people, mostly Lakwena's guerrillas, are said to have died in a fierce battle held over three days at Corner Kilak. The NRA used artillery and helicopter gunships against thousands of young rebels, who met with easy deaths.

Lakwena maintained leadership of the rebellion until the end of 1987 when, after a massive campaign that led her Holy Spirit army through much of Eastern Uganda, her advance was halted a few kilometres outside of Jinja. Getting inspiration from the Old Testament book of Judges, she foretold that only 300 of her fighters would reach Kampala to take power. Before that, they would cross River Nile in the same way that the Israelites crossed the Red Sea when it parted in front of them. It is difficult to determine whether these predictions would have come true, because the NRA struck a fatal blow against the HSM before it reached Jinja. Alice Lakwena fled to Kenya, where she died in a refugee camp in January 2007.

While Lakwena's army fled in disarray back to the north, the countryside of Kitgum district became a prime gathering place for gangs of thousands of well-armed Karimojong herdsmen. During the next couple of months this group swept through the Acholi villages, searching for cattle, goats, sheep and anything else they could find. In most cases the NRA did not intervene and simply watched with pleasure as "those stubborn northerners" lost the backbone of their economy. In a very short time an entire society was deprived of one of their more important means of livelihood, cattle. The Acholi were being raided not only by the Karimojong, but also by the rebels and government soldiers alike, who took every opportunity to steal cattle and other domestic animals from the common people.

Around 1987, the first formal attempts to negotiate a peaceful settlement were made, although as early as October 1986 three Acholi elders (Tiberio Okeny, Leander Komakech and Peter Odok) led a "goodwill mission" that established contact with the rebels and made some recommendations to the president for a peaceful end to the war. After several months of meetings between UPDA officers who were not under Lakwena's control and NRA top military men, a peace accord was signed in Pece Stadium (Gulu) in June 1988. Many of the UPDA fighters were incorporated into the NRA. However, the signed agreement did not signal the end of the war, which has always alternated between periods of widespread violence and periods of lull, even of near peace. Also, for different reasons, peace initiatives that normally lasted several months ended up collapsing and giving way to new waves of fighting.

After signing the Pece Peace Agreement in 1988, the remnants of Lakwena's forces regrouped under two leaders: in Kitgum district under Lakwena's father, an elder called Severino Lokoya, who called himself "Rubanga Won" (God the Father), and in Gulu under Joseph Kony, a young man in his twenties who had joined a Cwero UPDA in 1987. Kony was from Odek village, in Gulu district, and was said to be related to Alice Lakwena. Eventually, Kony took control of all rebel units, especially after Severino Lokoya was arrested by the NRA.

During the three years following the war, there was a phase of stagnation, with frequent abuses against the population committed by both sides. Violence became the order of the day and people had no choice but to live with that insecurity both day and night. In rural areas people often went to sleep in the bush, where they hid from the marauding rebels, who at that time called themselves Uganda Christian Democratic Army, although ordinary villagers continued to call them simply the "Holy".

In 1991, the NRA launched a very tough military offensive known as "Operation Simsim". Under the command of Gen. David Tinyefuza, the operation isolated the north by cutting off radio communications with humanitarian organisations, including the churches. Many civilians were shot dead when they were unable to produce any identification and 18 opposition politicians, among them Tiberio Okeny, were detained, charged with treason and ill-treated. As part of their counter-insurgency strategy, the government forced people living in rural areas to move around carrying traditional weapons like axes, spears and arrows to join in the hunt for Kony's guerrillas. This only angered the rebels further and they resorted to carrying out horrific mutilations on people suspected of cooperating with the government. In August 1991, the government announced that Kony had been defeated. Many thought that the nightmare was over, especially because from that time the north of Uganda was generally peaceful until the end of 1993. It seemed that at last Acholiland was beginning to enjoy a period of peace. The visit of Pope John Paul II to Gulu in February 1993 was an event of great significance that cheered many spirits. In Teso, where people had been put in concentration camps, the rebellion led by the Uganda People's Army (UPA) ended after a series of successful negotiations brokered by traditional, local and religious leaders. Some of their leaders, like Musa Ecweru and Max Omeda joined the government while their top commander Hitler Eregu fled to Kenya where he was later killed.

But peace has not lasted in Northern Uganda. During the second half of 1993, Kony's rebels, who now called themselves the Lord's Resistance Army or LRA, had re-grouped in areas of South Sudan, where they started receiving military support from the Khartoum government, as a tit-for-tat for Museveni's help to John Garang's rebels of the Sudan People's Liberation Army (SPLA). In this way the war in Northern Uganda became a part of the complex picture of a regional conflict that pitted Uganda against Sudan. Behind the scenes, and to complicate things further, the United States supported the SPLA in its effort to stop Khartoum's Islamic expansion.

When Kony's rebels resumed their attacks in Northern Uganda a new initiative was started by Betty Bigombe, Minister of State for the Pacification of the North. After several months of discreet contacts, some LRA commanders met in the bush several times with NRA officers like Toolit and John Mugume. An agreement was reached for a ceasefire, which was generally respected by both sides and, for the first time in many years, people could enjoy a peaceful Christmas. When it seemed that everything was about to end well and everybody thought that a peace agreement could be signed in a few days, Kony asked for six months to have time to gather all the LRA forces and prepare them for disarmament. On 6th February 1994, Museveni gave the rebels a seven-day ultimatum to surrender, which signalled the end of the peace talks and the resumption of hostilities. Many people still discuss what the reason was for the failure of the peace talks. Some say that a few politicians were envious of a woman receiving credit for bringing peace to the north. The government of Uganda has always reassured the public that they had reliable information that the LRA had started receiving great military support from Sudan and that they were simply using the peace talks to gain time to reorganise themselves, as indeed seemed to be the case.

With the failure of this initiative and Sudan's full support of the LRA, a new period that brought more terror on the population, started. Trapped in a cycle of violence, civilians have not been victims caught by chance in the crossfire, but real targets deliberately chosen as part of an evil strategy that seeks to control, humiliate and if - need be - destroy them, their lives and their culture. They have become human wrecks.

The LRA and their predecessors have always resorted to the abduction of civilians to beef up their forces, especially in moments of numerical weakness. In 1994 the massive kidnapping of boys and girls became endemic. Although different figures have been considered, UNICEF puts the number of children who have passed through this traumatic abduction experience at 30,000. For many years the same pattern has been repeated: several hundred LRA rebels infiltrate

Northern Uganda through the border with Sudan and, after splitting into many small groups that sweep through the countryside, they systematically abduct hundreds of boys and girls, who are tied up with ropes and led to the LRA's training camps in Sudan. Those who are too weak to walk are killed mercilessly. Girls, in addition to being forced to engage in combat, have to bear the humiliation of becoming sexual slaves for the LRA's commanders. The government of Sudan has greatly benefited from this endless reserve of child soldiers who have been sent to the frontline to fight against the SPLA. This tactic has spared losses among Sudan's own armed forces. Once abducted children have been trained they are brought back to Uganda to fight and to commit atrocities against their own communities. In this way they are instilled with fear. They are too afraid to escape since they think that they have nowhere to go. Different organisations that work with these children's rehabilitation estimate that roughly more than half of them have managed to run away. The children come back psychologically destroyed, heavily traumatised, often with serious gunshot wounds and incurable diseases that cause them extreme pain for many years. Thousands of parents in Northern Uganda have fallen into the most absolute desperation and grief. Some of them have seen all their children abducted in a single night, and the few parents who were courageous enough to follow the children into the bush have been killed, often by their own children who are forced to execute them.

Although the LRA has always attacked military targets, the group has shown a preference for what is euphemistically known as "soft targets" or "collateral damage", that is the civilian population, over whom they have maintained control with sustained levels of terror. Travelling on the roads of Northern Uganda has been a most scary experience for many years as passengers always risk falling into deadly ambushes. When the LRA ambushes a vehicle, they shoot to kill, bringing the vehicle to a complete standstill, then loot everything and burn the vehicle, regardless of any wounded passengers inside. They will abduct any survivors, some of whom will invariably be killed. Not even cars belonging to NGOs, humanitarian organisations or church groups have been spared.

In addition to these attacks on roads, the LRA has repeatedly attacked villages and suburbs of the main towns like Gulu, Kitgum, Pader, Lira and Kalongo. These assaults usually take place at night, and each time dozens or even hundreds of huts are burnt to the ground. Sleeping in the bush for fear of rebel attacks has become routine for ordinary people.

Among the worst atrocities committed by the LRA are the massacres that have been carried out to instill as much terror as possible. The list is endless. The first of these took place in April 1995 at Atyak, when more than 200 people were lined up on the bank of a river and shot in cold blood. The orchestrator of that killing was Vincent Otti, who was born in Atyak. After this mass murder, Uganda broke off diplomatic relations with Sudan (these were only restored in 2000). In July 1996, some 150 Sudanese refugees were killed in a succession of attacks in Acholi camp. During the first week of January 1997, four hundred people were clubbed or hacked to death in villages of Lamwo county. In July 2002, the LRA killed 90 people, most of them children, in Pajong village in Mucwini (Kitgum district), and 120 people in Amyel in October that year. In February 2004, they attacked Barlonyo displaced camp, in Lira, where they killed over 300 civilians, most of whom were burned to death in their huts. All these incidents have been extensively reported in the Ugandan press, but not so much in the international media. A detail that has often been overlooked is that in most of these massacres the UPDF has invariably arrived long after the LRA has disappeared. This has even happened in cases when the massacres took place over several days (this was the case in Acolpii and in Lamwo).

Since 1994, the government of Sudan has provided the LRA with anti-tank and anti-personnel landmines, which have added a new dimension to the suffering of the civilian population. One day in 1999, as I was travelling from Gulu to Kitgum in a small Suzuki Samurai vehicle, I was stopped by some unfortunate villagers who asked me to take a young man who had just stepped on a landmine to the nearest hospital. I quickly removed, from the vehicle, several boxes of books that I had bought that morning and accommodated the man in the best way I could. He was bleeding profusely and screaming in pain. Despite the fact that the road was rough and the vehicle was old, I maintained a speed of 100 km per hour until we reached the mission hospital, where doctors managed to save his life but had to amputate both of his legs. While the number of landmine victims in Acholi has not been high - hundreds rather than thousands - the psychological impact it has had on the population has added to their trauma. Also, in several visits to the north of Lamwo district, I have heard stories from villagers from the nearby camps of Agoro, Paluga and Potika of how, in 1999, they saw the UPDF planting landmines in areas close to the border, making it impossible for the villagers to return to their homes.

What is clear from this list of atrocities is that the LRA is much more than a handful of crazy armed men and abducted children who are led by an irrational, savage Kony. Behind their extraordinary brutality is a well structured organisation, united under an unopposed leader who is believed to be endowed with supernatural powers. In fact, the LRA is divided into five brigades, each with its own name: Sinia, Gilva, Trinkle, Stockree and Control Altar, with the latter under the direct command of Kony. In the LRA there are officers in charge of tasks such as coordination of strategies, finance, medical services, intelligence, political affairs, religious affairs, training and more.

In 1999, Northern Uganda enjoyed another long period of quiet that lasted eleven months. During that time the LRA stayed in their camps of Arua and Jebelein, near Juba. It was rumoured then that the Sudan government would soon suspend support for the rebels and that there was internal fighting among the rebel ranks. Part of those rumours were true, because in November that year Kony executed his second-in-command Otti Lagony (not related to Vincent Otti) after he learned of Lagony's plan to come to Uganda to negotiate a peaceful surrender with the government. At that time, the Carter Center was also carrying out intense diplomatic mediation between the Ugandan and Sudanese governments and in December 1999 a peace agreement was signed in Nairobi. One day later, the Parliament of Uganda passed the Amnesty Bill, which granted a blanket pardon for all fighters who agreed to lay down their arms, no matter how many atrocities they had committed. Nevertheless, despite efforts by the Carter Center to involve the rebel leaders in the negotiations, the LRA seems to have perceived this accord as a threat to their own safety, and two days before Christmas Day in 1999, when people were beginning to think that the war was approaching its end, a group of rebels led by commander Charles Tabuley invaded Acholi once again. The usual spiral of violence resumed through ambushes, killings, night attacks, abduction of children, etcetera. As if this was not enough, a few months later an outbreak of Ebola occurred in Gulu and for the following four months Northern Uganda was more isolated and helpless than ever.

This is the way things were in 2001 when we started some of our peace contacts with the rebels and when commander Onekomon and his boys left the bush.

3

Iron Fist

The sun descended softly towards the horizon, sending its last rays over the giant golden statue that represents a fish at the Olympic harbour in Barcelona, and as night approached, a great calm came to rest on the shoreline. The pedestrian avenues filled with people who walked in a relaxed way, enjoying the cool evening breeze.

I had been in Spain for a little more than one month, and I was planning to spend at least one and a half more. After two years in Northern Uganda without any holiday, bearing the pressure of an ever increasing workload and undergoing some tense moments in Gulu, including the months of the Ebola epidemic, I was beginning to notice the benefits of this period of rest in the company of my family and friends in Spain. I had gone out for supper with my sister Carmen and Florentino, an old novitiate classmate with whom I enjoyed the deep charm of his Soria villages on so many occasions. Next to us, the sea gently rocked the many boats and ships anchored in its deep waters. The quiet talk at the restaurant, the grilled fish and the glasses of cool beer were divine gifts for our senses.

I must acknowledge that I have always dragged my feet when it comes to paying bills, maybe because I seem to always wear trousers with torn-out pockets in which money does not last long. When the bill came and Florentino took out his wallet I did not rush to tell him "No, come on, man, let me pick up the bill…" or "Let me foot half of it". The pleasant environment invited us to prolong our enjoyment of the Mediterranean night and so, when we passed by an Irish pub, I said:

"You know, I have never tasted a glass of Johnnie Walker Black Label, and I would not like to leave this world without having ever tasted one... Let's go in."

I felt that I should be the one to pay for the next round. We stayed at the pub for some time, chatting and enjoying the music before returning home. This time my sister paid for the drinks, and I thought that definitely I ought to be ashamed of myself.

It was nearly two in the morning when we reached the house of the Comboni Missionaries, in the upper part of Barcelona. I know that being in such a state is not always the best way to go back to a religious house, but I had only been doing this once every two or three years. In any case, as a friend of mine from Andalusia is fond of saying:

"Catholicism is the best religion, because it allows you to do almost everything, and if you ever commit some kind of excess you can still be forgiven."

I walked into my room and I was surprised to find a handwritten note on my desk that said: "Fr. Giulio wants to talk to you urgently. Call him as soon as you arrive, no matter how late."

Giulio Albanese, an Italian Comboni missionary from Rome, was one of those close friends that one keeps for life. We had been classmates during my first years in Uganda, in 1984 and 1985 and we had both followed courses of journalism soon after finishing our theological studies. In 1998 he founded the MISNA (Missionary Service News Agency), a Rome-based media initiative which gathered information from countries in the southern hemisphere. The agency's "correspondents" were mainly missionaries who were "on the ground" and who knew what was going on since they could provide the point of view of the people who suffered most. MISNA's philosophy was to "be the voice of the voiceless" and was one of the very few international media houses that had so far given preferential and constant attention to the problem in Northern Uganda.

I dialled Giulio's phone number and on the other side of the line Giulio's drowsy voice greeted me. He went straight to the point.

> "I have been talking to Tarcisio. He has told me that ever since the LRA returned from Sudan a month ago the situation is simply horrifying. He has some reliable contacts with the rebels and there are good prospects for peace negotiations. Tarcisio, and also Archbishop Odama, would like to know when they may anticipate your return."

After exchanging some more phrases I told him, without thinking twice, that I would come back immediately. When I hung up I went to sleep wondering whether my decision was solely a result of my enthusiasm for the cause of peace, or if it may not have been influenced in some way by the two glasses of whisky I had just had next to the sea. Nevertheless, God really works in mysterious ways. In any case, I have not taken any more Johnnie Walker Black Label ever since.

The following day, after talking to Fr. Tarcisio and Archbishop Odama on the phone, I returned to Madrid. Two days later I was on a plane on my way to Uganda, feeling a most strange excitement.

Several months had passed since Onekomon and his boys had come out of the bush. Numerically they represented a very small fraction of the LRA, but their successful story proved something we had longed to show about the conflict in Northern Uganda: that dialogue with the rebels was possible and sitting to talk to them was a solution worth trying.

In December 1999, the passing of the Amnesty Bill, which granted a blanket pardon to all rebels who denounced rebellion and laid down their arms, was the fruit of a wide consensus in the Acholi civil society. One of the pillars of this traditional society has always been the peaceful resolution of conflicts and the restoration of broken relationships.

Religious leaders from Acholi, who had formed the umbrella inter-denominational organisation, Acholi Religious Leaders' Peace Initiative (ARLPI) the previous year, and the cultural leaders, the *Rwodi*, with their own organisation known as *Kal Kwaro Acholi*, had a considerable influence in the crafting of the law, which was approved at around the same time that the governments of Uganda and Sudan signed a peace agreement mediated by the Carter Center.

President Museveni took a few weeks to sign the new law. When he did, in January 2000, he publicly expressed his skepticism about its success. Like a chorus, he and his generals emphasised their belief in a military solution to the problem. All the same, at the end of 2005 statistics from the Amnesty Commission showed some hopeful figures: more than 10,000 people had received their amnesty certificates in Acholi. Most of the beneficiaries were individuals who had been abducted and forced into the rebel ranks, but also among them were top LRA officers. It is only fair to point out that even before the existence of the Amnesty Law, the UPDF generally treated all rebels who surrendered, and even those captured in the battlefield, humanely. I never heard of any of them being dragged to court to answer for their crimes.

The implementation of the Amnesty Law has not been easy. Despite the fact that the law had existed since the end of January 2000, it was only in 2001 that the Amnesty Commission could begin its work with offices in Gulu and Kitgum, offices that were financed by the European Union.

Nevertheless, there were cases of abuses within this process. Since most of the young rebels who escaped did so during battles with the UPDF, they had to pass through a military installation for some time. In some cases the length of stay could be prolonged for several months.

During this time many minors who had left the rebel ranks came under considerable pressure to join the army.

This was the case with practically all the boys who had come out of the bush with Onekomon. Once they returned to their homes they received frequent visits from soldiers sent from the 4th Division headquarters, who insisted that the boys join the army. In January 2002 the Justice and Peace Commission of Gulu wrote a letter to the division commander requesting that the boys be left alone. I found the case of the youngest of all the boys, the one who had a crippled hand as a result of a gunshot wound, particularly painful. We had started paying his school fees at a primary school in Gulu, but again and again he was discouraged because he could not hold a pen properly. He ended up joining the army at the age of 15. Although he could not hold a pen, his disability did not prevent him from being able to pull the trigger on a gun.

In 2002, Africa began to feel the consequences of the "total war on terrorism" declared soon after the events of 11th September, 2001. The United States had set its eyes on East Africa as one of the bastions of Islamic terrorism and the US State Department, in its updated lists, had included the LRA among the armed groups considered as terrorists. This left those of us who advocated for peaceful dialogue in a very uneasy situation. The Ugandan government was to reap great benefits from buying into the US's dominating ideology. In January 2002, everyone in Gulu and Kitgum could see unusual movements of big military convoys with tanks and pieces of heavy artillery. Uganda had just signed an agreement with Sudan to allow the UPDF to cross into Sudanese territory to carry out military operations against the LRA. The Sudanese government, on its side, was anxious to improve its international image and to cast off its tarnished image as a state sponsor of terrorist groups. At the beginning of March that year the

UPDF launched "Operation Iron Fist" in a bid to dislodge the LRA from its bases inside Sudan and to pursue the rebels. At that time, Kony's rebels were hidden in the difficult terrain of the Imatong mountains, not very far from the Ugandan border.

During the first months of Operation Iron Fist, the only source of information about what was happening in Sudan was the UPDF. As usual, the army assured us over and over again that the LRA had been defeated, that the LRA was about to disappear and that they would "soon be history". But things on the ground were far more complicated than what we were hearing. The government of Sudan has always made it a point not to stick to its word, or to act deviously to say the least. The UPDF could not go beyond a "red line" that had been drawn by Khartoum near Juba. Since the UPDF had to notify the Sudanese Armed Forces every time it intended to carry out military operations inside Sudanese territory, this meant that Kony was always well informed about the movements of the Ugandan army and could react accordingly.

For ordinary people in Northern Uganda, Operation Iron Fist was a total disaster. In June 2002 the LRA poured into Uganda and launched a violent backlash against the government and the population on the ground. The rebels were not a "ragtag army fleeing in disarray", but a well-organised army of several thousands who attacked with new military equipment, plenty of ammunition and even brand new military uniforms; all of these had been supplied by the Sudanese Armed Forces that continued to support them despite the peace agreement signed with Uganda at the end of 1999. The districts of Gulu and Kitgum experienced a wave of brutal violence never seen before. Arson attacks against displaced people's camps, ambushes and mass child kidnappings became the order of the day.

It was the urgency of this situation in 2002 that had drawn me back to Uganda, cutting short my trip to Spain.

It was nine o'clock in the morning of 17th July 2002 when we boarded Tarcisio's white pickup truck. I was standing in the back, holding the bars of the frame, together with Rwot Oywak and another contact person. Archbishop Odama travelled in the front of the pickup with Fr. Tarcisio. After leaving Pajule we took the Kitgum-Lira road and headed south. Two kilometres later we took a right turn and followed a narrow dirt track towards Koyo Lalogi. Once again the tall grass opened up in front of us as a new Red Sea stretched before us to allow us, as if we were Israelites faced with a challenge, to cross on dry land; only that this time Pharaoh's soldiers were not chasing after us. We were going to encounter them ahead.

At that time, John Baptist Odama was 51 years old and he was Uganda's youngest prelate. Born in West Nile, in Rhino Camp village, he had been rector of Pokea Seminary in Arua Diocese and of Alokolum major seminary in Gulu before becoming Nebbi's first Catholic bishop in 1996. One of the stories that he was fond of telling about his difficult years in Alokolum was how he was reluctant to build a fence around the compound to protect his seminarians. "The best fence," he would say, "is a good relationship with the people who live next to us." In 1999, when the Vatican created three new metropolitan sees in Uganda, Odama was appointed archbishop of Gulu. Since that moment he did not stop saying that his priority was to work for peace for the people he had come to serve as a pastor. Odama was a born peacemaker. His friendly character and his great simplicity and humble character endowed him with the best qualities a mediator could ever have. But he was more than that. Odama had a solid spiritual foundation and he would spend long hours in prayer in the chapel of his residence. His trust in God made him a person who lived in austerity. During the five years I lived with him I do not remember having seen him wear more than three different shirts, and he would often travel to Kampala by public instead of private means. On his pastoral visits to the most remote corners of his diocese he would not mind sleeping in a mud hut. Living with him, I learned that a leader's poverty can make people trust him/her more, since poverty can be a sign of authenticity.

Our meeting with the rebels was to take place in the abandoned school of Koyo Lalogi, 17 kilometres from the main road. We knew what lay ahead of us, since the rebels had asked Tarcisio to supply them with the names of our delegation and had cautioned him that we would have to go through several security checks. Despite knowing this, however, nothing could have prepared us for what we were going to meet a couple of kilometres before reaching the school.

After covering a good stretch of road without seeing a single person, ahead of us there emerged, like a ghost, a young man wearing a military uniform, a rosary around his neck and gumboots on his feet. He had a rifle slung over his shoulder and he was holding a jerrycan of water. Raising his hand, he ordered us to stop.

When Tarcisio slowed down and we all mumbled some words as a greeting, the youngster did not answer, but tilted his jerrycan, and sprinkled abundant water on us while he walked around the car. He was one of the LRA "controllers" and he was making sure that we were being purified before entering their inner circle of pure and uncontaminated beings. The LRA is more of a cult with religious-like practices than a rebel group with political aims. It is this cultic character that has always isolated it from the rest of the world. Groups that consider themselves a holy, pure remnant living in a sinful world often commit the worst atrocities and the most repugnant horrors against the rest of humanity, all in the name of their alleged superiority. They regard the rest of the world as dirty and corrupted.

The young rebel who had ordered us to stop was around 20 years old. Once again I watched his cold and expressionless face with eyes that once must have shone with joy becouse of his mother's tender care or with excitement while playing games at school. Maintaining a scrupulous silence and carefully avoiding eye contact, he waved us through. We began moving again.

All of a sudden, six young rebels came out of the bush in perfect coordination. They all pointed their guns at us. The one who seemed to command the group seemed older and had the hardest look in his eyes that sent a cold chill down my spine. He wielded a rocket propelled grenade (RPG) launcher and with a furious expression, ordered us out of the vehicle. Two children in fatigues searched the car, even looking under it and under the seats, while two others carefully searched our bodies. Tarcisio had no better idea than to say.

"What do you think, boys? Have we not been punctual?"

The tall man shouted an order.

"Remove your shoes!"

Feeling numb, I obeyed him and the soles of my shoes were carefully examined. When the boys reached Archbishop Odama he laughed heartily.

"If you want my shoes, here they are. What are you looking for in them?"

Perhaps the presence of an archbishop, with his white cassock and pectoral cross, inspired some respect from the rebels, because the tall man answered.

"You could have a bomb hidden in them."

After this group of young rebels had finished with us, we continued towards the school, passing through two more roadblocks. When we reached the last of them, just outside the school compound, a rebel knelt in front of us with a shoulder missile launcher pointing in our direction. I wondered if he would really ever think of using it against us.

Several circles of young men, well armed with assault rifles, machine guns, RPGs and rocket launchers, monitored the school compound. Discreetly I counted fifty of them. They all were wearing brand new uniforms. The carefully hand-sewn pips on their shoulders with embroidered stars and religious symbols (in particular the bible and a heart surrounded by wreaths) caught my attention. It was clear that they had a reliable source of military supplies.

In the middle of the compound, under a big tree, three LRA commanders waited for us. I recognised one of them, Charles Tabuley, because I had seen his picture before and you could not mistake his frog-like eyes. Tabuley stood and came to shake our hands cordially. Tarcisio repeated his greeting-question.

"Have we not been punctual?"

I had my blue bag with me, and in it I was carrying a notebook, a pen, a bottle of water and a digital camera. One of the rebels took it from me, as well as my watch.

"Can't I take pictures?" I asked.

"Another day. Today we shall take them ourselves," answered Tabuley.

But Tarcisio, whose spontaneity does not always observe protocol, was not used to asking permission. While I surrendered my bag he stood at a distance taking video footage as though he was at a holiday resort. He had hardly captured a few seconds' worth of footage before the rebels stopped him. Days later, when I watched those few seconds of footage I could only see the image of Tabuley raising his hand against the camera giving orders to stop the filming. We were assured that all our belongings would be returned at the end of the meeting, but I was allowed to take out my notebook and my pen in order to take notes during the meeting.

The other two rebel commanders introduced themselves as Lieutenant Colonel Livingstone Opiro and Major Dominic Ongwen. The three commanders were adults, but all of them had been abducted at the beginning of the war. Tabuley and Ongwen were kidnapped from their homes in 1987, when they were still children, and now they were men in their mid-twenties. Opiro, who was older, had been a nurse working in Anaka Hospital when he was abducted. Because of his medical skills he had become the chief of medical services for LRA.

The meeting, which took place in Acholi, started with a prayer led by Archbishop Odama. Tabuley and Opiro talked at length during the meeting. Ongwen did not say a single word. He had a big rosary in his hands and he spent all the time quietly passing the beads between his fingers while he looked at the sky as if he was in another world. An older officer was standing and recording in a note book everything we were discussing, while another rebel took pictures from different angles. The jerrycan boy had not forgotten us (how grateful I would have been if he had) and continued to sprinkle us with abundant water to make sure that we were properly purified and cleansed from our sins, something which we surely badly needed, as we were in the company of those men who apparently shone with holiness.

It was clear that the rebels were taking advantage of our meeting, turning it into a public relations exercise. Their well organised presence and their display of new weapons showed that they were going to great pains to give a different image from what had been portrayed about them as a wild rag-tag army of crazy guys.

"Look at us," they seemed to say. "Here we are, smart and civilised, highly organised and well armed. Do not underrate our capacity and take us seriously," seemed to be their message.

The irony of being a mediator is that it often puts you in uneasy situations in which you can easily be turned into an instrument that gives legitimacy to groups that commit heinous crimes. Unfortunately, there is no straightforward way to avoid this and it can lead to some other dilemmas.

After his prayer, Archbishop Odama highlighted two ideas that he wanted to make clear. First, we had come mainly to listen to them and, second, everything that they would say would be reported faithfully to the president. He also said that there was something important that we, the visitors, needed to know:

> "What we are going to hear from you in this meeting, are they just your personal views? Or does it represent the official position of the LRA high command?"

In answer, Tabuley gave an order to connect their radio call. In a matter of seconds, one of the young rebels threw a cable connected to an air antenna and it landed on the branch of a tree. The radio set, which was connected to a solar-powered battery, was switched on. We heard the voice of the LRA's second-in-command Vincent Otti, whose words made us tense.

> "Is the archbishop playing with us? Is it not enough what we told you in the meeting last week?"

At that point I did not understand what he was referring to. A few weeks later I would come to find out that Odama, who participated in these mediation activities with maximum discretion, had three days earlier taken part in another meeting with four top rebel commanders: Caesar Acellam, Sam Kolo, Tolbert Nyeko and Vincent Otti. The meeting had taken place in the Guru-guru hills, in Gulu district, and it had lasted seven hours.

One of the many lessons I have learned from these mediation meetings is that, generally, the least important parts of them are the rhetorical statements that are made when the rebels list their grievances and proclaim the causes for which they say they are fighting. Tabuley and Opiro insisted that the LRA was an organisation that fought for democracy and the human rights of the oppressed people of Northern Uganda. I bent down and took notes quickly while I felt waves of anger come over me. For many years I had witnessed the extreme cruelty of the LRA towards innocent people: children abducted and subjected to the worst forms of physical and psychological abuse, women and elderly people beaten or burned to death, massacres of hundreds of civilians at a time, travellers who ended their days in a volley of bullets in a road ambush. In a smooth but direct manner, the archbishop made the rebels see the contradiction between their beliefs and practices, and, at the end of the meeting, asked them why they killed innocent people. Opiro cut him short.

> "That is not true. We only kill soldiers when they attack us, and we kill
> their collaborators. We only kill in legitimate defence."

There was not much use in arguing with people who simply denied everything. But Odama insisted and pleaded with them to respect civilians and to stop laying ambushes on the roads. Tabuley assured us that from that moment onwards all roads would be free for travel.

When we ended the meeting, I took advantage of the more relaxed atmosphere. I took Tabuley aside and told him something that had been on my mind since the day before.

> "Today we have become friends. Let me ask you a favour. Release some
> of the children you have in your custody. If you do, people will take
> you seriously."

Tabuley did not answer my request and so we returned to the group. Opiro recorded our phone numbers and asked us to provide him with airtime cards for easy communication. I promised that I would do so and that I would also give them a copy of the minutes of the meeting, which would be sent also to the president. The main purpose of this meeting had been to request a ceasefire from the rebels.

Before leaving we got back our personal belongings. We gave the rebels one sack of maize, two sacks of beans, some boxes of biscuits and two crates of sodas that we had brought. The day before, the military had given us permission to take these items to them.

The journey home was marked by a spirit of euphoria, maybe because despite the unusual situation (in a remote place and among fierce men with guns) we were treated with some respect and this had increased our level of hope. Everything had gone well. All the same, however, Archbishop Odama reminded us that we needed great doses of prudence. Before reaching the main road he asked Tarcisio to stop the vehicle so that he could tell us something important.

> "For the time being it is better not to say anything to the media. If anybody asks you anything about what we have spoken about with the rebels, tell them that I am the only spokesperson for this group."

When we reached the mission many people had gathered. They all had great expectations and waited anxiously to hear from us. Odama called the district and military authorities and informed them that all had gone well. When he was pressed, he made it clear that he could not reveal the content of our conversation with the rebels.

> "Let me put it this way. I am only a man who has been asked to take a letter to another person, in this case the president of Uganda. While I am still on the way I cannot open the envelope and reveal its content to others."

After a hurried lunch we took the road back to Gulu. When we arrived I pulled out my notes and, typed the minutes on my computer so that they would be ready the following day when Archbishop Odama had an appointment with President Museveni. Our evening ended after midnight, and I felt really happy and relaxed, ready to rest during a quiet night. But our optimism crumbled when we received the news that on that very morning when we were having our peace meeting in which the rebels told us their good intentions, some 70 kilometres south of Koyo Lalogi, in Alito, another rebel group had ransacked the Catholic mission there. I went to bed thinking? "Who can understand this".

During the next few years my life was going to be marked by an endless succession of unexpected and painful events that would often make me ask myself that same question. Who can understand this? As we tried to make sense of the road to peace in Northern Uganda, we were beginning to be submerged in an ocean of incomprehensible facts.

4

Monica, the Rebel Girl

The wide visitor's room of the archbishop's residence in Gulu, where the morning rays of the sun filtered through the white curtains like a rare sign of calm in an environment that was getting more charged with violence by the day, was a busy place where many people came to attend daily meetings. The day after our meeting with Tabuley and his men, the main religious leaders working with ARLPI came to put their heads together. Archbishop Odama insisted once again that confidentiality was essential in these contacts with the LRA. After a phone call to the minister of the presidency, Gilbert Bukenya, Odama arranged for an appointment with President Museveni for the following day. The ARLPI group decided that Archbishop Odama, Bishop Baker Ochola and Rwot Oywak should attend.

Ochola had been an Anglican bishop of Kitgum for a number of years and, after reaching the age of 65, had retired in February 2002, as is required in the Church of Uganda. After his retirement he continued to devote himself fully to the cause for peace in Northern Uganda. I remember vividly how one day in 1997, while I was working in Kitgum, he came to see us in the Catholic mission and convinced us to work together with the three main religious denominations, Anglicans, Catholics and Muslims, to form a joint peace initiative. The group started in a very modest manner, with a peace rally in the streets of Kitgum on 15th August 1997. The event attracted thousands of ordinary people tired of seeing how the war continued unabated in the face of the indifference of the international community and, to a certain extent, the rest of Uganda. The group of religious leaders

51

started to document different abuses against the population and published public statements. In our effort to do advocacy, we also tried to meet with diplomats.

That same year, 1997, Bishop Ochola's wife, Winifred, was killed as the vehicle he was travelling in was blown up by a rebel-planted landmine on the Kitgum-Madi Opei Road. Ochola has said often that he felt "like a tree struck by lightning from the top to the roots". Ten years earlier one of their daughters had committed suicide a few days after being gang-raped by a group of soldiers. Ochola was a great enthusiast of the Acholi cultural traditions, which he knows thoroughly, and an advocate of the *mato oput* reconciliation process. He often said in public that he forgave the people responsible for the deaths of his daughter and his wife. This sincerity gave him great moral authority in the community.

Odama and Ochola, together with the cardinal of Kampala, Emmanuel Wamala, had previously met with President Museveni on 5th July. It was important to begin this peace initiative with the go-ahead of the country's highest authority, since the media those days was full of inflammatory statements, purportedly official ones, informing the public that the government would never talk to criminals. After receiving the president's authorisation to initiate contacts with the rebels and work out the modalities in coordination with the military authorities at the UPDF Gulu-based 4th division, the first meeting took place with four top rebel commanders in Guru-guru hills on 14th July. Archbishop Odama was accompanied by one of his priests and two Acholi MPs, Reagan Okumu and Michael Ochula. The meeting was a breakthrough, because no meaningful peace overtures had taken place for many years. It lasted seven hours and it went on well into the night.

The meeting with President Museveni that followed our encounter with Tabuley in Koyo-Lalogi took place in a cordial atmosphere. The president showed great interest in the explanations that Bishop Ochola gave about the *mato oput* reconciliation process. After going through the minutes of the two meetings with the rebels, the president immediately wrote a letter of response. The terms of his reply were rather hard, but he offered a proposal for peace negotiations in four uninhabited zones of South Sudan, far away from populated areas, where the LRA could not commit abuses against civilians.

During those days we made frequent journeys, like a "shuttle diplomacy", carrying out our peaceful mission in a war zone where everything was unpredictable and there were ambushes almost daily. Ours was indeed a risky enterprise. From the very beginning, we tried to work under four principles: good coordination with frequent meetings among the religious and cultural leaders; no paid remuneration (not even allowances) for our work, which we wanted to be free from financial strings and purely for the love of the people; no armed escorts so as to guarantee our impartiality; and lastly, confidentiality, which we stuck to where possible.

The day after the meeting with President Museveni, Odama and Ochola went to the bush in Langol (near the Gulu-Alero Road) where they met with rebel commanders Tolbert Nyeko and Sam Kolo and delivered the president's letter. These rebels wrote their own response. The two MPs attended this meeting. Three meetings with top rebel commanders in one week was an indication that the process was moving in the right direction and that there were reasons to be optimistic. Maybe we were too optimistic at that time, for one of the things that experience teaches in peace processes is that one has to anticipate at least three or four different scenarios or outcomes, and at that time we could only think of, or hope for, one way of success. We were ready to put in as much effort as was necessary and for however long it would take to achieve peace. Indeed we were not going to be in short supply of tough moments, but we hoped that peace would be at the end of the road we were beginning to travel.

While the two bishops maintained the contacts in the west of Acholi (Gulu), part of our strategy was for Tarcisio, Rwot Oywak and I to do the same in the east (Kitgum and Pader).

On 22nd July, Rwot Oywak received a letter signed by Tabuley asking us to pick up 18 women and 13 children who they had just released in a village near the school of Koyo Lalogi. Was this the answer to my request to Tabuley at the end of our meeting with him days ago? Without much time for this or other questions, Rwot Oywak, Fr. Peter Olum and I prepared a pickup truck and off we went to Koyo Lalogi the following day. The vehicle was too small for the task, but we did not have anything better. After reaching the school we proceeded some six kilometres further on foot, passing through villages and fields with very few people in sight.

After walking for one and a half hours we reached a village deep in the bush where we found the girls, many of them with small babies in their arms. Their reception of us could not have been colder.

Rwot Oywak knew the girl who commanded that group since she was from Pajule. Her name was Monica and she had been abducted in 1997 when she was 13 years old.

I tried to present myself as relaxed and calm.

> "Dear friends, we are very happy to see you. We have come to help you. We shall take you to the mission and we will take care of you and take you back to your homes with your parents."

Monica bent her head towards the ground. When she answered, she did not raise it an inch.

> "That is not true. You will take us to the soldiers and they will kill us."

I am afraid I have never been a very patient person. I have always admired Africans for their patience, and in this situation, Fr. Peter Olum and Rwot Oywak taught me a lesson I needed to learn. We had to wait for as long as it took.

And so, we sat near the trunk of a fallen tree and chatted casually about nothing and about everything. I did not have trouble waiting patiently, but I started thinking about how we were in a very remote place in the bush in a dangerous war zone where anything might happen unexpectedly. The girls, as though they did not mind our presence, were busy washing their clothes and feeding their babies.

We may have been waiting for two hours when, out of the blue, Monica gave a laconic order and in a matter of few seconds all the girls collected their belongings and formed a single line without leaving any trace of their presence in the compound. Such swiftness showed that they were well trained and that they were used to dismantling their camps without delay.

And without delay we left the village.

Like many thousands of other abducted children, Monica had been kidnapped by rebels as she was going to school. She was taken to Sudan, where she underwent military training in the LRA camp of Jebelein, near Juba. She was 14 years old when she was given to Kony's second-in-command Alex Otti Lagony, to be part of his "family". Lagony had lost a leg in combat and walked with difficulty with the help of an artificial limb that had been provided to him by the Sudanese Army. In 1999, soon after the passing of the Amnesty Bill by the Ugandan Parliament, Lagony worked out a secret plan to leave for Uganda with the intention of trying to negotiate a settlement with the government. Kony, however, did not want to hear about such an idea and, as soon as he was tipped off about Lagony's plans, ordered his arrest and execution. Monica, like the rest of Lagony's "family", came under suspicion and was arrested and held for two months. She was then given to another commander.

While we walked towards the vehicle I asked her whether she would like to continue with her studies. Her answer, which I was going to hear many times from returned child rebels, left me very sad.

"Those of us who have been with Kony are useless for studies."

A few months later, Monica would request us to send her to a tailoring school. We paid for Monica's three years at a tailoring school in Gulu, run by the Sisters of Sacred Heart. She passed the course with great success and was at the top of her class, finishing with a certificate in fashion design.

At the end of 2006, renowned fashion queen Sylvia Owori offered her an internship at her workshop in Kampala where she spent one month learning new techniques. Since this opportunity, her modest tailoring workshop in Gulu has kept her going.

As we went on with our march away from the village and towards our pick up truck, I continued to talk with Monica and tried to gain her trust. She knew Onekomon and the other young rebels who had come out of the bush with him the year before. The official version of the story that Kony had told his fighters was that as soon as they surrendered in Uganda the UPDF had killed all of them. Isolated and without any possibility of cross-checking facts, the young rebels in Kony's ranks continued their pitiful existence under the assumption that escaping would invariably lead to death.

When we reached the school compound where we had left the pickup truck, we saw some villagers who had come there out of curiosity. No sooner did the girls catch sight of them than they began to run scared in disarray, thinking that we had led them into a trap. We had to run after them and convince them that they had nothing to fear. Finally, they approached the vehicle cautiously while we unloaded some crates of sodas that we had brought. The girls refused to drink the sodas.

It was around two in the afternoon when we finally reached Pajule, carrying the 31 girls and babies packed like sardines in our vehicle. At the mission we were received by some of the Pader district authorities. Two Caritas aid workers had also arrived to help us provide the girls with water, food, clothes, medical attention and psychological counselling. Fr. Tarcisio had come too, and after a couple of hours he returned to Kitgum with a girl who was in need of medical attention. She had an ugly gunshot wound in her hand, which she received after the group she was with was attacked by a UPDF combat helicopter earlier in the mountains near the border with Sudan a few days earlier.

It was a moment of great joy and euphoria that was not to last long. War perpetuates the most absolute and illogical reign of hatred and grief, and the rare moments of consolation do not last long, but instead fade away leaving us with the impression that such moments are but mirages in a hot, sandy desert. In this case, euphoria gave way to downheartedness on the following day when once again we felt the choking of the troubled waters in which we were submerged.

Early the next morning we were struck by shocking news. The night before the LRA had massacred at least 60 people in Pajong village, near Mucwini. Most of the dead were women, children (particularly babies) and the elderly. Everything started when a boy from Pajong, who had been abducted two years earlier, escaped with a gun and a radio communication system, which he surrendered to the UPDF. The enraged rebels launched a most brutal retaliatory attack which was led by Dominic Ongwen, the rebel we had met at Koyo Lalogi who had worn a sort of mystical expression on his face as he looked at the sky and passed the beads of his rosary through his fingers.

It was a most repugnant and cowardly massacre. Many babies were picked up by their legs, hit on the ground or on trees and smashed to death. Some terrified women were forced to kill their children by pounding them in the mortars they used for grinding food.

Three years later, when the International Criminal Court would issue its first arrest warrants for war crimes and crimes against humanity by the LRA, one of the five commanders indicted would be Dominic Ongwen, the main suspect in the planning and carrying out of this revolting mass killing.

At eleven in the morning the UPDF intelligence officer from Pajule came to see us. He told us that he had come to collect all the girls for questioning at the military barracks. We tried to explain that they were still in a state of trauma and that interrogating them could be counter-productive. We also feared that if the rebels found out that we had handed the girls over to the UPDF it would be detrimental to the trust we were trying to build with them, and ultimately this could affect the peace process. Ours were beautiful words and intentions that were very far from the intelligence officer's interests and only solidified his position more. In the end, he told us that he had received orders to send all of the girls to the Gulu 4th division headquarters.

We decided to speak directly to the officer in charge of the Pajule detach, Lt. Col. Sheriff Gava, who until that moment had not missed any chance to show us how unsympathetic he was to our cause. Although he had on several occasions granted us permission to meet the rebels in the bush, he had made no effort to hide his low opinion of our initiative. He was convinced that dialogue with the rebels was a pure waste of time and that the only solution was to fight until all of the rebels had been wiped out to the last rebel; such a task, he told us, had been calculated to take about two or three years.

Assessing our situation as one where we were in "hot soup", we decided to use our satellite phone to call Archbishop Odama. The British embassy had provided us with two handsets the month before and was also meeting the cost of airtime for easy communication. But the archbishop could not do much to help us.

At six in the evening a military vehicle entered the Caritas compound in Pajule. The intelligence officer was there with some other soldiers and the fact that they had all brought sticks did not augur well with us. No sooner had they descended from the car than all the girls started screaming. We stood between them and the girls and made it clear that if they had come to beat the girls they would have to beat us first. After some tense minutes they went back to the car and left, cursing us and saying that the following day military authorities from Gulu would come for them. It was clear that ours was not a victory, but rather a first skirmish in which we had somehow managed to be successful, at least for the moment.

In the meantime, the two Caritas aid workers, Tom, a German psychologist and Carolyn had been examining the girls and children individually. They realised that eight of them were in need of serious medical attention. The following day, very early in the morning, Tom and Carolyn took these eight girls to Kitgum. However, as soon as they reached the gate of the mission hospital they were stopped by the "military authority" from Gulu that we had been told about. One of the officers had no qualms about snatching the girls away and taking them to the Kitgum barracks, ignoring the aid workers pleas for the priority of humanitarian law.

That afternoon the intelligence officer returned to our compound to take the rest of the girls once and for all. He arrived in the company of the "military authority" who had taken the girls to the barracks in Kitgum earlier. He definitely seemed to have more "authority", for he served us with a long speech in which he accused us of having gone to meet "the enemy" without any permission, and of instigating the girls against them. We could no longer do anything and hated having to convince the girls to go with them to the Gulu barracks, assuring them that we would come to visit them soon and that they would be treated well. We had no choice but to swallow our anger and frustration, and wonder whether we could ever trust anyone in such a maze of brutal force.

The next morning, authorities from the Pader district came to get information about what had happened when the military came to take the girls to Gulu barracks. As usual, they came when the storm was over, when there was nothing more to be done and above all when it was safe.

The next day, to make the situation even worse than it was, we received a letter from the rebels threatening to launch a retaliatory attack on Pajule should the girls not be released immediately.

I rushed to Gulu in my small white Suzuki. During those days we lived under continual strain and stress. We often found ourselves in situations that resulted in plenty of unexpected, complex and delicate moments in which we had to make quick decisions under considerable emotional strain. We knew that any mistake could lead to the loss of human lives. Under these circumstances Archbishop Odama was our point of reference. As soon as he received the information we had gathered, he called the 4th division commander in Gulu, Col. Andrew Gutti , a man who always treated us well, did everything possible to help us and who favoured our moves for negotiation. Despite his support, we however sometimes wondered how much power he really had. Gutti wasted no time in inviting us to come promptly to the barracks to meet with the army commander Maj. Gen. James Kazini. In the meantime, Bishop Ochola went to Radio Freedom FM and read a statement appealing to the rebels to be sensible and show restraint in their attacks on people. At that time Radio Freedom FM was the main radio station in the north, and we knew that the rebels listened to it regularly.

Whether they listened to Ochola's plea or not, that night Pajule was attacked and three soldiers died in the exchange of gunfire. I was sad to think that the loss of those three human lives could have been prevented if people had been a bit less proud and instead had used more common sense.

In the barracks, our meeting with Maj. Gen. Kazini was cordial. He assured us that he was in favour of initiatives for peace negotiations, but he advised us to consult the military more before going to the bush to meet with the rebels. At the end of our meeting he told us that we could take the girls back to Pajule.

We went to the part of the barracks where Monica and the other girls were being held. It was a simple building called "Child Protection Unit". When Monica and her companions saw us they were overjoyed. The captain in charge of their custody did not look so happy, and despite the fact that the army commander had given instructions to hand them over to us, he mumbled that he still had to prepare some documents and that they were not ready to leave. Since it was late in the evening we had to leave without the girls.

Soon after we left the barracks, though, we had a different reason to rejoice. Late in the evening, Radio Freedom FM broadcast a message sent by Tabuley. Mentioning me by name, he asked me to collect a second group of 55 abductees in Atanga.

The following day was a hectic day. Very early in the morning Bishop Ochola and I went to Radio Freedom FM to read a message addressed to the rebels in which we thanked them for the gestures of goodwill and we asked them to keep up the spirit.

Even amidst these hopeful, positive events, however, we suspected that the rebels' actions were nothing but a dishonest game they were involving us in without giving us a choice. The LRA was releasing captives and showing a compassionate, reasonable face, while at the same time they continued with their massive abductions and cruel attacks against the population. Every night 40,000 terrified people took refuge behind the walls of Lacor hospital. It did not take us long to realise that the rebels were releasing the weak and sick abductees who had become a burden to them, and replacing them quickly with new, younger and stronger recruits. In such a situation, did we not run the risk of providing legitimacy to a gang of criminals who we were indirectly helping to spread propaganda?

We had too many questions and too few answers.

Before returning to Pajule we still had to go back to the Gulu barracks to pick up the girls. We arrived at ten in the morning but were denied entry. This was another game the military made us participate in without giving us the option to refuse. We explained that we had an appointment with the captain in charge of the Child Protection Unit and we were told that he was in the security office of the district. At the security office, we were not received in a very friendly manner. The regional security officer lectured us about how we were wasting our time. The captain seemed surprised to see me and asked me to give him my phone number. Although he assured me that he would call me, I knew that he would never do so.

I went back to the archbishop who called Col. Gutti. The colonel told us to go back to the barracks. On the way there Archbishop Odama uttered a phrase by way of comment that I never forgot.

"When you are working for peace you just have to set your eyes far, on the place you want to reach, and do not mind about anything else, even if it makes you stumble and fall one thousand times".

Once we were in the barracks, Col. Gutti apologised to us for the confusion and told us to go straight to the Child Protection Unit. When we mentioned to him that Tabuley had sent a message the evening before calling us to collect 55 more captives, we asked him whether the military could help us. It was a chance to turn the bad spirits of the last few days into a new exercise of cooperation. He said that he would send a military lorry to collect the people released and that they would be taken to Pajule.

When we reached the Child Protection Unit, the unfriendly captain from the day before still tried to make things as difficult as he could, forcing us to wait three more hours. We sat and waited patiently, trying to control our emotions, knowing that at most he could only delay us, but not prevent us from taking the girls away. Finally we were allowed to leave with the girls at three o'clock.

When we reached Pajule we were welcomed with great joy. The contrast between the spontaneous joy of simple and ordinary people, who could smile because of any little sign that gave them hope, and the bitterness of some military and security officers, who could only rejoice at the death of "the enemy", really struck me.

It was time for evening prayer at the parish church. We all entered the church. Half an hour later a military lorry arrived and stopped just outside the church. We all came out singing and clapping our hands, and surrounded the big green Tata lorry while we danced. The driver came out and opened the back of the lorry, revealing scores of children and young people dressed in rags, some of them emaciated and with fear in their eyes. That vision of humiliated and abused human beings contrasted starkly with the party that was going on around the lorry. Slowly and painfully, they all descended one by one and were received by a sea of open arms.

Half numb, but filled with emotion, I noticed a man wearing a military uniform who approached me to tell me that he was entrusting us with the 55 people. I raised my head, only to to see that the speaker was the intelligence officer who two days earlier had tried to collect the girls using sticks. I was dumbfounded.

That night, after many days of unbearable tension, we had a peaceful night of sound sleep in Pajule. But the Pandora's Box had just been opened, and the surprises were not yet over.

The following day, one of our contact persons arrived in Pajule with a pretty 17-year-old girl called Betty. When we sat down with them, he pulled out a letter from his pocket. It was signed by Tabuley and he asked us to take care of the girl and to look for her parents. He also wanted her to be tested for HIV.

It was clear to us that Betty was immersed in a state of complete mental confusion, which gave us an idea of how deep the brainwashing suffered by the abducted children was. She could not stop repeating again and again that she wanted to go back to Kony. She assured us that the angels from heaven had descended to boost the rebels' morale and instructed them to go on fighting until they had overthrown the government. We feared that she could take advantage of any moment in which we let down our guard to escape back to the bush, so we put her in a car and drove to Gulu, where we hoped to find her parents.

When we reached the archbishop's residence we had supper together, gave Betty a room to sleep in and let her rest for the night. It did not take us very long to locate her parents, who were excited and overjoyed when we broke the news to them that their daughter was alive and well. Soon, however, their joy turned into immense grief.

I realised then that in many cases an early encounter between parents and their returned abducted children could be counter-productive unless both parents and children were given counselling first. Without any warning, the psychological shock could be brutal. It had been five years since Betty had been kidnapped by the LRA from her home village. After such an experience she was not the same innocent and charming little girl any more. Her parents did not believe their ears when she described, in an angelical and animated voice how she had taken part in deadly attacks against her own community. Forcing abductees to perpetrate heinous crimes against their own villages and communities was a satanic tactic Kony used to make the children sever ties with their places of origin.

> "I did not like to kill people using a machete, because the spirit of the slain man could come back to haunt me. But when I had to use the gun I really enjoyed it, because it was not me, but the gun that killed the people rejected by God. What I enjoyed more though was to see the blood flowing…"

When I heard this I interrupted Betty and told her parents that they would have plenty of time to be with her the following day. I went to the Caritas office and arranged for Betty to begin long-term counselling therapy to help her recover from her deep traumas.

Betty was just one of many of the returned abductees who needed counselling and other services when they left the LRA. We struggled to secure funding to help some of the children who were returning from the bush to continue with their studies. And the number of children was increasing by the day. Similarly, Pajule was becoming an important hub for our peace activities, and the quick succession of events was beginning to become overwhelming. Archbishop Odama and Bishop Ochola were busy, with frequent contacts with LRA top commanders Tolbert Nyeko and Sam Kolo. They also kept President Museveni constantly updated. Our group of religious leaders met frequently to compare notes and coordinate our actions. We felt that we were making progress and that our work was making a lot of sense.

After spending a few days in Gulu I returned to Pajule.

It was not yet 10 o'clock in the morning when I was stopped at Puranga, the southern gate to Acholiland through Pader district. Crowds of anxious villagers were moving up and down along the road. They informed me that before dawn they heard loud explosions coming from the Acolpii refugee camp, some 40 kilometres away. Since 1993 Acolpii was home to approximately 20,000 Sudanese refugees. In July 1996 it had been attacked by the LRA, who massacred more than one hundred people. Before this event, some UN officials had not liked the idea of setting up a camp in a dangerous war zone, but in the end the thousands of Sudanese who had fled the war in the south of their country were placed in the camp as there was no other option.

After waiting for a short while, I continued on my journey to Pajule. For the next 20 kilometres I did not see a single person on the road, only thick bush on either side. I started to feel scared. When I finally reached the next inhabited centre, Rackoko, I was stopped at a military roadblock where I was told that I could not proceed any further.

As I came out of the car, I saw a tragic picture in front of me. Columns of thousands of terrified people were advancing towards Rackoko, from the east. Most of them had nothing in their hands. A few of them had managed to flee carrying a few belongings including old saucepans, blankets, plastic sheets and empty jerrycans. Some desperate women wept while they told of how they had left their babies and small children behind. They did not know whether these children were alive or dead now.

A few days earlier, the rebels had sent a warning letter to the military in Acholpii, warning people of their intention to launch an attack, but the army had not taken the warning seriously. The LRA group, led by Tabuley, had launched a pre-dawn attack soon after. After chasing away the few soldiers stationed there, the rebels had burnt down the UPDF barracks and killed 60 Sudanese refugees. On the day following the attack, a picture was published in the newspaper of a dead Sudanese mother with her live baby still strapped to her back, amidst the smouldering burnt huts of the camp. This picture touched the hearts of many who still looked at the war in the north as a distant affair that did not concern them.

I spent four days between Pajule and Kitgum, where day after day the number of displaced people who had fled their villages for the relative safety of the town increased. They did not receive help from anyone except their already impoverished relatives in the slums of Kitgum. One morning I went to greet the women who ran a reception centre for abducted children called KICWA (Kitgum Concerned Women's Association), a local NGO that was started in 1998. There, among the recently arrived children, I met a 15-year old boy who told me that he had seen me during the meeting with Tabuley in Koyo Lalogi. He said that after we left, Tabuley gave orders to leave the place immediately without collecting the sacks of beans and maize flour that we had brought for them. They feared that the food had been poisoned.

On my journey back to Gulu, on 8th August, I still found plenty of Sudanese refugees trekking along the road towards Lira, carrying some of their belongings on their heads. Three days had passed since the deadly attack on the camp, and the people I saw from my car were the elderly, weak and sick. I experienced a great sadness when I stopped and could offer only four of them a ride to town. As soon as I reached Lira I went to the offices of UNHCR and pleaded with them to send some lorries to collect those unfortunate people. After checking with me about the security situation they assured me that they would.

Two days later, Rwot Oywak called me late in the evening to tell me that they had just received a letter signed by rebel commander Raska Lukwiya. The letter asked us to collect some more women and children the following day. We wasted no time and Archbishop Odama and I went to the barracks immediately to get assurance of safe passage when we went to pick up the abducteees. Col. Gutti assured us that we could go safely.

Once again I left very early in the morning. When I reached Pajule, at 10 o'clock, a big group of women and children was already seated on the verandah of the mission eating porridge. I noted with happiness that the girls serving the steaming bowls to the new arrivals were the very girls we had brought out of the bush a few days earlier, led by Monica.

The new group of returned abductees consisted of 64 women and 30 small children. For Caritas it was a real struggle to provide decent accommodation, food, medical services and counselling to the 160 vulnerable people who had landed at the mission during the past few days.

On 23nd August, a much-awaited political breakthrough came. In the evening, President Museveni arrived in the studio of the recently opened Radio Mega FM in Gulu. There he read a statement expressing his readiness to declare a one-week suspension of military activities in certain areas in order to facilitate peace contacts, so long as the rebels stopped their acts of violence against the population and released all children recently abducted. He mentioned the names of some areas he was proposing for peace meetings. The most important part of his message was the list of several leaders who would form his "presidential peace team": Eriya Kategaya (the leader), Minister Gilbert Bukenya, Gen. Salim Saleh, Attorney General Francis Ayume, and MPs Betty Akech, Norbert Mao and Reagan Okumu. The team also included some members of the opposition. Museveni's announcement was welcomed with joy by the population in the north.

The following day, in the midst of that atmosphere of optimism, I wrote an article for publication in *The Daily Monitor*, in which I recalled our experience one year earlier with Onekomon. My article also defended the peaceful option as the best way to end the war.

Two days later I accompanied Archbishop Odama and Bishop Ochola to another meeting at Gulu barracks with General James Kazini. Kazini insisted that we should convey to the rebels the message that they should stop abducting children and shooting at vehicles on the roads. It was the only way to make the peace process succeed.

At the end of that meeting Odama and Ochola proceeded to Langol for another meeting with LRA commanders Nyeko and Kolo. That evening Fr. Tarcisio called me from Kitgum to say that he had just made another appointment with the rebel commander Captain Topaco, whom he had met the year before in the bush. Tarcisio had contacted the military authorities in Kitgum, to ensure that our meeting was in order and there would be no problem. I was pleased to learn that my friend Giulio Albanese had just landed in Kampala and intended to arrive in Gulu the following day. Tarcisio wanted Giulio and myself to come with him for the meeting with the rebels that he had set for 28th August.

When Archbishop Odama returned from his meeting in the bush I told him everything about Tarcisio's phone call and our plans. He was happy to hear about these plans and he told me not to miss such an opportunity.

Things were moving. But future events were going to get in the way of our intended direction.

5

The Trap of Tumangu

The morning of 27th August was a hectic one. Fr. Giulio arrived at around 10 am when I happened to be in a meeting with Archbishop Odama and Bishop Ochola. We were busy preparing a working document to take to the president, who Odama and Ochola were going to meet soon to have a meeting. A great feeling of optimism and freedom came over me as we prepared for the appointment we had made with the rebels for the following day. Before I left for Kitgum, I had a final consultation with the archbishop, who encouraged me to go ahead with the meeting with the LRA in Kitgum. Fr. Tarcisio and Fr. Giulio were also to attend it.

Before I left I met with Rwot Oywak, who gave me a letter from Kacoke Madit in London. The letter was signed by its coordinator, Dr. Patrick Oguru Otto, and addressed to LRA commander Charles Tabuley. Written in Acholi, the letter encouraged the LRA to attend peace negotiations and stop all acts of violence, particularly ambushes and abductions; the contents were in line with what we wanted to tell the rebels face to face.

The next day Fr. Giulio and I travelled to Kitgum by road and arrived at around 3 pm. I was rather tired and decided to spend the afternoon at the mission while Tarcisio and Giulio went to meet with the resident district commissioner (RDC), Okot Lapolo, who gave them a personal letter for the LRA.

Fr. Tarcisio told me he had met with two UPDF intelligence officers and the RDC the morning before. The RDC had told him that everything was in order for us to meet the rebels and that they had no objection to supplying Topaco, an LRA commander, with a course of antibiotics.

That night I could not sleep, for I was so excited. I was about to attend my third meeting with the LRA, and as usual it looked as though I would spend the night before in a state of vigil, as though the lack of sleep prepared me to be better disposed to enter the unreal world of the rebels.

The next morning I rose before dawn, went for prayers in the church, and had a spare breakfast. Afterwards I headed straight to the parish office where some people were already waiting. Such is the beginning of a normal morning in a rural African Catholic Mission. The liturgy of that day, 28th August, was in honour of St. Augustine.

One of the first visitors to the parish office of Kitgum Mission that day was "Brown", a man from the military intelligence who had worked in Kitgum since the early days of the NRA, in 1986. He had come to see Fr. Tarcisio to say that he was well aware of our intended meeting with the LRA in the area of Tumangu, some 15 kilometres from Pajimu, and that everything was in order.

Soon after, our catechist Franco Okello came by bicycle. He worked as a catechist in Alone, a small village located 25 kilometres from Kitgum, deep in the bush. I knew his village well since I had been there many times during the nine-year period I had spent in the Kitgum Mission. I always felt a great fascination for the scattered homesteads of the African bush, where friendly and simple people stick to their traditional culture, have plenty of time to talk and welcome visitors as a blessing from above.

Franco Okello had been the contact person between Fr. Tarcisio and Topaco. Okello, like most peasants who lived in remote settlements in Northern Uganda, lived between two fires. He and his family did not want to abandon their home and their land to end up languishing in one of the displaced people's camps where, at that time, more than one million destitute refugees sank in a hole of emptiness, desperate and lacking essentials. But that choice meant having to live at the mercy of gangs of cruel rebels who arrived unexpectedly and committed all sorts of atrocities. Often, after the rebels invaded, it was the patrols of government soldiers who harassed and threatened them.

Two weeks earlier, when some LRA fighters commanded by Topaco came to Okello's homestead, the young commander entered Okello's hut unceremoniously and noticed a good number of religious books. After declaring that he was a catechist, Topaco said:

"Do you know Fr. Tarcisio?"

"Of course," Okello answered. "He is my parish priest. "

Topaco then scribbled a letter to Tarcisio asking for a dose of drugs for his personal use. The young commander still had memories of that meeting in the bush the year before, when he met with the old missionary near Pajule. This is how the connection between the priest and the rebel came about. Coincidentally, on Sunday 25th August Fr. Tarcisio encountered some rebels as he was travelling to Kitgum Matidi to celebrate mass. One of the rebels fired a shot in the air and Tarcisio stopped and courageously talked to him. Tarcisio took the opportunity to ask the rebel to go and confirm with Topaco that they could meet on Wednesday morning at Okello's home.

On the day of the meeting, as we waited, Okello told us that when he left his home some two hours earlier there was no sign of any LRA movements nearby. This meant nothing, since rebels would often turn up unexpectedly, when they were totally sure that the people they wanted to meet were in close proximity and it was safe for them. We then boarded a pickup vehicle from the mission and set off. Soon afterwards we set out for the meeting place.

Once again there I was, in the back of Tarcisio's pickup, talking to Okello. Tarcisio was in front with Giulio. About 12 kilometres later we reached Pajimu trading centre and branched west towards Alone Primary School. We took the narrow track only taken by villagers on foot or by bicycle. We had hardly driven one kilometre when we found a UPDF road block. We stopped. We were absolutely convinced that everything was in order and that we had followed the right procedures, so we had no problem talking to the two soldiers standing there. We answered all their questions and repeated over and over that we were attending a meeting with the LRA near Alone Primary School and that we were taking some drugs, dry cells and two letters to the rebels. We also had some recent newspapers and two digital cameras with us to take pictures of the meeting if we had a chance. After being showered with the same questions again and again and wondering whether it was a technique the soldiers learned at military academies for whatever purpose, the two soldiers told us that we could proceed. Our appointment was set for eleven, so we were in so much of a hurry, afraid to miss this chance, that we did not realise that the soldiers had taken our plastic bag containing the drugs and dry cells.

Some twelve kilometres later we reached Alone Primary School, a simple building that had been abandoned a few months earlier when children had stopped attending lessons because of insecurity. The road we were taking ended near the school, and we continued until the track became too rough for our vehicle. We stopped, left the car and proceeded on foot. After a few minutes of walking, we met Santina, Okello's wife, who told us that she was going to the market and that so far she had not seen Topaco, but that she had heard that a group of LRA rebels were in the house near their homestead. We parted from Santina and continued on our way until we reached the house of another man. He quietly pointed at some trees in the distance.

"They are there," the man said, "I heard they arrived this morning. I can escort you."

The man lived in the village called Tumangu, a name that in Acholi means "the beast's sacrifice". Little did we suspect that something that matched that name was about to take place.

I was so afraid that we would miss our appointment that I hurriedly followed the footpath and walked ahead of the man from Tumangu, while Tarcisio and Giulio followed at a distance. We encountered two armed young boys in military fatigues that were too big for their small bodies. They pointed their guns at us and ordered us to stop and to sit down on the ground. They asked who we were.

"We are three priests." I said "Our names are Tarcisio, Giulio and Carlos and we have an appointment with commander Topaco."

"Are you carrying any guns?" asked one of the boys.

"We do not have any weapons."

The boys ordered the man accompanying us to remove our bags and leave them on the ground near them. After one of them finished inspecting them he looked satisfied.

"Are you coming with any soldiers?"

"No," I said, "it's only the three of us and one catechist."

We were ordered to stand up and follow them. After a few metres we came across a scene all too familiar and sad in Acholi: about 20 young boys in uniform and armed with guns, held several groups of terrified women and children captive. They may have been abducted that very morning, but we were unsure. They all seemed very surprised to see us, but one of them broke the silence and said that he remembered seeing us the month before during the meeting with commander Tabuley. Among the captives we also met Matthew Obote, also a catechist from the Kitgum Mission, who forced a smile when we came to greet him. There was no sign of Topaco and we started to suspect that we had happened upon his group of rebels by accident. Nevertheless, we took our time to move around cordially greeting everyone one by one, despite the fact that not one of them made any effort to respond to our extended hands.

Three of the rebels who seemed to be the ones in charge told us to come closer. Somebody brought several folding chairs for us and set them under the generous shade of a big mango tree. When Tarcisio explained that Matthew was also one of our catechists he was allowed to sit with us.

They seemed to be rather mystified by this unexpected encounter. Tarcisio, displaying his usual friendly manners, asked them to begin the meeting with a prayer, which he led. Then we introduced ourselves. They did not tell us their names, but a few days later we came to understand that we had been in front of self-styled Lieutenant-colonel Francis Oyat Lapaico, who would be captured by the Ugandan army four years later.

Maybe because I am a slow learner, and so many years in Africa have not taught me that it is a good idea to begin slowly and talk somewhat casually at the beginning of a meeting or conversation, I went straight into the business we wanted to attend to and asked them whether they were aware of the president's message broadcast on Mega FM five days earlier. They said that they had heard something about it but that they were not very sure what the president had said. Then I continued and told them that we were at a very critical moment and that it was essential to stop acts of violence in order to have a real ceasefire and allow peace dialogues to take off. In this respect, I told them, the LRA must end abductions and ambushes.

Then Lapaico spoke. The coldness of his speech, combined with the fact that he stuttered, created in me a fear of being in front of a man ready to do anything. He said that Kony had ordered them to suspend all attacks and abductions, but that it was the government who did not want peace because it followed them constantly with combat helicopters and foot-patrols. His threats, pronounced with sharp jerks, were menacing.

> "We-e wa-ant pe-eace…," he stammered, "but if Mu-useve-eni does not wa-ant pe-eace, we-e shall no-ot leave any-ybo-ody a-ali-ive…"

When he finished his angry remarks I opened my mouth to say something, but I could not even begin a word as the first gunshot rang out a short distance behind us.

In less than a second I saw fear in Lapaico's face, and all the rebels picked up their guns as quick as lighting and darted out of the compound, running for their lives, and leaving no trace of themselves.

Then all hell broke loose.

In an instant, and all around us, there was an all-out barrage of gunfire, explosions, and bullets flying above our heads. The noise was deafening. I threw myself on the ground feeling numb and confused. My first thought was to stand up and run. Hardly had I started flexing my muscles than I was stopped by the thought that I could not possibly run faster than bullets. Tarcisio and Giulio were in a better position, down on the ground and behind the big tree but I found myself exposed in a place that had no protection, at the mercy of the endless gunfire that came from an advancing line of government soldiers.

I realised I was next to the man who had guided us to that village. Like snakes biting the dust, both of us dragged ourselves to a nearby hut and went in. Then a second thought came to me. The hut's thatched roof could easily catch fire and fall on us. No sooner had we come out of the hut than it burst into flames. The burning dry grass fell everywhere around us, making me feel an unbearable choking, dusty heat. Not knowing what to do next, I felt helpless, closed my eyes and waited for the worst to happen.

Then I saw the deepest darkness in front of me. Never in my life have I been so struck by grief. I was convinced that a bullet would hit me any moment and my only worry was whether my death would be slow and painful or instantaneous. My thoughts took me by surprise and I found myself doubting the existence of the hereafter. Why did God not do something to stop all of this violence? Did God really exist anyway? I do not know how much time all that lasted, but it seemed endless to me. The noise was so deafening that I stopped hearing or seeing anything. I did not even realise that my right elbow was burnt and that tiny spots of blood dotted my neck, back and arms. The shower of shrapnel had mercifully missed me, only leaving a scratch mark.

When I finally opened my eyes I saw the soldiers advancing towards me while the gunfire continued. I raised my hand and one of them signalled to me to drag myself slowly towards the tree where my two companions had taken cover.

The gunfire was still going on, although it was beginning to die out. I noticed that Tarcisio had his rosary in his hand. With his eyes closed he was praying, half in Italian, half in Acholi, and throwing in some Hail Marys with an interesting variation.

"Holy Mary, Mother of God, pray for us sinners, now and in the hour of our death," he was saying, "but let my death be another day!"

Giulio pointed at my head and told me that my face had become dark as charcoal and that my hair was charred.

A few soldiers strode towards us with rather unfriendly faces.

"Who are you?" they asked "What the hell are you doing here?"

"We are priests, and we were here for a peace meeting" we responded.

One of the soldiers removed my blue bag in which I had a digital camera, my notebook, three newspapers, some religious books and two letters (the one from RDC Lapolo and the one from Kacoke Madit). When I told him that the contents were mine he assured me that I would get the bag back later.

Another soldier shouted angrily.

"Stay with your face down. Do not raise your head!"

He cocked his gun while he pointed it at us.

I could not stand it any more and I shouted.

"Please, no..!"

He came closer and yelled.

"No what?"

Then he jumped on the three of us, one by one, kicking us on the back with his strong boots. When he finished, as though he wanted to carry home a souvenir, he pulled out his camera and took our photo. It was not the first time I had seen soldiers on military operations carrying pocket cameras. This soldier could one day boast in front of some friends in a bar how he had captured three priests in the bush. He would even be able to add that he had caught us red-handed in the company of terrorists.

But what I saw next hurt me much more than the kicks that we had just received. Some soldiers took a group of women and children out of a hut and started beating them with sticks as they shouted at them.

"Did we not tell you to leave this place and go to the displaced camp? You are too stubborn..."

They were abducted by the rebels at dawn that very day, then beaten up and abused a few hours later by the very soldiers who were supposed to protect them. Such was the life of ordinary people in this forgotten corner of the world. We could not stand it any more and the three of us shouted loudly to the soldiers asking them to leave those poor people alone. Then one of the soldiers removed our watches and my glasses. He dug into his pocket and, with an air of triumph, waved a small box of drugs in front of us.

"Where is the terrorist for whom you were carrying these medicines?"

The little box he waved was the one we had carried for Topaco. We realised that it had been removed from our car at the roadblock two hours earlier. Then it dawned on us that the roadblock had been part of the snare laid to trap us. We had revealed all the details of our plan to the military, trusting them, and they had taken advantage of our lack of malice. It was only too easy for them to follow us and use us as a bait in a raid against the LRA.

After some few minutes they ordered us to stand.

"If you run away we'll shoot you!"

I felt sorry to see the two catechists and two young men who had been abducted from that area earlier in the morning tied up with ropes. We tried to explain to the soldiers they were abductees and not rebels, but our efforts were in vain. The signaller picked up his walkie-talkie and radioed a message to their base.

"Sir, we have just captured four enemies."

I looked again at our two catechists and the two poor boys and I thought of the words of a certain American senator: "When war comes, the first casualty is truth." These words have become a blueprint for all conflicts. So, this was how the army spokesman could dispatch daily releases saying that the UPDF had captured or killed so many rebels.

I tried to gather my strength as we started the long march that awaited us. It was maybe midday when we took a bush path towards Pajimu. The hot sun accompanied us as we moved in two long lines. During the first half hour the soldiers – I counted about one hundred of them – walked slowly, as if fearing an ambush at any moment. Some of them scanned the horizon with their binoculars, looking for any sign of rebels. Each time they did this, they signalled for us to take cover and lie down on the ground. The tense waiting was unbearable.

We continued for about six hours. It was hot and we were beginning to feel thirsty. Some soldiers gave me water to drink from their canteens. My arm was getting swollen and was beginning to hurt, but I was more worried about my companions. Giulio, who had been suffering from kidney stones for many years, preferred not to take any water which may not have been very safe for him. Tarcisio, 68, and having undergone two heart by-pass surgeries already, had also undergone a major operation recently in which a part of his intestine and spleen had been removed.

Halfway through our march, two intelligence personnel came by motorcycle to talk to the soldiers.

Fr. Tarcisio asked for a lift but they refused. Then he stopped walking and sat under a tree next to the dirt road.

> "Get up and continue with us," one officer said. "If you remain here the rebels will take you."

His answer made them all the more upset.

> "Let them take me. At least they may treat me better than you!"

I was surprised to see this interaction between Tarcisio and the soldier. Despite everything we made an effort to talk and be friendly with the soldiers, even though some of them took every opportunity to mock and taunt us. Some even referred to us as "Al-Qaeda" terrorists. Others argued that it was a waste of time to talk peace with the rebels and that the only choice that remained was to kill them all one by one.

During our conversations with the soldiers, I found out that during the shootout a woman had been hit by a bullet in her head. The soldiers had left her bleeding at the compound. A few days later, when we were back in Kitgum, somebody told me that she had been collected by her husband, who carried her on his bicycle to the mission hospital where the doctors managed to save her life.

On our march, though, the sun was beginning to go down in the forested savannah when we reached Pajimu military barracks. The people who lived in the mud houses close by looked at us in silence. Two women, came to us with bowls of cool water. I drank it to the last drop. Giulio was still afraid to drink. He was wailing and gasping with excruciating pain in his kidneys.

Pajimu barracks was a cluster of metallic huts, called unipots, and mud shacks. Located on a hilltop, it was a privileged strategic point where soldiers could observe any movement from far off. We all sat on the ground, asking for more water in vain. As we waited, the man who had pointed his gun at us and jumped on our backs came to our two catechists and started slapping them. We shouted at him to leave them alone. He turned his back and went away.

Another soldier came with an old exercise book and told us to write a list of the personal items we carried in our bags that were still in their custody. I lost count of how many times we asked for water. They did not give us a single drop.

It was beginning to get dark when a green military vehicle arrived carrying two men in fatigues, both with the pips of captains. I knew one of them from some meetings I had attended with district officials. When I mentioned this to the one I recognised he did not even bother to answer. We were ordered to sit quietly when he told us to get into the vehicle.

We took the road to Kitgum at breakneck speed and after two kilometres we branched off and took the same narrow road we had taken that morning towards the forest. Then I felt the grip of fear. On that lonely road and at night, without any witnesses, anything could happen. And anything could be reported afterwards.

"What is this? Where are you taking us?" I demanded.

After a moment of uneasy silence, one of the soldiers in the car whispered that they were taking us to the place where we had left the vehicle. If that was true, it was tantamount to suicide. Giulio could not stand it any more and shouted at the top of his voice.

"Stop now! We are not going there!"

The driver stopped abruptly with a jerk. Giulio did not think twice, opened the door and stepped out. His determination made me shake. Tarcisio and I got out too.

The two officers looked surprised. I tried to calmly plead with them.

"Please, please. It is dark and, honestly, we have no interest in recovering the car. This can be very dangerous. Please, why can't you take us to the mission hospital?"

As I was talking, one of the officers took his camera and snapped a picture again. I thought that firms like Kodak, Nikon or Sony could increase their business if they did more publicity in military barracks in countries at war, and did not just focus on film and cameras for tourists on holidays.

I felt relieved when I saw the car turning around. We boarded it again and Tarcisio and Giulio started chatting in Italian about whether they had left some bottles of beer in the fridge that morning, and how RDC Okot Lapolo was going to hear their complaints. I remember that the day before I had brought a bottle of wine from Gulu, with the intention of opening it after the meeting with the rebels, but I suspected that we were going to drink neither beer, nor wine, nor anything at all that night.

As the car gathered more and more speed the dizziness I had been feeling melted and was replaced with dismay. My fears were confirmed when we drove past the corner where we should have made a turn to go to the mission. Instead, we took the bridge access to Kitgum town. This was definitely not the end of the nightmare. In fact, things had just started. Giulio went into a rage and shouted loudly at the soldiers, firing swear words in his native Roman dialect which, fortunately for all of us, the Ugandan officers could not understand.

We entered the military barracks located in a Kitgum suburb called Gang Dyang. There we were ordered to sit on the ground again. There were some other men, without shirts or shoes, accused of being rebel collaborators. Once again we pleaded in vain for water.

Next, we were ushered into a metallic shack. There was nothing inside but the bare dirty ground.

> "Excuse me, sir," I said to the soldier in the shack. "Are we under arrest?"
>
> "You are," he replied.
>
> "What is the charge against us?"
>
> "Our boss will tell you."

Another soldier came in, recorded our names and ordered us to remove our shirts, shoes and belts. When I removed my light shirt I realised that most of it was torn. I was overcome with fear, a feeling that up to that moment I had somehow managed to keep under control. I asked him again why we had been arrested.

> "Because you were in the wrong place, talking to the wrong people."

He went out and slammed the metal door, bolting it from the outside. Once again we implored the soldiers to bring us water. The answer we got was not very encouraging.

> "You pigs!" they shouted.

Giulio could not stop wailing in pain. Tarcisio seemed to have passed from his usual euphoria to a state of depression.

> "They will execute us by firing squad. At midnight. Let us give one another the absolution."

Not without some strange spark of humour, when I drew the sign of the cross on my companions' heads, I thought that God must have forgiven them already for having called me to Uganda the night I was at the Olympic port in Barcelona.

I was numb but the pain in my arm was just increasing. I tried to maintain a clear mind. Yes, we had been too naïve, and the soldiers had taken advantage of us, laid a trap and mistreated us, but I could not believe that they could kill us just like that. If that had been their plan they had had plenty of chances to do it earlier without any witnesses. At the same time, I was beginning to think that there was a part of the events we had not considered. There were some military officers who loathed the idea of negotiating peace with the rebels and they would try anything to end our efforts.

The metal hut we were in had a small window. Outside I made out the shape of a soldier. I dug into my pockets and I was surprised to find a 20,000 Ugandan shilling note.

> "My friend, we are badly off. Why don't you give us some water?"

His face came closer to the window until he almost touched mine. He whispered.

> "Our superior has given us orders not to give you any water."

I passed the note through the window bars and he silently gave us a plastic bottle containing 250 ml of mineral water. Each of us took a small sip, that left us worse off than before.

> "Take the empty bottle," I begged him, "please, give us more water."

But the soldier told us that he had no more water. I had just paid the equivalent of ten euro. Not even in the most luxurious hotel on earth would anyone pay so much money for a small amount of water.

None of us managed to sleep that night. Every time we asked the soldiers to let us out for our natural needs they told us to keep quiet. We had to do everything inside the hut. Tarcisio was getting dehydrated and started suffering from diarrhoea. Desperate, he hit the door, and one of the soldiers outside opened it angrily.

"What do you want, mzungu?"

"Please, let me go to the latrine."

"You have to wait. Wait for the order."

"Which order?"

The soldier pointed at a building, probably the officers' mess hall.

"The order comes from there!"

Tarcisio put his hands on his belly.

"But my order comes from here!"

The soldier slammed the door and bolted it again, and poor Tarcisio had no choice but to use the dirty floor inside our hut as his latrine.

When the first rays of daylight filtered through the hut's small window the next morning, we felt somehow relieved. But our thirst continued to torment us, making us feel weak as we wailed with even weaker voices. In war, everything is good that makes the enemy suffer and humiliated. We were perceived as part of the enemy.

"We do not have water here. There is only waragi!"

These retorts were met with laughter from their comrades.

At nine o'clock in the morning the metallic door opened. The air was unbearable and we were dehydrated. The night had been a real session of refined torture. Rather unwillingly, a soldier gave us a plastic jerrycan filled with water and a dirty cup. The three of us drank with anxiety, without stopping, until the soldier grabbed the container and locked us in again.

At ten o'clock we were summoned for questioning. They took us separately. The strong sun fell on us. We were barefooted. Giulio saw his shoes under a tree and put them on. Then the man in charge of the barracks, Major Kazoora, shouted at him.

> "Who told you to put on your shoes?" he asked "You are a prisoner. We are fed up with you!"

Our two catechists, Franco and Matthew, were also seated under the tree, waiting to be interrogated. When I came to greet them they told me that they were worried about us. When I told them that we were denied water the whole night they answered that they had suffered the same mistreatment, and they were beaten as well. Ordinary people in Northern Uganda suffered much more than us.

Seated under a tree, some security operatives asked us to make our statement. They recorded our words with an exasperating slowness, and I found myself talking to them as a teacher who dictates the lesson for primary schoolchildren.

It was midday when RDC Okot Lapolo turned up in his car. He was the one who had given us a personal letter for the rebels. When we started talking to him he cut us short and said that he had something urgent to do in his office and that he would come back. He sent his driver to buy some cakes and sodas for us, but we never saw him again.

We were wondering what would happen next when a big military chopper landed at the barracks and we were ordered to board it.

I have always felt a lot of curiosity about helicopters, but in those circumstances the thing I fancied less than anything was getting into one of them. The aircraft was loaded with ammunition boxes and bombs but there was still some space for us to sit. I noticed that the two pilots were of much lighter skin, which could have meant that they were either Arabs, or Eastern European or from only God knew where. Mercenaries perhaps? The two doors were open and at each of them was a soldier with binoculars scanning the ground below, looking for possible signs of rebels, and another military man with his hands ready to operate a heavy machine gun. I prayed with all my strength that no combat would start as we were being carried to Gulu barracks.

Once we landed we were taken to a room. A captain came and took our order for lunch before going to one of the hotels in Gulu to look for our choice of meal. Interesting, I thought, since a few hours earlier we had been desperate, on our knees, begging for a glass of water and had been denied these requests. Now we were like VIPs being asked for our choice of food. I suspected that the "bad cop, good cop" strategy, often used to make prisoners soften their emotions, was about to begin.

Except for the few morsels of hard cake brought to us at the barracks in Kitgum, we had not had anything to eat for the last 24 hours and we could feel the pangs of hunger. When we finished our lunch we were taken to the office of the 4th division commander, Colonel Andrew Gutti. He was the first officer who treated us humanely and kindly. Next to him was Brig. Kale Kayihura, who had just arrived from Kampala. Answering their queries, we insisted that we had been on a peace mission with the rebels as part of the religious leaders' initiative to mediate in the conflict. We further explained that we had permission from the authorities in charge of security, as the Kitgum RDC's letter proved. Somebody brought my blue shoulder bag, but that letter (and everything else, including my digital camera), was no longer there. And, we were informed, the RDC had denied writing any letter for the rebels.

My feeling of being under the "bad cop, good cop" strategy intensified and I realised that after having gone through a near-death situation we were in a moment of great emotional vulnerability. First they kicked, threatened and humiliated us. Second they treated us with such an exquisite protocol, perhaps to encourage us to say what "they" wanted us to say and, finally, when they released us, we would come out of captivity bowing down and warmly thanking them for having allowed us to live.

But we also wanted to make it crystal clear that we would never give up in our struggle for peace. I got the impression that in the UPDF there were some top officers who were in favour of negotiating, but there were also some others whose only aim was to finish the war by "killing the enemy up to the last man". I wonder if they ever thought that when they were "wiping out the terrorists" many innocent children who had been abducted died too. And it could not be ignored that, as it happens in nearly all wars, there were some army officers who clearly benefited from the situation by making money from it. For a good number of years the Ugandan press reported on the much talked-about case of the "ghost soldiers", which filled the pockets of some big army men with salaries of non-existent servicemen. Also, ever since the Iron Fist operation had started in Sudan some army lorries regularly carried a most unusual cargo: big logs of valuable teak trees from the forests of Eastern Equatoria, just across the Ugandan border. The Acholi Inn, Gulu's best and most upmarket hotel was undergoing serious renovation after being bought by Colonel Charles Otema, chief of the military intelligence in the north. On one occasion, when I happened to share a glass of beer with a United Nations official with much experience, he told me:

"I have worked in many conflict zones in four continents and in every town at the epicentre of a war you invariably always see the best hotel being owned by some big military officer."

Since my arm was still in pain and swollen, I was taken to the military hospital inside Gulu barracks. The nurse who treated me and bandaged my skin burns told me that she had met me in 1986.

The captain who had brought us lunch said that they were preparing a room for us to spend our second night. So, we were still prisoners after all, I thought. They were treating us well, yes, but we were undoubtedly not yet free men.

That evening we received a visit that cheered our spirits. Mgr. Matthew Odong, vicar general of the archdiocese of Gulu, Fr. Cyprian Ochen, with whom I worked in the office of the Justice and Peace Commission, Sister Dorine Tadiello and Bro. Elio Croce, from Lacor Hospital, came to see us. Politely but firmly, they made it very clear from the very beginning that they would not leave without us. The presence of these dear companions gave us a much needed sign of hope. The messy situation we found ourselves in was not the result of a personal adventure of ours, but the consequence of having been faithful to the church's work for peace among the suffering people.

As it was getting dark we were still receiving contradictory messages. First an officer told us that they were going to prepare a room for us to spend the night. Then, after a while, another man in uniform told us that we could spend the night in the Catholic mission so long as we reported back to the barracks the following day.

Around nine in the evening we were taken to the office of Maj. Gen. James Kazini, the army commander. With him was Brig. Aronda Nyakairima, commander-in-chief of the Iron Fist operation who smiled the whole time but did not say a word. Kazini insisted that we should have sought permission from the 4th Division Commander in Gulu before meeting the rebels in the bush. He handed us a statement to sign. The document stated that we had not followed the right procedure and that we had not informed the UPDF. We were also strongly cautioned not to act in that way again. We answered that Fr. Tarcisio had informed the UPDF in Kitgum, but to our surprise, Maj. Gen. Kazini told us that the authorities in Kitgum had denied granting us permission for the meeting.

In the statement there was no apology for the dirty attack that could have ended our lives, or for the way we had been tortured the night before by being denied water to drink.

Once again, I found myself in a most stressful situation: deeply traumatised and confused, in pain and fearful of what I could face once we were out of the barracks, including deportation from the country. I found it repugnant to sign that statement, but I was also worried that the whole peace process would be in jeopardy if we did not. We struggled to keep our cool and mumbled that we would have preferred the statement to be put in a different way. However, we had not been called there to negotiate the contents of the statement. Instead we either signed or rejected the statement. We could not foresee the consequences of either decision.

No sooner had we signed the statement than we were told that we were free. Our companions took us to Lacor and that night I had the most delicious cool beer of my life, and probably the deepest sleep too.

Before leaving, Maj. Gen. Kazini had offered us a lift to Kitgum by helicopter to collect our belongings. The following morning, after a change of bandage for my arm, we returned to the barracks. Some people tried to advise us against doing this, assuming we were naïve enough to walk into the trap again. Despite everything, however, I have always felt that the UPDF deserved some trust and up until then I had never thought that there was any plot to kill us. Maybe to discourage us or to scare us, but not to end our lives.

As we passed through Gulu town, we could see the newspaper headlines of the day: "Army arrests three white priests".

I hurriedly bought *The New Vision,* the government owned paper, and was angered by the way they reported our story. The army spokesman, Captain. Shaban Bantariza, stated that I had been detained by an army patrol when I was found driving a vehicle carrying three armed rebels and transporting "an amazingly huge amount of drugs". He also affirmed that I had three communication systems for the LRA. I called the paper to deny the allegations.

I also gathered some more interesting information from the local papers. The day we were detained (28th August), *The daily Monitor* had published a lengthy article written by President Museveni in which, using rather tough language, he rejected an article I had written a few days earlier in favour of peace talks.

"Fr Carlos' arguments, like the ones of all pacifists, are erroneous and induce confusion," he wrote.

For a good number of people, the fact that our detention and the publication of that article happened on the same day was not a coincidence. Despite everything we went through, I personally am still inclined to believe that it was.

But what worried me most was a line in the *New Vision* that stated that "some official sources spoke of a possible deportation of the missionaries". It was indeed a serious possibility and not to be taken lightly. For some years after I was going to live almost permanently with that fear and it was going to affect me more than I could have thought.

We entered Gulu barracks, but this time not as prisoners. We were greeted cordially and with smiles. We boarded the helicopter to Kitgum, chatting more casually and in a more relaxed way with the very soldiers who had treated us with mistrust the day before.

It was like being born again into the world. Never before had I enjoyed so much the small things of everyday life: breathing fresh air, sleeping in a bed, feeling the water of a shower fall on my back, drinking cool fresh juice, chatting with friends. It was as though everything was new. During the next several months, however, I would have to undertake a hard struggle against a new enemy: post-traumatic stress disorder. I began to suffer from unexpected fears, nightmares, sudden headaches and depressions which started to take their toll on me. Even years later, in Madrid, I have found myself waking up in the middle of the night agitated and bathed in sweat after dreaming that I was being chased by a gunman from Puerta del Sol to Gran Via.

One or two days after our experience Giulio and Tarcisio boarded a small plane fleeted by the Italian Embassy and left for Kampala. Giulio went back to Italy, where he continued working as director of MISNA for several years, letting the world know what was going on in Northern Uganda. Tarcisio remained in Kampala for a much-needed rest. Despite the fact that I am not Italian, the people of the embassy were very kind to offer me a seat in the same plane. I declined the offer even though I was in great need of rest.

But things were not over for us, particularly not for me. Almost every day somebody was pumping out negative propaganda against me in the media. A government official who had previously been an RDC in Gulu referred to me as "a thug with a cross" and made up a most interesting biography about me, saying that I was a deserter from the Spanish army, where I was once a sergeant, who came to East Africa as "a soldier of fortune". Radio Simba promoted me to the rank of colonel with some rebel group in Spain. I sensed that if I left Gulu at that time, some people would say that I was quitting. So, I simply tried to prove them wrong by being more stubborn than they were and by going on with my daily work as normally as possible.

The day after we were released was a Saturday. I spent the whole morning writing down everything I had gone through. After midday I was happy to meet Archbishop John Baptist Odama, who had just returned from Kampala. I had enough time to tell him everything that had happened in detail. From the beginning I knew that he supported us. Two days later, as the campaign of lies against us, headed by the army spokesman, was in full swing, the archbishop published a press release in which he defended us and said that we had acted in a correct manner. Most importantly he made it clear that we were not going to abandon the peace process because of what had happened.

On Sunday I went to my parish in Minakulu, 30 kilometres south of Gulu. I was wearing a bandage on my right arm, which was still hurting, but I managed to drive along the lonely road. The gospel of that Sunday included Jesus' words: "He who wants to come with me, let him deny himself, carry his cross and follow me." I have always stuck to the custom of writing the main ideas of my homily, but with so much hassle that Sunday, I had no time. I needed no notes, though, since I had a sermon written on my body. I celebrated mass in Minakulu and in the displaced people's camp of Bobi. I looked straight into the eyes of my congregation and realised that the events of those last few days had taught me more than I would have learnt in many years. I gained new insight into the daily suffering of the people I had come to minister to and who attended the church services to find words of consolation and encouragement. I have never felt as united with them as I did during those glorious days.

When I took the road back to Gulu I came across two tanks moving along the road. I pulled over to the side to let them pass. A few minutes later I heard several loud explosions and, with my body shuddering all over, I relived the hell of Tumangu.

6
Listen to God

"When I am in Spain during holidays and I hear fireworks I get very nervous, I get scared and the first thought that comes to my mind is to throw myself to the ground and look for cover."

"I see. And does that prevent you from having a normal life?"

"Eeh… Not really. No, I do not go to parties very often, anyway."

"Keep going. Would you like to tell me more?"

"And when I walk through a very open field, a flat plain I panic and I can't stand it… I think that is called agoraphobia…"

"Right. I ask you the same question. Does that prevent you from having a normal life?"

"Certainly not."

"Then there is no reason for you to worry."

Tom, the German psychologist working for Caritas, who had helped us so much when we organised the counselling centre of Pajule, had been listening to me patiently for two hours. When he finally took the time to make some remarks, he told me that putting in writing everything I had gone through in that traumatic experience with the UPDF, as I had done, had certainly been an important factor in helping me take control of the situation, and not become a "victim". It had helped me to overcome the trauma. He assured me that many people who go through similar experiences close themselves off from the trauma completely and do not talk about how they feel or what they experienced, and this always has negative consequences that can return even years later.

Tom was surprised when I told him that so far I could sleep well and without nightmares, although he cautioned me not to be too confident since, after, some weeks, I was likely to begin having problems sleeping. He told me that when people go through "near-death" experiences, they can overcome the trauma better if they have strong motivation to do so and if they enjoy the support of good friends. There was no doubt that I was very fortunate. During the previous few days I had received numerous visits from many good friends who came to show sympathy for me. If I walked down the streets of Gulu, people I had never met would stop me and embrace me warmly. These acts moved me deeply, since many of them had surely passed through trials much harder than mine. Even the LRA commander Sam Kolo called me one evening to ask about my health. Although I was surrounded by all this support, Tom also told me not to let down my guard and insisted that I should be on the alert about situations and persons that could make me feel anxious.

Indeed, the more difficult moments would come after a few months when, for a period of about two years, I would learn a lesson the hard way: that discouragement, threats and feelings of being betrayed can hurt deep inside much more than grenade explosions. When I started noticing the first symptoms I considered the possibility of undergoing therapy at a centre for victims of war trauma outside Uganda, but the day I met the director of the centre, a priest from the United Kingdom, I changed my mind. As I chatted informally about my near-death experience at Tumangu, his comment was that he was pretty sure I had thought of committing suicide. I was surprised and told him that sincerely speaking many thoughts had passed through my mind but not that one. The man insisted, telling me that a few years earlier he had worked in Sudan in circumstances very similar to mine and that he had come close to taking his life. Shrugging my shoulders, I asked him whether he had ever tasted Rioja wine from Spain. Poor man, I thought, living in such cold weather without ever enjoying the warmth of the sun and without ever tasting Rioja wine (he told me that he was a pioneer) no wonder he had such desperate thoughts. Life, with all its complexities and even with its unsolvable problems, has wonderful moments that consist of good friends, beautiful places, great music and books, all of which cheer up our drooping spirits and make us feel God's blissful presence. And there are times when some of the most tragic situations can be transformed into new beautiful stages of life that spring up and bloom.

"Do exercise regularly," Tom advised me.

I nodded and I have since taken this piece of advice very seriously.

"And go on doing your work. The work we do helps us take control of difficult situations, so that we do not go adrift being tossed around by circumstances."

This was an interesting reflection and very perceptive, especially coming from a German psychologist. Maybe if I had followed therapy with, say a Brazilian psychologist, he may have given me some other not less useful instructions, like samba dancing or vacationing on some tropical beach, certainly something more rewarding.

Those days I realised that I had to make extra efforts to be the master of my life and the circumstances that surrounded it. It was not easy, especially keeping in mind that every day I had to listen to many well-intentioned people, who had no shortage of good "advice" which often made me doubt everything: you must leave Uganda immediately or you'll be a dead man before next week; go away for a few months until things cool down; go to Kampala and hide yourself there for a while; remain in Gulu but sleep in a different place every day; give up the peace work; remain in Gulu but stay indoors always and do not go to the Parish because you'll be shot on the way…

If I had paid attention to each and every thing I heard I would have truly run mad.

But the hardest part of the whole situation was what I had to read about myself in the newspapers almost daily. After Archbishop Odama published his press release supporting us, the army spokesman responded in his usual defamatory style calling us liars. Some letters sent to the government owned newspaper *(New Vision)* asked for our deportation, and the Soroti RDC referred to me as "a thug with a cross".

In the meantime, and like a ship sailing through a rising storm despite the troubled waters, we continued with the fragile peace process, which was showing its first signs of stagnation. We wrote letters to the president and to the rebels, begging them to make extra efforts to overcome their mutual mistrust and to come back to the exchange of communication, lest the flickering flame of hope for peace be put out.

But things were not getting any better. On 14th September we heard rumours that Opit Catholic Mission had been attacked early that morning. Apparently, the rebels had stormed Opit in a pre-dawn attack and abducted scores of children who had sought refuge in the church. When the two Italian priests came out to plead with the rebels, they were taken too. One of them, Fr. Ponsiano Velluto, had been in the north of Uganda for more than 40 years and this was his third time to be kidnapped by the LRA. As for his companion, Fr. Alex Pizzi, this was his fourth time, and this time he was abducted in his pyjamas.

The man who commanded the rebel group, Okot Odiambo, took them a few kilometres inside the bush and made them talk by radio with Kony who, as usual after a brutal attack showed his best face and insisted that he greatly trusted the mediation of the religious leaders.

Kony said he wanted Archbishop Odama to continue the process, and to involve Cardinal Wamala and even the Pope. The fact that Kony claimed to have a direct hotline to his spirits made him flip back and forth between presenting himself with exquisite kindness one day and with cruelty beyond belief the next. This made him totally unpredictable. At the end of his radio communication with the priests he told Odiambo to release them, but Ponsiano and Alex put their feet down and made it absolutely clear that they would not leave without the children. In the end, most of the children were released with the missionaries.

That same day Sam Kolo called Archbishop Odama and made an appointment to meet him in the bush the following day. Kolo asked Odama to come with me. As usual, Odama contacted Colonel. Gutti, who assured him that everything was in order and we would be given safe passage.

Some of my friends told me that I was reckless to accept that rendezvous, but I must confess that I felt excited once again, like a child going to a birthday party, when I entered Odama's car and we took the road to Langol.

As we rode on, we were not surprised to meet people who constantly signalled for us to stop. Everyone in the area around Gulu knew the archbishop's car well. One of them literally stood still in front of us and raised his arms anxiously.

"Please, turn back immediately. Don't you know that the rebels are ahead?"

Of course we knew it, this was why we were going there, but we were not supposed to tell anyone.

"Thank you, my friend," we answered. "Just pray for us."

And we moved on.

Hardly anyone had used that road since the rebels had launched their violent backlash in June. Three months had passed and the grass was overgrown, preventing us from seeing anything beyond the narrow path in front of us. We reached a junction where the road was crossed by railway tracks. The train had stopped coming here at the beginning of the war in 1986. We turned right, wading through a sea of thick bush until the archbishop, who seemed very familiar with the area, pointed at a spot where the terrain rose. There we stopped the car. We got out cautiously and looked around, scanning the horizon but we did not see any sign of human presence.

We waited in silence for about half an hour. Nobody turned up and we started getting concerned. Slowly we opened the doors of the car, got in and started the engine.

Once we were back in Gulu, Archbishop Odama contacted the military, who answered him ambiguously. From what we gathered, it was not clear whether or not they had withdrawn their forces from that area. Most likely, if the rebels had smelled trouble, they did not risk coming close to a situation they could have detected as dangerous for them. Everything seemed to indicate that we had run a serious risk, and that we had simply been lucky this time.

During the following days the escalation of violence did not augur well for peace. One of the incidents that prompted more controversy took place in the Gulu prison where one evening a group of soldiers commanded by Colonel. Otema came to pick up some suspects accused of collaborating with the rebels. The suspects had been held for several days, waiting to be taken to court for trial. When the soldiers told them to board the lorry outside the prison, some of them resisted. In the scuffle that followed Colonel. Otema reportedly opened fire, killing one of them. The incident created a great deal of uneasiness among the civilian population who saw how, day after day, they were caught between two fires: the rebels and the military.

Three days later, during the night, in the downward spiral of tit-for-tat, scores of rebels entered the village of Pece Acoyo, five kilometres west of Gulu town, and took away fourteen men who were asleep in their homes. When they reached the main road they tied the men with ropes, made them lie face down and clubbed them to death. The next morning, the few travellers who ventured on that road found the men lying in a thick pool of coagulated blood.

That same day, Archbishop Odama was visited by two UPDF intelligence officers, who informed him that Kony had given orders to kill him. Odama, despite receiving multiple death threats, never accepted to have bodyguards or travel with armed escorts. Despite the obvious danger in which he lived he never showed the slightest sign of fear, tension or irritation. Thursday was his only day off in a very busy schedule, and he invariably spent it in long hours of prayer in the chapel of his residence.

During the afternoon I met with Tarcisio, who had just arrived from Kitgum and was on his way to Kampala for a medical check-up. He told me how he had met some terrified eyewitnesses from Tumangu who narrated to him how, on the day after our arrest, the UPDF had returned to the same village and attacked another rebel group. When the soldiers arrived, two schoolchildren from Palabek Gem who had been abducted a few days earlier by the LRA raised their hands, their small bodies shaking. The soldiers shot them dead at once. They were still wearing their school uniforms.

That very day we tried contacting the rebels to ask them for an explanation for the massacre of Pece Acoyo, but none of the numbers went through. None of the rebels bothered to call us either. Then we decided to try other ways of making our voices heard.

On 29th September 2002,we organised a demonstration that took us from Gulu town to the very spot of the massacre in Pece Acoyo. On the banner at the head of the group was written in English and Acholi: "Listen to God. You shall not kill!" This message would surely be provocative to the people who called themselves the Lord's Army, but who did exactly the opposite of what the Lord had commanded us to do.

Some intelligence officers tried to convince Archbishop Odama not to participate in the demostration, reminding him of Kony's death threats that were not to be taken lightly. But Odama was adamant that he be involved.

Some one thousand people walked the six kilometres to the spot of the massacre. There we prayed next to the big stains of blood still visible on the road. We visited the nearby homes to console the victims' families and we prayed beside their tombs. During his sermon, Archbishop Odama spoke loud and clear:

"I am making a new appeal to the government and the LRA to sit down and talk peace. Words cannot kill anybody. These must be the last human lives that we lose due to violence. If I do not say this here God will hold me accountable one day."

That very evening, Radio Mega FM broadcast a message - an ultimatum - from the UPDF addressed to all the population of Gulu, Kitgum and Pader districts. They were given a 48-hour deadline to vacate their homes and move to the displaced people's camps without delay.

"We have discovered that the terrorists use the people's homes to hide in the bush," went the release, clearly threatening the civilian population reluctant to obey the order. The UPDF's message made it clear that anyone found in his or her home after that 48-hour period would be considered to be part of the enemy and therefore treated as a legitimate military target. It is not difficult to kill innocent people in wars. All it takes is simply the use of the correct language and, instead of calling civilians human beings, rename them "the enemy", "legitimate targets", or (when they are murdered) "collateral damage". Once people's identities have been changed in this way, two schoolchildren can be shot dead in cold blood as though nothing has happened.

The army's abrupt announcement fell like a heavy stone on the depressed population. Those who continued to suffer the worst part of this war were the most vulnerable part of society: women and children.

The beginning of the systematic displacement of the population in the north of Uganda can be traced to September 1996, in Gulu district. Peasants living on their homesteads in the bush started receiving orders from UPDF mobile patrols telling them to leave their homes, within 48 hours and go to the trading centres along the main roads. When some of the local councillors (LC1s) came to the district headquarters to ask for an explanation, the district authorities just answered that they had not been informed and there was nothing that could be done. Washing their hands of the situation and avoiding any conflict with the UPDF seemed to have been a constant trend among the civilian authorities who chose not to put up a fight against these commands.

At that time, people were told by the soldiers that the military was about to launch a well-planned operation that would completely wipe out the rebels in about two or three months, and because of this plan the military needed the rural areas to be totally empty of civilian population. In many cases, people were told that should they not follow these instructions they would be considered rebels. To prove these threats, many zones where people resisted were bombed with artillery and helicopter gunships.

During the days that followed these edicts, thousands of peasant families were abruptly woken up before dawn, beaten up and chased away from their homes, without time to collect their few belongings. In many cases, whenever people ventured to return to their hurriedly abandoned homesteads to collect food, saucepans or clothes, they found their huts and granaries burnt and their foodstuffs gone. There were reports of the army using combat helicopters to transport sacks and sacks of food that people had left behind.

When people reached the trading centres, they were forced to build tiny huts where entire families had to live. Husband, wife and seven or eight kids packed like sardines in a tin, slept together in congested spaces of hardly ten square metres. The lack of privacy in these displacement camps became one of the most humiliating trademarks of these concentration camps, euphemistically called "protected villages" at that time. Again, it was just a matter of changing the name to make something acceptable. The Acholi population were compelled to live in appalling conditions that destroyed their traditional culture and values, the backbone of their very existence.

In the trading centres, there was nothing to enable people to live with a minimum amount of dignity. In the beginning, there was no relief food distribution, no water or sanitation, and no medical provision, since everything was done so haphazardly and without proper planning. International help from humanitarian organisations took its time to arrive. No one will ever know how many small children died during those first weeks or months of forced removals.

How protected were the so-called protected villages? Very soon the frequent rebel attacks, usually at night, would prove that these settlements were not protected at all. The outer edges of the camps were more exposed, and therefore particularly vulnerable to the LRA attacks, which always left dozens of people dead. In some cases, the military detach was built in the centre of the camp, making one wonder who protected whom. With their proverbial sense of irony, the Acholi soon started calling these settlements "protected barracks".

Many months after the first camps were formed, it was clear that the war continued unabated, without any sign of ending. Clearly, people had been taken for a ride. Behind that strategy of evacuating villagers from the country side there was an inhuman ideology that played with the control of the population as a core military strategy. Mao Tse Tung had said that guerrilla warfare could be compared to a fish that needs water to survive. Rebels cannot live without a supporting population that provides them with water, food, shelter, information and recruits. Remove the water (the civilian population), Mao said, and the fish (the rebel army) will die. The army seemed to believe that the people in Acholi supported the LRA although it was not politically correct to say this in public. The military seemed to act in such a way that revealed the conviction that the only way to win the war was to leave the rural areas empty of people.

All of this happened in 1996, in the face of a passive international community. Not a word of protest, nor an official public release of concern was made. The UN High Commission for Refugees (UNHCR) did not have, at that time, the internally displaced personas as part of their mandate. UNHCR's offices in Gulu only opened in 2006; too little, too late.

In Kitgum, the massive displacement of the civilian population started in January 1997, in not less tragic circumstances. During the first four days of that year, several hundreds of rebels, commanded by Raska Lukwiya and Matia Lakati, poured into Lamwo county (the northern part of Kitgum district) from their bases in South Sudan and swept through village after village clubbing, hacking and beating to death over 400 people, most of these in Lukung, Padibe and Palabek.

It was surprising for some, and unsurprising for many others that the army arrived on the fifth day of these cruel attacks, when the rebels had already left Uganda, leaving behind them a trail of death and destruction. Tens of thousands of people fled their homes in sheer terror, moving towards the trading centres and to Kitgum town. There was no need for the army in Kitgum to repeat what they had done a few months earlier in Gulu, since the rebel massacre provoked a spontaneous wave of mass displacement.

In 2001, the total number of internally displaced persons (IDPs) in the districts of Gulu and Kitgum (Pader was carved out of Kitgum district during the year 2001) rose to 400,000, according to data from the World Food Programme. In April of that year ARLPI and the Gulu Justice and Peace Commission published a report about the IDP camps and their living conditions entitled "Let My People Go". We elaborated on personal stories in the report, based on several group interviews in 40 IDP camps, and it came out clearly that the official version of the story, that all displaced camps were created by spontaneous and voluntary movement of the population was simply not true.

When the UPDF gave another 48-hour ultimatum for people to vacate their homes on 29th September 2002, it was the third time that internal displacement was being caused. Two months later, the number of IDPs in Acholi doubled, reaching a total of 800,000 people uprooted from their homes.

During the following year, internal displacement continued to increase, particularly when the LRA spread their campaign of terror to Lango and Teso. At the end of 2003, the number of IDPs in the north of Uganda reached two million, making it the world's highest figure of displacement. A report published in 2004 by Civil Society Organisations for Peace in Northern Uganda, (CSOPNU) a consortium of humanitarian organisations for Northern Uganda, stated that one thousand people died in the IDP camps weekly as a result of violence and the appalling living conditions. Some outstanding international personalities, particularly the UN special rapporteur for children in armed conflicts, Olara Otunnu, spoke of genocide in Northern Uganda.

One of the world's best war photographers of our days, Reza Deghati, described the reality of war in these terms:

War consists of destroying people's soul, changing their lives, their culture, smashing their links, their identity, all.

This is exactly what those massive displacements achieved. It was one of the most repugnant aspects of the war in Northern Uganda.

> "This life in the camp has dehumanised us", a man in the Alero IDP camp told me during one of our field visits in 2001 when we were gathering data for the "Let My People Go" report. He continued: "In a house you have a family weeping and mourning because one of their sons has just died, while in the hut next door others are having a party, dancing and getting drunk."

A visit to any of the IDP camps in Northern Uganda would not leave anyone indifferent. Unattended children, women busy distilling local waragi (a strong brew) or burning charcoal that was purchased at five hundred shillings (20 cents of euro) per basin, men seated idle and drunk the whole day… these were some of the more common and depressing sights. Venturing beyond the perimeter of the camp was a risky enterprise that could lead to a deadly encounter with the rebels or with a mobile army patrol.

Rates of suicide increased drastically. In Acholi traditional culture, suicide was considered an abomination, and used to be extremely rare. A number of cultural rituals are performed whenever a man hangs himself, and the tree he uses has to be uprooted and totally burned to ashes. Sadly, most of the people who killed themselves in the IDP camps were young women, and it was not unusual to have six or seven such cases in a camp of hardly 20,000 people in a week. For many youth, with no prospects for their future and the most absolute of miseries, one of the few alternatives they had was to join the local defence unit (LDU) forces or homeguards, which were usually used in the frontlines when the LRA carried out deadly attacks, particularly at night. Despite this, the monthly salary of 40,000 shillings (about 16 euro) was attractive enough to convince a 15 or 16-year old boy or girl to join the LDUs.

The lack of hygiene and the great congestion hit the senses. A study carried out by Médecins Sans Frontières in 2004 revealed that most of the displaced persons consumed an average of three litres of water per day, far below the minimum of 20 litres recommended by United Nations. The stench of open latrines, heaps of rubbish rotting under the scorching sun and the ubiquitous waragi being distilled in the homesteads penetrated deeply into the nose and remained inside long after one left the camp.

People who once lived in open lands, with visible horizons, walked for many hours in the beautiful wooded savannahs, and enjoyed a freedom and a closeness to nature, were now confined to a miserable jail, serving a sentence of uncertain duration for a crime nobody knew or understood.

On 1st October, we received two important visits at Archbishop Odama's residence. First, we met a delegation from the UN Office for the Coordination of Humanitarian Affairs (OHCA). As soon as they left, a delegation of diplomats from the European Union, headed by the EU head of mission in Uganda, Sigurd Illing came. Illing was one of the first diplomats to take a great interest in involving the international community in searching for a solution to the tragedy of Northern Uganda. We were beginning to see the first signs of a growing interest in our problem, an interest that would greatly increase over the following three years.

One of the activities to which we devoted more time in ARLPI was the gathering of information for publication in a daily incidence report. This document helped us analyse the situation on a continual basis. As with most war situations, the army tried to have total and exclusive control of the information, something that they failed to do, primarily because the daily press releases from their public relations officer sounded so ridiculous that nobody took them seriously. The Ugandan government, assured the international community constantly that everything was under control, that the rebels were "fleeing in disarray" and that "soon Kony would be history". But its credibility and good image fell to very low levels with the disbelief of its population and, increasingly, of the international community. Army Commander, Maj. Gen. James Kazini, went as far as to say that if the war was not over by the end of 2002 he would resign. The end of 2002 came, the war did not end and the army commander did not give up his post!

Soon after my arrest in Kitgum, the Spanish ambassador in Nairobi called me to ask how I was. According to him, the embassy had worked hard to have us released. When he asked me whether I needed anything, then and on successive occasions, I always answered the same: "We would very much appreciate a visit from your side so that you can see for yourself how people in Northern Uganda are suffering." During my years in Acholi I saw diplomats representing many different nations, especially from the European Union, Canada, United States, South Africa, Japan and others, but no Spanish ambassador ever took the trouble or time to come to Gulu. This caused me great shame.

In 2004, while I was in Madrid, a Spanish MP who helped us finance some scholarships for formerly abducted children took me to the office of the Ministry of State for International Cooperation.

There I told the official who received us that Northern Uganda needed attention from the Spanish government. She just opened a book where she showed me the list of African countries that Spain considered to be of top priority: Senegal, Namibia, Sudan, Angola, Mozambique and some others. I understood immediately. Those African countries are of interest to Spain for two reasons: either they sent an influx of illegal immigrants on fragile boats, or they have long coastlines where Spanish ships caught huge amounts of fish. "As you will understand," she continued, "we cannot be everywhere." This final remark indicated to us that the visit was over.

But let us just wait and see. Now that it has been discovered that Uganda has huge reserves of oil under Lake Albert I would not be surprised if, very soon, Uganda was included on the list of countries that are priorities for Spain's foreign policy.

In addition to the visits we received from the different foreign organisations, on 1st October, the *New Vision* flashed an interesting headline on its front page: "Museveni asks the bishops not to see Kony again". When some of the visiting diplomats questioned Archbishop Odama about this detail he just smiled.

Perhaps he guessed what was about to come. It was two o'clock in the afternoon when a military vehicle arrived at the archbishop's residence. One of the president's secretaries came out of the car. She gave us a big envelope containing a letter from Museveni that invited us for another meeting with him two days later. Also in the envelope was eight million shillings in cash (about 3,400 euro) as a contribution to help us pay for expenses in our peace initiative.

Meanwhile, the rebels had extended their campaign of terror to Lango, where they were burning down hundreds of homesteads every day. These attacks were made particularly in the outskirts of Lira, and thousands of people were fleeing from their homes. On 27th September they destroyed the premises of the Catholic station, Radio Wa. The army, despite having been tipped off about the imminent attack, did not come in time to defend the place. Neither did they do much to repel the rebel attacks from the suburbs of Lira. The Acholi and Lango, two neighbouring communities that speak practically the same language and have very similar cultural patterns, saw how the relationship between the two groups quickly deteriorated because of the war. Aware of these rising tensions, we paid a visit to the religious and cultural leaders of Lira to express to them our solidarity and sympathy.

On 3rd October we arrived in Gulu barracks for our appointment with President Museveni, who had pitched camp at the centre of military operations against the LRA. Archbishop Odama, Bishop Ochola, a representative of the Muslim community, Rwot Oywak, Rwot Achana (the paramount chief of the Acholi) and I made up the delegation.

After four hours, Museveni brought out a military map and he proposed that we continue our peace contacts with the rebels in an area north of Palabek, bordering Sudan. Before we left, he gave us a letter he had written and a detailed map of the zone. During the next few days we made every possible effort to send both documents to the rebels; however, we never obtained a response from them saying they had received the letter and map.

Soon after I went to Spain for a five-week break. At the time I was arrested in Tumangu there was no way I could communicate with my parents, who got the shock of their life when they learnt about my ordeal on the radio. My mother, who had been suffering from cardiac insufficiency for some time, worsened significantly and was about to lose her life. The timely help of some good doctor friends, who put her on treatment in time and fitted her with a pacemaker a few months later, saved her life.

Like any other peasant in Atyang village, Matthew and his wife lived off the land. Matthew also volunteered with the church as a catechist three days a week; he led Sunday services, visited the sick in their homes and gave catechesis to groups of young people who wanted to be baptised. He and his family owned about thirty acres of a fertile land that yielded enough crops to support their seven kids and send them to school. In Atyang, eight kilometres from the main road, most people had simply ignored the army's ultimatum. Only a few had left their mud and wattle huts to move to the nearest camp in Palenga.

Atyang and Palenga were two of the 15 rural communities that I visited regularly in the Minakulu Catholic Parish. For people like Matthew, who braved the situation and lived a few kilometres inland, staying at their homes in the bush carried the considerable risk of being placed at the mercy of armed men. The less serious misfortune that could befall any of them was to be abducted by the LRA to be compelled to work as their porters for a few days. Children always suffered the worst since the LRA preyed on them, forcing them to become rebel soldiers, and for the girls it was worse since in addition to being soldiers, they were forced to be sexual slaves. It was not unusual to hear from returned abducted children that it was better to be an adult than to be a child; at least grownups were normally released a few days after being kidnapped, or were used as porters. If they were not strong enough to carry the heavy loads, this weakness could cost them their lives.

Matthew experienced this after a group of rebels stormed his village on 1st December and looted everything. When they did not find any children in his homestead they were infuriated. After beating him cruelly in front of his desperate wife they forced him to accompany them. From his village of Atyang the rebels proceeded to a neighbouring village within Bobi sub-county. Richard, a young, strong man in his thirties, was a member of this village and someone Matthew knew well. When they reached Richard's home, the rebels forced him to carry a heavy sack of maize flour that they had just looted. After several hours of marching under a scorching sun, Richard could not stop himself from falling to the ground under the weight of his heavy burden. An adolescent dressed in combat fatigues who commanded the group made a sign to the other child soldiers, two of whom ended Richard's life by hitting him hard in the back of his head with axes. All the captives were forced to watch the execution, as a warning of what would happen to them if they delayed the group or were not strong enough. Such killings were routine for the LRA, who referred to the murder as "sending the tired man to sleep".

Matthew was luckier than Richard. After three days he was released, but when he returned to his homestead it was abandoned. His wife had taken their seven children to Palenga IDP camp, a place with a population of 20,000 that continued to increase by the day. When I learned that he had returned I went to see him but he was not in Palenga. He had gone to see Richard's father to inform him of his son's death.

Like Matthew, many hundreds of thousands of people in Acholi and Lango, unable to stay at their original homes, languished in the squalid IDP camps, where they were somehow safer; other predators like idleness and a lack of hygiene, however, posed a dangerous threat to their lives.

To say that Christmas 2002 was a sad one would be an understatement. It would be more accurate to affirm that, since 1986, nobody in Northern Uganda had enjoyed a happy Christmas, indeed not a single day of happiness.

In another sub-region of Northern Uganda, West Nile, people had more hope. West Nile is where Idi Amin and many of his henchmen hailed from, and since he had been overthrown in 1979 a handful of rebel groups started by some of Amin's former soldiers had caused intermittent insecurity from their bases in Sudan and the Democratic Republic of Congo (formerly Zaire). One of these insurgent groups known as Uganda National Rescue Front (UNRF), led by Brigadier Ali Bamuze, had fought for some time alongside Kony's LRA. In 2002 the UNRF entered into negotiations with the Ugandan government, a dialogue in which many local leaders and elders played a crucial role. The government gave the rebels a demilitarised zone where peace talks could take place under sensible security conditions. The talks were funded by some donor countries; the United States' contribution was made through its international cooperation agency USAID.

On 24th December 2002, the government of Uganda and the UNRF signed a final peace accord in Yumbe. The pictures of President Museveni and Brig. Ali Bamuze, both wearing military fatigues, inspecting a heap of 800 rifles surrendered by the rebels, and shaking hands, graced the main pages of the newspapers on Christmas Day. The inhabitants of Gulu who walked the streets on their way to the churches that day stopped to look at the newspaper photos and wondered whether they would see similar images signalling the end of the war in their region.

On 31st December, Archbishop Odama, Anglican Bishop Nelson Onono, the Muslim Khadi Sheik Musa Khalil and the head of the Orthodox Church in Acholi, Julius Orach, led a massive peace demonstration on the streets of Gulu, marching behind a banner with an eloquent slogan: "Stop fighting, start talking". Every last day of the year since 1997, the religious leaders of the main denominations organised a peace march and prayer.

On this day, several thousand people marched in an orderly fashion, demanding the end of the war. They flowed towards Boma Grounds, a large arena just outside Gulu town. From the stage, the warm and sharp voice of Roselyn Otim, a popular Acholi singer based in London, rose above the crowd with a song that in those days blared from radio sets frequently, to the point that it was almost becoming a hymn.

Ganwa tye ka to, wadok kwene, wadok kwene, wadok kwene...

(Our home is dying, where shall we go, where shall we go, where shall we go..?)

7

A Sad New Year 2003

"UPDF kills 19 rebels" was the main headline of *The New Vision* on 7th January 2003. Quoting the army's spokesman, the government newspaper assured its readers that four days earlier two helicopter gunships had bombed a large group of rebels in Pella, a few kilometres from Namukora, in Kitgum district, putting 19 of them "out of action".

Fr. Tarcisio knew the place very well. A few years earlier, when he was parish priest of Namukora, he had built a chapel there. Namukora is a fairly remote place, with its unreliable rain and frequent raids from neighbouring Karamoja. It has always been one of Uganda's poorest places. Fr. Tarcisio left simple chapels, classrooms, dispensaries and boreholes that gave abundant clean water after he was transferred from Namukora to Pajule.

The terrified villagers who lived in the surrounding area fearfully trekked to the site on 4th January, the day after the bombing. As the news spread, many other people arrived. Some had walked distances of 60 kilometres to get to the site. Parents of children who had been abducted a few days earlier confirmed their worst fears when they found the corpses of their children. They collectd the bodies, shedding tears and silently taking them back home for burial.

Tarcisio too was among the first to reach the scene. His arrival was providential, since he was able to take some of the children who had been injured to hospital, in Kitgum. Among these children, there was a girl whose right arm had been severed by a bomb blast. Her cries pierced

Tarcisio's heart as he drove her, and the other injured children, to Kitgum , a 55 kilometre drive on a rough and often dangerous road.

After leaving the wounded children at the mission hospital, Tarcisio returned home where he reviewed the footage he had hastily taken with his small video camera. Something unusual caught his attention. He pushed the pause button and zoomed in to see more detail. What he saw sent a cold chill down his spine. There, among the bushes, was the blurred but clear enough image of a severed arm, the same limb that the little girl he had just left in hospital had lost. A few days later I would have a chance to watch the footage myself. There was no doubt; almost all the corpses that appeared were of children, most likely the ones who had been abducted a few days prior to the helicopter attack. Some of the wounded I visited in the mission hospital told me a similar story to the ones I had heard many times before. As soon as they were abducted by the rebels they were tightly bound with ropes in groups of five. When the rebels sighted the military helicopters, the trained guerrillas took cover while the scared kids moved in disarray and fell like flies when the bombs exploded.

A few days before that incident, the army's spokesman stated that there were only 500 rebels left and that the war was practically over; soon they could proclaim final victory. Interestingly, the same spokesman would say one year later (at the end of 2003) that during 2003 the UPDF had put 1,200 rebels "out of action". During a seminar organised in Gulu about the conflict in the north I had a chance to ask him during one of the sessions how the army managed to "kill rebels four times over".

Each time I read the official army releases I recalled Otto von Bismack's famous words: "People never tell so many lies as before an election, after a hunt and during a war".

Unlike other recent or concurrent conflicts in other parts of the world like Bosnia, Kosovo, the Middle East, Afghanistan, to name a few, the war in Northern Uganda was still an invisible tragedy ignored by the world press. The Ugandan media was duly cautious to avoid saying anything that could enrage the military. In September 2002 the independent paper *The Monitor* ran a front-page story in which it reported that the LRA had shot down a combat helicopter in Pader district. The government did not take long to react. The offices of *The Monitor* were raided by security operatives and the paper was closed for three weeks. Frank Nyakairu, the journalist who wrote the story, was detained for several days. In the end, and after considerable pressure from donor countries, *The Monitor* resumed its publication but only after it apologised for having published "false information". Needless to say, *The Monitor* and other Ugandan media were extremely careful following this incident; they made sure to cool down the tone of everything they published about the war in the north. Most of the times, nothing could be published without consulting the army spokesperson first which, in practice, amounted to a degree of censorship of pieces of information concerning the war.

Perhaps because of this and some other reasons, many serious atrocities happened daily in the north and went unreported. For instance, on 12th October 2002 the LRA brutally massacred over 100 villagers in Amyel, a remote centre of Pader district. From 22nd to 24th October, at least 17 people died when the vehicles in which they were travelling were ambushed by rebels in Atanga, and on 12th November more people died in an ambush in Okinga, a small centre halfway between Kitgum and Gulu. There were also reports of seven civilians who were killed by the UPDF in the aftermath of a rebel ambush in Ngora, a hamlet halfway between Kalongo and Patongo. Everything started when the rebels destroyed a UPDF armoured personnel carrier on the road. Soon thereafter a lorry full of soldiers arrived on the scene and they went on the rampage around the nearby villages, combing the zone in search of rebels. A catechist from Patongo Catholic Parish called Elia Okello and his wife were killed during that incident.

A few days later, on 13th January, the rebels infiltrated the east ward of Kitgum township under night cover and abducted 27 children. Incidents of this kind happened every day, but none of these got two lines in the local press or in any international news agency. MISNA, the Rome-based missionary agency that Fr. Giulio Albanese continued to run, however, tried to acquire and publish daily, a first-hand account of the events; by people who were aware of the great risk in exposing the truth to the outside world. Other international journalists who made a choice to take the same risk, like the BBC correspondent Will Ross or *The Economist's* Lambert Blake, ended up being something close to *persona non grata*.

The killing of the 19 children in Pella during the helicopter attack also went unreported. In one of the statements published by ARLPI at the end of January this conclusion was made:

> "Two Palestinian children killed by the Israeli army can become the first headline in the world news, whereas 20 children killed in Northern Uganda do not deserve even two lines."

Renowned writer Ryszard Kapucinski, master of reporters and considered by many the 20th century's best journalist, described this situation in his book *The Shadow of the Sun*.

> Many wars in Africa are fought in the absence of any witnesses, secretly, in remote and inaccessible places, in silence, without the world taking notice or devoting the slightest attention.

And this was the way it was in Northern Uganda.

Will Ross, who was the BBC correspondent in Uganda during those years and who certainly did everything possible to make the world know about the tragedy unfolding there, commented to me once that one of the reasons for the absence of news of this conflict in the international media was what he called its "monotonous character". I thought his was an interesting reflection. It was a boring war, yet today's world information has become, in many ways, a form of entertainment. In this conflict there were no clear frontlines and events took place in an illogical and unexciting manner: an ambush with ten killed one day, twenty children abducted another day, an attack that left two dead the following day... Everything was the handiwork of a strange rebel group who killed their own people, who proclaimed to be fighting for the Ten Commandments but who systematically broke them wreaking havoc on the population. If a journalist arrived today and sent two or three news dispatches relating these and other similar atrocities, he would surely find a repetition of the same events if he returned five or six months later. In this information age, news consumers demand to be served with stories that are more interesting, more comprehensible and "new".

In the meantime, we began to see a few hopeful signals that the stagnation, in which our peace initiative found itself, might lead to resumed contacts with the rebels. On 9th January, Rwot Oywak attended a meeting with the top brass of the LRA: Vincent Otti, Raska Lukwiya, Charles Tabuley and Tolbert Nyeko. During this contact, which took place at Ibong hills in Pader district, Oywak was put in radio communication with Kony, who complained bitterly about the government's constant provocative deadlines to "kill the terrorists". Kony further told Oywak that very soon our religious leaders' team would receive an official communication from the LRA declaring a unilateral ceasefire in order to resume peace negotiations.

Two days after that meeting Oywak came to the archbishop's residence to inform him of this new development. He was accompanied by Rwot Lugai, Rwot Oryang Lagony and the paramount chief David Achana. It was agreed that the traditional leaders would send a letter to Kony and that Archbishop Odama would inform President Museveni of this latest move.

On 16th January, Kony's father died in a Kampala hospital. In Acholi traditional culture, the father's death is considered a fitting chance for peacemaking whenever there has been a period of conflict and unresolved division in the family. Perhaps because it was felt that this was an opportunity that could be grasped, the government asked Archbishop Odama to preside over the funeral at the Catholic parish in Gulu town. His conciliatory gesture did not end there. A few days later Odama entrusted me with a letter of condolence addressed to Kony, inviting him to reflect on his father's death as a chance to reconsider the peace dialogue to end the war. Without thinking too much about any possible risks and happy to see that things could get moving again, I got into my old Suzuki Samurai and off I went to Pajule, a place I was beginning to miss.

Pader seemed to have become the epicentre of the war. There, like everywhere else, the number of displaced continued to rise. IDPs doubled from 400,000 to 800,000 in a matter of weeks and it took time before World Food Programme could provide food rations for all of them. The new arrivals had no option but to sneak back to their original villages deep in the bush to collect whatever food they could find, a most risky venture that could involve running into gangs of marauding rebels or mobile army patrols. Often, people found their homesteads burnt down, their granaries empty and even their fruit trees cut down, a drastic act that the UPDF put into practice much too often.

Our three main contact persons had been arrested by the army and accused of being rebel collaborators. This circumstance made it very difficult for us to establish a reliable contact with the LRA.

When I reached Pajule I went straight to Rwot Oywak's home and delivered the letter written by the archbishop to Kony. In the Catholic mission I met Fr. Robert Obol, a young priest who had just been ordained the year before. He showed me the Caritas Centre, which hosted 68 women and children who had either been released or escaped from the LRA. Since July 2002 some 600 abductees had passed through this mission's reception centre. In the whole of Pader district there was no other operational NGO except Caritas. All the others had left because of the rampant insecurity.

The following day I took a small motorbike and rode the 23 kilometres between Pajule and Pader. The road was deserted and gave me a heavy heart. Given the high number of ambushes that took place in the area, because it was infested with rebels, the army only allowed movement of vehicles between 11 am and 4 pm. The strong sun, the dusty wind that carried ashes from charred bushes and the presence of rebels frightened me and would have chilled the soul of the most courageous of human beings.

The RDC of Pader had been away from his office for the last five months. His deputy, Sylvester Opira, braved the situation and remained there doing what he could. I went straight into his office and informed him of the steps I was taking on behalf of the religious leaders. He promised to arrange a meeting with the military authorities for better coordination and to avoid any possible suspicion.

I returned to Pajule by 4:30 pm and went back to see Rwot Oywak, who had already found a way of sending Odama's letter to the rebels. He showed me a handwritten note signed by commander Tolbert Nyeko, who assured us that we would meet with them very soon.

I did not know that I was going to meet them much earlier than I thought.

Shortly before dusk I found myself more relaxed than usual. I sat under a tree in the mission compound to watch a football match between some young former rebels from the Caritas Centre and some soldiers from the local detach. Next to me, a soldier cheered his comrades. I noticed that he was in that kind of euphoric state that was one point short of being tipsy. He took a long look at me while he smiled.

"Don't you remember me?" he asked.

I looked at him closely and told him that I could not recall his face.

"That night in Kitgum barracks when you were prisoners. I gave you a bottle of water. I do not like to see men of God suffering."

Of course I remembered that, although the darkness of the night had not allowed me to notice the face of the soldier who gave us some little relief for a few seconds. My face brightened and I thanked him. That sentry was the only one who had shown us a little kindness in the midst of so much brutality. I also recalled, however, how I had given him a 20,000 shilling note in the hope that he would bring us some more bottles of water. Instead had just pocketed the money. I did not mention this detail in our conversation, though. Instead I asked where he was from. He told me that he was from Kigezi, and that he was a Muslim.

"If you are a Muslim you should not drink any alcohol," I advised him.

"I know. But it is five years since I last saw my family, I am fed up to the teeth with this war and I am dead scared of being killed, as has happened to so many of my friends. Every evening, before the sun sets, I have to drink some *waragi* to calm down."

No sooner had I entered the parish house after leaving the soldier by the football field than gunshots rang out in close proximity. I glanced at my watch. It was 6:30 pm.

In no time thousands of people from the IDP camp started running in all directions. Two children dashed inside our house and hid under the bed in one of the rooms. Latigo, the deaf and dumb mission cook, was coming to me with a wide smile holding a tray of pork *muchomo* he had just prepared for our supper.

He must have seen the deep fear reflected in my face because his smile froze. He left the tray on the table, raised his arms and started making gestures as if he was holding a gun and pulling the trigger while he looked straight into my eyes. When I nodded he too darted out of the dining room to look for a hiding place before it was too late.

After securing the metal doors and bolting them with iron bars, Fr. Robert and I sought refuge in the same room where the children had hidden under the bed. Lying down on the cold floor, my heart was beating faster by the minute and I struggled to find the air I lacked. The deafening noise of gunshots, grenade and rocket explosions and machine gun bursts was increasing and I found that to shut my ears was a futile exercise. I closed my eyes and my whole body and soul started vividly reliving everything I had gone through hardly five months earlier in Tumangu.

The rebels did not seem to share our fear. Every time a volley of bullets was shot at them, I heard them singing outside.

Dolotiya, Dolotiya, Dolotiya nkwagala…

Dolotiya, by the popular singer Jose Chameleone, was Uganda's top song that year.

Some very loud bangs hit the metal door and startled us. Outside, somebody shouted at the top of his voice, increasing our fear.

"Open now or we shall throw down the door with a bomb!'

I tried to get up but I could not. It was the first time in my life that I experienced total paralysis from sheer fear. Robert stood up at once and then answered the door.

"Wait. I am the priest. I am coming to open now."

I remained in the room in darkness, under the bed, with the two terrified children. Before two minutes passed the door was kicked wide open and the room was flooded with light from several torches. They pointed them at our faces, so that we could not see anything.

The three of us were pulled out from under the bed. I heard a voice telling us to sit on the bed and we obeyed. I slowly raised my head and saw four boys in front of me, no older than 12 or 13, wearing military fatigues and pointing their guns at me. One of them took my watch and I offered no resistance. A few months later, when I would return to Spain for a few weeks of holiday, my mother would ask me about the watch, which she had given to me as a gift the year before and I would tell her that I had given it to a child. I answered with a clear conscience that I had not told her any lie.

The rebel boys grabbed one of the children who was with me. His name was Joseph and he was 14 years old. Numb and frightened, I mumbled some words to ask them to leave him. Joseph's words came out much more strongly than mine.

"Do not risk," he said. "Let me go. God will help me."

I thought of acting more decisively, but I was overcome by fear. There I was, the outspoken advocate of human rights, the defender of children in Northern Uganda, completely scared, seeing a child abducted in front of me and not doing anything to stop it. That experience was going to cause me numerous moments of unbearable remorse. One year later Joseph would escape from the LRA during a skirmish in Soroti and be brought back to his home. For two years afterwards I paid for his studies at Pajule Technical School, seeking to clear my conscience.

"Take care of my brother," said Joseph before disappearing into the darkness.

He was pushed forward at gunpoint by children younger than him, they themselves abducted a few weeks or months earlier.

His little brother was four years old and seemed to be staying outside the hell that was unfolding in front of us. I hugged him, while the young boys in uniform told me not to move. They brought two big sacks and pillaged the room. They asked me for a backpack and I told them that they could take mine from the next room. We moved there hurriedly and I gave it to them. As soon as they left the room I crawled under the bed, with Joseph's brother. The gunshots went on outside unabated.

Then I heard the first mortar blasts, which were much more deafening than the grenades. The rebel attack had taken the soldiers by surprise; they did not really put up a fight against the rebel infiltration, but simply took refuge in their detach from where they could launch light artillery. People called that kind of military strategy "to whom it may concern". It would have been worth laughing about was it not for the fact that the use of grenades and mortars during a rebel attack in a congested IDP camp where thousands of desperate people were crammed often resulted in fires and deaths among the civilian population.

From under the bed, I heard some rebels walking on the house roof, removing the solar panels. The mortar explosions seemed to have little effect on them, for they laughed loudly and continued with their singing.

"Dolotiya, Dolotiya, Dolotiya wi lobo..."

They were asking for trouble, and I got even more scared thinking that one of the bombs could fall on the house.

Half an hour later the door of the room opened again. I held my breath. After a few seconds somebody spoke.

"There is nothing here. Let's go."

Then I noticed that some other rebels were outside my window and, in the courtyards, busy bringing old newspapers while somebody asked loudly for a matchbox. I shivered when I thought that maybe they were planning to burn down the mission house and I grew angry at the memory of poor Raffaele being burnt to death inside his car. I wondered if this would also be my death.

But the rebels had other intentions, for they were busy burning a car that was parked outside. They would have done the same with my Suzuki had Fr. Robert not pleaded with them not to.

I spent the whole night awake, trembling with fear under the bed while the little child slept peacefully and snored as if what had happened had nothing to do with him. As the hours passed the gunshots subsided, giving us a false impression of returning calm. Every few minutes a loud bang of a mortar shell froze the blood in our veins. Some rats came to share our hiding place, chewing my hair and nibbling at my clothes. I used my hands to cover my ears and to send them off.

It must have been around 6 am when I heard some voices outside again. I stood up and came out of the room slowly, staggering. I felt a great relief when I saw Robert alive and well. He had just come out of some bushes where he had spent most of the night. The parish house and the nearby community of sisters had been ransacked. The saddest part of everything was that they also entered the Caritas reception centre where, after looting everything they could lay their hands on, they shot and killed a 14-year-old child who had escaped from them a week earlier. As they ransacked the place, they also smashed the body of a baby who was only a few months old. We found his mother weeping loudly over the tiny corpse.

At nine in the morning the soldiers arrived at the mission, when the damage had already been done. I opted to keep my mouth shut and stay away from them, for I would have sent them to hell if I had not been careful.

Robert and I went to the trading centre in Pajule. From different corners of the centre columns of smoke rose to the sky. The rebels had burned down 30 huts and their unfortunate tenants were now busy trying to gather the few belongings that remained. Near the market a bomb had fallen inside a house, killing two small children who had been inside.

A heavy sadness filled the air and people walked slowly, heads down and in silence, crushed by so many humiliations. We took the path towards the mission cemetery, where we buried the four children, the casualties of the attack. Wearing alb and stole, I lead a prayer for those innocent victims. As I tried to mumble some words of consolation, but I could not stand it any more and my speech drowned in a flow of tears.

I prepared for the journey back to Gulu. I asked Robert if he wanted to come with me. The rebels had stolen everything he had and he had remained with nothing except the clothes he was wearing. He quietly told me that he preferred to remain.

"After my experience last night I understand my people better," he said.

The windscreen of my Suzuki had been smashed and during the trip to Gulu the hot air hit me mercilessly in the face. I carried with me a 12-year-old girl from the Caritas Centre who had a bullet lodged in her back. During the four-hour journey she did not stop crying. In the first two hours, before reaching Lira, I did not see a single person on the road.

I arrived in Gulu exhausted and depressed. After taking a long shower I sat at my computer and wrote everything in detail. Then I slept soundly for a long time.

8
Another Chance at Peace

We were really stubborn. We expected a phone call from the rebels, late in the evening on 28th February.

After the brutal attack on Pajule, the month of February had abounded in promising and encouraging events that boosted our morale. On 11th and 12th February, a delegation of diplomats from the European Union, led by their head of mission, Sigurd Illing, visited us. Three days later the Nuncio came, accompanying the bishops of Luweero, Hoima and Arua. The Vatican Ambassador, Pierre Christophe, was an outgoing and friendly Frenchman who, since being appointed to his post in Uganda, understood the magnitude of the problem in the north and went the extra mile to do all he could to help us. He was the foreign diplomat who visited us most often and stayed more days than any other. The Catholic Church in Uganda, whose bishops were divided when it came to political and social issues, simply reflected the north-south divide that has plagued the country since the time of independence. The same was true for the Anglican Church of Uganda. For many years Christians in the north had felt aggrieved because of what they perceived as a lack of interest on the part of their bishops and the congregations in the south, for whom the war in Acholi was a remote affair that did not concern them much. Making use of his fine diplomacy, and at the same time using paternal firmness, Archbishop Christophe was a master of moving things behind the scenes and he knew how to push bishops from other parts of Uganda to come and show solidarity with their brother, Archbishop John Baptist Odama. Christophe insisted that the war in the north was a problem that concerned the whole church and the whole society in Uganda, not only the ones who lived in Gulu, Lira or Kitgum.

On 19th February Rwot Oywak met with the LRA top brass in a location near Atanga. It was the first time that the rebels seemed to come out with some concrete proposals: they wanted a ceasefire effective on 1st March, the involvement of the United Nations in the peace talks, and the demarcation of some de-militarised zones for peace contacts. In the meeting were a number of people, including a young man who had recently joined the LRA ranks called James Opoka. He was an ambitious politician who had been chief of the electoral campaign in Acholi for opposition leader Kiiza Besigye during the presidential elections in 2001. At that time Besigye's party, known as Reform Agenda (and later called FDC) denied having a member in the LRA and dismissed the allegation as an attempt by the government to tarnish their image. But Opoka was at that meeting, wearing military fatigues, bearded and wearing spectacles, and sitting with the LRA top commanders. Hardly one month later he was executed on Kony's orders, because he feared that Opoka's political influence could challenge his leadership.

As usual, Oywak informed the top religious leaders about the meeting. Aware that a new phase of peace contacts was about to come about, the religious leaders decided that when the rebels called us, three people should go to meet them: Rwot Oywak, Rwot Lugai and myself.

On 24th February, a man who said he worked with the political branch of the LRA in Nairobi visited us. His name was Paul, and he had been a valuable contact person for the *kacoke madit*, the powerful Acholi international peace lobby. For the next few months Paul would be very instrumental in helping us make contacts with some of the LRA main commanders. Things were beginning to look up.

I received a phone call from Fabio Riccardi, an official from the Community of Sant'Egidio in Rome. He had been in phone contact for some time with the LRA's second-in-command Vincent Otti. This prestigious peacemaking Catholic community, well known for their mediation efforts in many parts of the world (particularly in Mozambique), had been discreetly working behind the scenes to find a peaceful solution for Northern Uganda. Fabio Riccardi, brother of Sant'Egidio's founder Andrea Riccardi, offered the possibility of supporting the peace process with logistical arrangements for direct face-to-face negotiations between representatives of the government and the LRA in their headquarters in Rome.

Oywak and I travelled to Lira on the evening of 28th February. We were put up at Ngeta's Catholic Mission. As soon as we arrived we did something very important in any peace process – something that would occupy much of our time in successive years; sitting and waiting.

The much-awaited phone call arrived finally at nine o'clock in the evening. Vincent Otti's unmistakably rough voice summoned us to a meeting the following day. We immediately called our people at the ARLPI's office so that they could inform the military to ensure a safe corridor for the meeting.

Very early the next morning we went to Lira to buy items that the rebels had asked us to buy for them: some soap, radio batteries, children's clothes and photo film. The army had told us in our meetings with the LRA we could give them items considered to be humanitarian help, for confidence building, but not anything like gumboots that could be used for military purposes. Once our hasty shopping was over, we drove the 70 kilometre stretch of road that separated us from Pajule. There we were joined by Rwot Lugai. We liaised with the UPDF intelligence officer, although he answered our questions with such ambiguity that it was impossible for us to check whether or not he had been informed by his superiors in Gulu about our impending mission.

For the third time I drove the 17 kilometres between Pajule and Koyo Lalogi's abandoned school compound. This time I drove faster, not only because we were at the highest peak of the dry season and the tall grass had been burnt, but also because I felt invaded by an optimism I had never known before.

When we reached the familiar spot we stopped and parked the car. The place was deserted.

Immediately my heart sank. Were we going to have a repetition of what had happened in Langol in September the previous year? Not knowing what to do next, we got out of the vehicle and slowly walked along a footpath in front of us. No sooner had we gone a few metres than we sighted three adolescents in military uniform, carrying rifles and wearing the usual cold expressionless faces I have never gotten used to. My optimism vanished when I remembered that a few months earlier we had been told that Kony had given orders to kill any of the religious leaders who came to meet with his commanders. Was the order still in force or had Kony forgotten his anger?

After communicating some messages in low voices using their walky-talkies they made signs for us to follow them. We walked for about one hour in the open savannah before we reached a forest where we encountered an emaciated child with a sad face, holding a gun that was too big for him. Soon we saw groups of silent women and children seated under the shade of almost every tree, being watched closely by young armed men.

It appeared as if we were passing through different concentric security circles, until we reached the centre. There, seated under the shade of a big mango tree, we found the commanders. Tabuley was flanked by Col. Alphonse Lamola and Maj. Okot Ayoli. Some other junior officers stood next to them. A few metres away, as if prepared for an exhibition, we found a line of middle-range light artillery, canons, machine guns and shoulder ground-to-air missiles. Some of those weapons, we were assured, could destroy a tank or shoot down a helicopter. It was clear that the Sudan government, despite all their statements, was still the LRA's effective source of military supplies enabling the LRA to continue spreading terror in the north of Uganda.

Tabuley got up from his folding chair with a big smile. Unexpectedly, he walked towards me and embraced me warmly. Without thinking much, I spoke my mind.

> "You did very well to release all those women and children. I hope you shall continue doing…"

He cut me short and did not acknowledge my comments. Instead, he told us to sit quickly as he took a radio set out of a sack.

> "Today you are here to talk to our chairman Joseph Kony," he said, tuning the radio.

After some few seconds of background noise, we could hear the strangely modulated voice of Kony. Part of the mystery about him is the fact that pictures, recorded messages and video footage from him are rare. Ugandan news papers still ran Kony's photographs from 1993, which were taken at the time of the peace talks with Betty Bigombe. Some of his speeches in Sudan have been recorded, dubbed onto old tapes and circulated clandestinely in Northern Uganda. I recognised his strange voice on the radio. It was a queer mixture of amusement and aggressiveness. Perhaps it was the peculiar sound of his voice that made it hard to forget once you had heard it.

> "Who are those people who have come?" Kony asked.

Tabuley gave him our names.

"What do they want?" Kony continued to probe. "Have they been sent
by Museveni?"

The question, asked with an unfriendly tone of voice, left us frozen.
What did he mean by asking what we want? They were the ones who
had called us to this meeting. Sensing danger, the three of us shook
our heads repeatedly. It was not a very encouraging beginning for a
conversation held in a remote corner of the bush, surrounded by many
young rebels armed to their teeth and commanded by unpredictable
people used to cruelty. Kony was a master over the life and death
of the people under his control, and whether we liked it or not we
were now in his hands. The fact that we were communicating with
him, without seeing him, added to our anxiety. Perhaps he wanted to
begin the meeting by putting us in a state of mind that would be easy
to manipulate. In any case he was making it clear that we were in his
hands.

However, Tabuley came to our rescue.

"They are saying that they have not come representing the government,
but as neutral mediators."

Kony replied.

"Let them wait. Let me consult."

A tense, uneasy silence followed. I tried to break the tension by uttering
friendly comments to change the mood, but one of the officers looked
at me while he put one of his fingers over his mouth, motioning me
to be silent. I wondered whether Kony would be consulting with his
spirits, and I prayed that they would not inspire him with an action
that would go against our physical integrity.

Those few minutes became an eternity for me. At the other side of
the line, Kony's shaky voice sounded again.

"Are those people still there?"

What on earth did he mean by asking whether we were still there or not, I wondered.

> "Let them get closer," he ordered. "There is something I want to tell them and I want them to understand it very well."

Slowly, we moved closer with our folding chairs.

> "I am very happy that you have come" Kony said energetically, and then he began to laugh loudly.

The conversation lasted about one hour. After a few minutes I realised that Kony easily switched from a highly aggressive tone that froze us with fear to the friendliest cordiality. It was a most unpleasant combination, and in that environment of madness it made me feel as if I was floating in a cloud that was about to fall. The conversation with Kony was an emotional roller coaster designed to make us feel under his control by manipulating our feelings. If that could happen to me, I thought, how would it be for the thousands of children and adolescents he kept in his ranks who obeyed him blindly. That day I understood why many of the children who escaped could live for years with the belief that Kony still saw them and could even read their thoughts.

I took notes on the conversation while Rwot Oywak recorded it by cassette. Kony's main message was that he was declaring a unilateral total ceasefire from that very moment. He asked us to broadcast his message on Radio Mega FM. I passed on to him Fabio Riccardi's message about the possibility of having peace talks in Rome, but Kony was not enthusiastic about such a possibility.

> "First we shall begin with peace talks at home, in Uganda," he said, "and later on we shall think of going to other countries."

Rwot Oywak asked him to be more explicit about the meaning of his ceasefire.

"From this moment no more attacks, no more ambushes, no more abductions," he assured us.

Kony also requested a first meeting with some government representatives in a place not far from where we were. He wanted his mother, Norah Ating, to be present in that meeting so that he could talk to her by radio. We assured him that we would transmit his request.

Towards the end of the conversation he asked me whether I had a rosary with me. I told him I had one.

"I want Fr. Carlos to pray with my people five rosaries for peace," he said.

This is the way Kony was. One day he asked you to pray the rosary, the next day he quietly ordered his fighters to massacre women and children, or to mutilate people with the worst display of brutality.

"If it is because of peace I shall pray ten," I answered.

Once our conversation was over and the radio had been switched off, we tried to hang around with the rebels for as long as possible. In peace negotiations informal, unplanned moments are usually the most important. We posed for pictures together, but I refused to stand next to the pieces of light artillery on display.

One of the young officers present came to greet me. I noticed that he had two stars on his shoulder pips that denoted he was a lieutenant. He asked me to record his name so that I could alert his mother that he was alive and well.

"My name is Moses Rubangangeyo," he said.

His name, which in Acholi means "God is the one who knows," struck me and I was sure I would never forget it. I looked at his face. He might have been 21 or 22. His eyes had the usual expression that denoted cold hardness, although when he mentioned his mother I thought I caught a glimpse of a smile.

I asked him for his mother's name and address, but at that moment some other rebel officers came closer to us and Moses withdrew. One of them also told us his name: Okot Ayoli. One year later he would display great bravery in abandoning the LRA, with 60 fighters plus some women and children. He reported to the UPDF detach in Pajule. Moses would also leave the LRA. Tabuley and another officer called Kitara, who pestered me at the end of the meeting to give him my watch, died in November that year fighting fierce battles in Teso. As for the rest I would not hear anything about them again.

Once again, the way back to Gulu was marked by the highest state of euphoria at the seeming success of our meeting. It was Saturday and when we reached Lira we slept there, tired but happy.

We left Lira very early the next morning and at eight o'clock we were at the ARLPI office. I sat at the computer and recorded the minutes of our meeting (or rather, teleconference) with Kony.

After our personnel from the ARLPI had decided what to do next, we were told to go to the paramount chief Rwot Achana's home, which was on a hill on the outskirts of Gulu. When we arrived at eleven o'clock, a military vehicle bringing Gen. Salim Saleh, one of the members of the presidential peace team appointed in August 2002, was also arriving. The chief of military intelligence for the north, Col. Charles Otema, came with him. The LC V chairpersons of Gulu (Walter Ochora) and Pader (Jacob Komakech) were also in attendance. It had been two years since I had met with some of these officials.

Salim Saleh began the meeting with a tone of informality and cordiality. We needed it. He pulled out a cigarette.

"You will excuse me, but if I do not smoke I cannot think," he said.

We started the meeting by informing the officials of our encounter with the rebels the previous day. Not everybody had the same reaction. While Col. Otema showed very little enthusiasm for Kony's declaration of ceasefire, interpreting it as just another attempt to buy time, Salim Saleh insisted that we had to give the rebels another chance. Saleh's was a view that was enthusiastically shared by Jacob Komakech. I asked myself whether we were not watching another version of the bad cop, good cop strategy.

Finally Salim Saleh, who left the room periodically throughout the meeting, apparently to consult with his brother, President Museveni, concluded that they would prepare an official statement on behalf of the government. The statement would welcome Kony's ceasefire.

As far as I could remember, the chairman of the Presidential Peace Team (PPT) was Eriya Kategaya, who was at that time the minister of internal affairs, but he was not in Gulu. During the time that the PPT was in Gulu making this attempt at peace we did not see Kategaya. Although the PPT tried their best, I always wondered whether they had any written terms of reference about their mandate, who was in charge of their leadership in the absence of Kategaya, and what procedures they followed to make decisions.

At 6:30 pm we went to the Radio Mega FM studios. Part of Kony's recorded message was broadcast there, and it was followed by the official response from the government, which was read both in English and Acholi. The government's statement welcomed Kony's announcement of ceasefire. The news fell like fresh raindrops of joy on the listeners' ears.

We spent the following two days in meetings with the PPT, from morning until night. Two MPs from Acholi, Santa Okot and Norbert Mao, also took part in the discussions. During the meetings I noticed that with Eriya Kategaya absent and without a vice-chairperson, it was difficult to know who was in charge, whether it was Salim Saleh or Betty Akech. Under the circumstances, because we were living in a war zone, it seemed quite clear that Salim Saleh, who had a direct link to the UPDF – even though he officially retired from the army - and the president as a close person of reference, was in charge. Saleh's friendly and informal personality made it easy for all to talk freely and work together, although Saleh did not seem to be the most disciplined person in the world and seldom turned up for a meeting before midday.

At that time I had the telephone numbers of two young LRA officers who were often our points of contact with the rebels. I will call them Jimmy and Francis. These were the only phone numbers that were usually available any time we called. As we were preparing for the details of our next meeting, I called them several times to agree on several details. Almost invariably they answered me with some strange sound, or they told me that they would consult and get back to me later.

Finally, the meeting that Kony had requested was arranged for 6th March, at midday, at the place they had proposed near Koyo Lalogi.

During the endless meetings, however, I had the impression that many details were not being addressed and were being left to chance. We were going to pay dearly for the consequences because of this negligence.

We had agreed to meet at 10 am at the office that the PPT had started using in Gulu, next to the premises that the European Union had in the senior quarters. I was used to appointments with the rebels very early in the morning, and I kept wondering whether we were going to have enough time to reach the venue before midday. Also, we had proposed that the presence of two international observers was needed. Although everybody agreed in principle that it was a good idea, logistics were still up in the air. To complicate things even more, the day before some members of the PPT had insisted that they wanted to be accompanied by military escorts, something that the rebels were not very likely to accept. If the situation was not managed properly, it could degenerate into an explosive one.

At 10 am some members of the PPT arrived: Betty Akech, Santa Okot, Reagan Okumu, Oryem Okello, all of them Acholi MPs. The Permanent Secretary from the Ministry for Internal Affairs, Dr. Kagoda, came accompanied by a state lawyer. Salim Saleh sent a message saying that he would arrive later. I came with the Vicar General of Gulu Archdiocese, Mgr. Matthew Odong, and Bishop Baker Ochola. We agreed that Bishop Ochola would be the moderator of the meeting with the rebels.

When Salim Saleh finally arrived, he told us that we were going to travel to Pajule by helicopter but that before we did this, we had to meet with President Museveni at the Gulu barracks. The problem was that His Excellency, as we were informed, was still in Kampala, where some important matters were still detaining him, and we had to wait. I was completely dumbfounded, wondering whether somebody was working behind the scenes to delay our departure so that our meeting would flop.

In a new display of what seemed to be the use of improvisation in managing difficult situations, the PPT members suggested that it was important to wait and meet the president, and that in the meantime the religious leaders should take a letter to the rebels asking them to postpone the meeting to 10th March.

Then my telephone rang. It was Fr. Tarcisio calling from Pajule. He was alarmed and concerned. He told me that the army was going on heavy offensive against the rebels in the zone where we had agreed to meet with them. I informed Salim Saleh.

"It cannot be," he said.

Immediately, Salim Saleh called the 5th division commander, Col. John Mugume, in charge of military operations in Pader district, who updated him.

"Unfortunately it is true," he said as soon as he hung up.

To complicate things even more, my telephone rang and I saw Onekomon's number flashing. A few months earlier he had joined the UPDF, where he had been confirmed in his rank as major. But when I answered my phone I did not hear his voice, but the voice of another young man who assured me that he was an LRA officer. A bit startled, I decided to act as though I had not noticed this change in the phone's ownership. Once again, I thought that there were people in the military, particularly among the intelligence service, who were trying to make us fail.

At the end of those tense hours of confusion in which the situation changed continuously and at breakneck speed from one moment to the next, we ended up boarding a military helicopter. On the helicopter were Bishop Ochola, Mgr. Matthew Odong, Rwot Lugai, Salim Saleh and myself.

We flew to Acholpii, where the UPDF 5th division had its headquarters. There we met with Col. Mugume, who told us that he had neither received an order to stop his current military operations, nor been informed of our peace meeting that day. When Salim Saleh showed his intention to continue to Pajule, Mugume adamantly told him that he could not authorise that. I watched the whole scene in amazement. My experience with military affairs is minimal (I never served in the army in Spain during the years in which young men were drafted for compulsory military service), but all the same I have always felt a lot of curiosity about the way armies function and particularly how their ranks and hierarchies affect behaviour. Despite my ignorance, at that moment I could not understand how a colonel could deny permission to a full general. Definitely, there seemed to be things in the UPDF that did not match the way other conventional armies conducted their affairs.

The two top officers asked Rwot Lugai to take a letter to the rebels, telling them that today's meeting had been postponed, and that it would take place on another occasion. The traditional chief was driven to Pajule under a heavy military escort while the rest of us returned to Gulu, where Salim Saleh took us to his residence for supper.

During that day and the following days the military helicopter bombed the rebels who had turned up for the peace meeting in the proximity of Pajule. I could not stop thinking of the desperate women and children I had seen on 1st March in the bush with the rebels. Surely, many of them must have died.

The following day, the *New Vision* run a front-page story with this headline: "Kony dodges Saleh".

What a lie, I thought, while I felt once again that we had missed another chance. Somebody had worked hard to make sure it did not work and was surely rejoicing.

9

Difficult Days

"What exactly happened on the 6th?"

Was it really possible that he did not know? If that was the case, his informants were not exactly the most competent people in the world. Personally, I found it difficult to believe that the president and commander-in-chief of the armed forces in Uganda did not know about the fiasco that had made us fail to meet with the rebels three days earlier.

> "Your Excellency, we could not make it for the appointment we had with the rebels because we had planned to meet with your Excellency before and that was not possible since your Excellency was detained by some important matters in Kampala."

That was the explanation given to President Museveni by the Minister of State for Security, Betty Akech. At once, I raised my hand and I was given the floor.

> "Excuse me, Mister President," I began. "We could not meet with the rebels because a few hours earlier the army went on the offensive against them in the area where we had agreed to meet with them."

I breathed heavily when I finished those few words. I needed to point out the real cause of the blunder that had made us fail once again.

> "Do not worry," said President Museveni. "Now I am here coordinating everything and nothing like that will ever happen again. I want to finish this problem once and for all, so that the displaced people may leave their camps and return to their homes at the beginning of this rainy season."

As had happened the previous year when we fell into the trap that the army had set for us during our peace meeting with the rebels in Tumangu, I was stunned to see that a group of soldiers could sabotage an approved negotiation and get away with it, without the slightest sign of disciplining or demanding responsibility from whoever was responsible. There seemed to be no intention of investigating the mishap. Everything seemed to be glossed over lightly as if nothing had happened, or as if in the higher echelons of power there was some rejoicing over having successfully botched another attempt at peace.

Our meeting with President Museveni lasted three hours. At the conclusion, he accepted to sign a declaration of "temporary cessation of military operations", time-bound and space-bound in the area of Koyo Lalogi, and to facilitate peace contacts with the rebels. The next day we were given the letter signed by the president and it was extensively broadcast on Radio Mega FM.

After some shuttling by Rwot Oywak between Gulu and Koyo Lalogi, the new appointment with the rebels was set for 14th March. That day was also going to unfold in most unexpected ways.

Events leading up to the meeting were far from hopeful. On 13th March, LRA second-in-command Vincent Otti entered Uganda from Sudan with hundreds of well-armed rebels. The government of Khartoum continued to supply the LRA with all kinds of military equipment, even as they officially continued to deny this assistance.

On that day, I was in Kitgum, where I had gone to consult with Fr. Tarcisio and to update myself on events in east Acholi. At midday, one of the programme officers from ARLPI had called to inform me that military intelligence had tipped them off about a message from Kony giving orders to his men to kill me instantly should they meet me in the bush.

On the morning of 14th March I found myself full of doubt, fears and anxiety. All the same, I drove towards Pajule. I had barely left Kitgum town when I was overtaken by a Kampala-bound bus packed with passengers.

I had driven maybe five kilometres when I saw the bus again, in front of me, enveloped in a cloud of thick dust, driving at full speed. In a fraction of a second some of the scared passengers shouted for me to turn back immediately. They had just sighted a big group of rebels crossing the road, and on such occasions rebels could become very aggressive and shoot to kill.

I stopped with a jerk, trying to quickly compose my thoughts. I heard my good angel telling me: "You fear too much. If they are crossing the road, it means that they are going to Pajule for the peace meeting". Was it a well-founded optimism? Or was I just being naïve? One of the things that my psychologist told me often was that it was not a matter of thinking with optimism or with pessimism, but with rationality. Under such circumstances it was difficult to keep a cool head in order to think and act logically, simply because there was often too little time to make a decision.

After a very long minute I decided to resume my journey to Pajule whatever the risk. After one kilometre my phone rang again. This time it was Salim Saleh, who told me plainly that it was true Kony had given orders to kill me on the spot.

It seemed that spending my days being thrown around at the mercy of unexpected events and having to change plans all the time had become my lot, and it was beginning to take its toll on me. I turned the car around and returned to Kitgum, where I booked an airplane ticket for Gulu.

When I reached the airfield I was told that the flight had been postponed until the afternoon. I was still wondering what to do next when Rwot Oywak called, angrily telling me that I could not leave them.

An Acholi proverb goes like this: *Ka rac ki rac* and is translated to mean "if it is bad, let it be bad". A very prudent man would never subscribe to that mentality, but prudence has never been a very strong part of my personality. This may be the reason I was given the Acholi name *locoromoi* (which roughly translated, means bulldozer). Maybe because of that I guided myself by the Acholi traditional wisdom (assuming that it was wisdom to overlook caution) and in the end I drove to Pajule, arriving at 10 am.

I thought that I was late, but I was the first to arrive. The members of the PPT reached Pajule at midday, in a road convoy escorted by several armed personnel carriers. At the mission, our contact person told us that he had met with the rebels the previous day and that they wanted to know the names of the people in the government delegation. They had also warned our contact person that they were not ready to receive any delegation with armed escorts. Some members of the PPT objected to going into the bush without armed protection, while others preferred to go unarmed. After a few minutes of discussion a number of people volunteered to go without escorts: MPs Santa Okot, Reagan Okumu and Otto Odonga, Internal Affairs PS Doctor Kagoda and two secretaries who worked for Salim Saleh. Fr. Peter Olum, Rwot Lugai, Rwot Oywak and I accompanied them. Salim Saleh wanted to go without escorts but we all told him that while we appreciated his courage it could be too risky for him. Lars Eric, a retired military officer from Norway who worked for UN OCHA in Gulu, came with us, playing the part of an informal observer.

Without armed escorts, we left in several vehicles for Koyo Lalogi. When we had covered 10 kilometres we stopped. Rwot Oywak told us that he would continue alone by motorbike to make sure that everything was in order.

After one hour he returned to say that he had met some rebels, who told him that it was late and the meeting could not take place, but arrangements would be made for another day.

So, our attempt at another meeting flopped again. We returned to Pajule, where the PPT wrote a letter to the rebels.

That afternoon I sat in the mission compound, chatting with a group of UPDF soldiers. The intelligence officer from Pajule detach told me once again that I should take Kony's threat seriously. While I was there, other soldiers arrived with a tall young man dressed in new clothes that were too tight for him. As they came closer and greetings were exchanged I noticed that he avoided eye contact with me. I had a quick flashback and I recognised him.

He was the rebel officer who had made us remove our shoes at gunpoint in July 2002, when we went for the first meeting with Tabuley. His tough demeanour seemed to have vanished. Truly, our work was full of surprises and this one, at least, was a pleasant one; it was as if God had prepared these kind moments to compensate for the rosary of frustrations that filled our days.

This ex-rebel's name was Okema, he was 24 years old and he had been abducted by the LRA eleven years earlier. He had deserted the LRA the day before. The two young officers who had been our main contacts for several months, Jimmy and Francis, he told us, were about to leave the LRA too. That little trickle of junior commanders who were starting to abandon Kony was beginning to flow, and it would gather pace in the following year. These desertions would deal a severe a blow to the LRA, weakening their forces greatly. The young rebel officers with whom we had been in contact were the ones who left first. I began to wonder whether their leaving was the reason for Kony's anger against some of us.

A few weeks later we helped Okema enrol in a mechanics course in Gulu. Each time I met him on the streets, we stopped to greet each other and chat. After a firm handshake I always asked him with a whisper:

"Excuse me, sir, do you wish me to remove my shoes?"

Then we would burst out in long peals of laughter.

Eventually, President Museveni extended the ceasefire in Koyo Lalogi for another month. But our contact with the rebels did not produce any tangible fruits. Kony did not respect his own ceasefire and not a single day went by without people being murdered in attacks and ambushes. Abduction of children also went on unabated. On 18th March, eight people were killed when the rebels ambushed one of the rare means of public transport in Pamolo, a few kilometres from Kitgum.

That same day, as Tarcisio was in the parish tuning the radio call to talk to another mission station, he overheard a communication between the rebels. The LRA had looted so many radio call systems in their looting sprees against rural Catholic parishes that they were beginning to use the same frequency as the Gulu archdiocese. It was not unusual to switch on the radio at eight in the morning to hear the different LRA units informing Kony about their actions and receiving instructions for the day. Most of the times they used codes to communicate. These codes, abounding in figures, were impossible for us to decipher.

While listening to the LRA communicating with each other, Tarcisio recognised Tabuley's voice. Without hesitation, he quickly intervened and asked Tabuley if he could talk to Kony.

When Kony spoke to Tarcisio he was furious. The church was collaborating with the government, he accused, and accepting to serve as a bait to attract rebels to venues where later on they would be killed by the UPDF. He made it very clear that in the next few days there would be many more attacks and deaths, and that all vehicles were legitimate targets for them, including those belonging to church institutions.

Three weeks later, Jimmy and Francis, the two young LRA officers, began calling me every day. Eventually we made an appointment to meet at a location on the outskirts of Gulu town on 24th March.

After informing Archbishop Odama of this meeting, I arrived at the location with my old rattling Suzuki. Immediately I saw two young soldiers, with rifles slung over their shoulders. One of them introduced himself to me as Francis. They asked me to take them to the archbishop's residence.

Everything had happened so quickly that I did not know where Francis and Jimmy had come from or how. Once in the car, Francis spoke in a very aggressive voice as he bounced up and down in the back seat of the car each time we hit a pothole. He shouted at me and rebuked me for driving such a useless, uncomfortable car.

It was the same comment I had heard several times from the UPDF soldiers in Pajule. I consoled myself by thinking that at least the rebels and government soldiers could agree on one thing: my car was a ramshackle.

Later on I would learn that both Francis and Jimmy matched the most typical profile of young LRA rebels. Abducted when they were no more than 10 years of age, minimally educated and without families, they had found in Kony a father-like figure to follow and imitate. Such destructured youth found that the way to be promoted and to have power was to show cruelty. Even though life in the bush was hard, there were also incentives to stay with Kony. They had power and status. They felt important as they could decide on other people's lives, and they were rewarded with young girls as their "wives".

When the nuns working at the archbishop's residence saw us drive into the compound, they greeted us kindly with big smiles. Surely, they thought that I was coming to see the archbishop with two government soldiers. They called Odama, who invited us to sit with him in his visitors' room.

Every time I saw Archbishop Odama, a holy man of God, speak with great humility and sincere affection to rough armed men, it reminded me of St. Francis of Assisi preaching to the wolves. The rebel Francis told us that he, Jimmy and some other comrade-in-arms of theirs were entering into a deal with the army, who had authorised them to go to a military installation located in the outskirts of Gulu. They were free to go there, talk to the soldiers and return to the bush, although sometimes they stayed overnight. They were about to make the decision to leave the LRA for good.

Francis and Jimmy asked Archbishop Odama for some food and he instructed me to give them two sacks of foodstuffs. After loading everything into my fragile car we went back to the place where I had met them. They took the sacks and left quickly.

The following day I brought Francis and Jimmy to meet with the archbishop again.

The following weeks involved a succession of incomprehensible and illogical events. The situation would suddenly appear to be brightening up and then, just as fast, degenerate into the worst possible scenario.

During the period in which the UPDF respected the limited cessation of military operations declared by the president in Koyo Lalogi the rebels killed a former LRA officer whom the PPT were using as an emissary. His name was Okech Kuru and he was killed on 26th March. He had met with his former comrades on many occasions, but this comradeship did not stand in the way of them executing him by firing squad after receiving orders from Kony.

Despite the fact that the situation was getting worse, Rwot Oywak met with commanders Tolbert Nyeko, Raska Lukwiya and Onen Kamdulu again. On behalf of ARLPI, he handed the rebels some bags of maize flour which, for the first time, the rebels accepted. During the meeting Nyeko wrote a letter addressed to the PPT in which the LRA put their unilateral truce in writing.

During those days two officials from the Community of Sant'Egidio, Fabio Riccardi and Vittorio Scelsio, visited Gulu to become familiar with the situation on the ground. I introduced them to Paul, our LRA contact person in Gulu.

In the meantime the members of the PPT were busy addressing rallies in the different displaced people's camps. One wondered which message was being delivered to the desperate people who lived in the camps, especially when some members of the PPT talked openly about suspending their activities and withdrawing from the process. Archbishop Odama's position, though, continued to be the same. "We must be the last ones to withdraw", he repeated.

Unfortunately there were reasons for pessimism. On 10th April the rebels planned and executed a massive ambush in Atyak. They killed 13 civilians who were travelling to Adjumani. All their declarations of ceasefire, verbal or written, were just empty words.

On the same day, two ARLPI staff met again with Tolbert Nyeko and Raska Lukwiya in Koyo Lalogi and delivered to them some more bags with foodstuffs. Paul travelled with them and remained behind to prepare some documents. The intention of these food deliveries, for which we had permission from the military, was to convince the rebels not to take by force whatever food they needed, otherwise there could be no ceasefire. In practice, what happened for the next month is that the LRA continued to attack both soldiers and civilians and, when they were pursued, they returned to the demilitarised area where the UPDF had orders not to enter.

Two days later, Rwot Oywak and two ARLPI staff went back to Koyo Lalogi after being called by Tolbert Nyeko for some "consultation". Nothing could have prepared them for what happened next.

The boys in uniform who came to meet them in the bush ordered them to sit down on some old fallen trees and wait. After one hour Tolbert Nyeko, Raska and Paul arrived.

Nyeko called one of his escorts, who came with one of the maize flour bags that ARLPI had given to them and a plastic bag that carried some broken pieces of glass.

"This is what we found in the bags of food that you brought us" said Nyeko.

An uneasy silence followed. The three peace emissaries were dumbfounded. This was not possible.

"We always knew that we could never trust you," Nyeko went on in his cold voice. "You have accepted to act as a bait sent to us by the government to kill us with their helicopters. You deceive us by telling us that you are mediators but you come here to steal our boys and hand them to the enemy."

The emissaries' surprise began to turn to panic.

"You have tried to kill us, but God helped us and you have failed."

Tolbert Nyeko's calm and smooth voice gave to that scene a refined yet terrifying character. He must have learned that tactic from Kony.

"Rwot Oywak, have you come with your sat phone?" he asked.

The traditional chief could hardly mumble anything and his body shook with fear.

"Call the archbishop," ordered Nyeko "and tell him to come this afternoon to collect your dead bodies."

As though waiting for orders, several young rebels armed with guns and machetes surrounded the three terrified emissaries.

Several minutes of tense silence followed, occasionally punctuated by some unimportant comment.

"How is my mother-in-law?" Raska Lukwiya asked abruptly with a grin.

Raska Lukwiya, one of Kony's top and most trusted officers, had achieved a notorious violent reputation after he led a massacre in which more than 400 civilians were beaten or hacked to death in villages of Lamwo county in January 1997. The previous year, in October 1996, the LRA raided St. Mary's College in Aboke, one of the country's finest secondary schools run by the Comboni sisters, abducting 139 girls. Uganda held its breath as it was touched by the courageous witness of its deputy headmistress, Sr. Rachele Fassera, who boldly followed the rebels into the bush and pleaded with them, securing the release of most of them. The rest of the girls were taken to Sudan and given to the commanders as sexual slaves. One of them, who was called Charlotte, had become Raska's forced concubine. She was the daughter of Angelina Atyam, a nurse from Lira who was the elected chairperson of the Concerned Parents' Association (CPA). The CPA's first members were the parents of the girls abducted in Aboke. Over time, the CPA had become a very powerful international lobby group working for the release of all the abducted children in Northern Uganda. When Lukwiya asked about his "mother-in-law", he was asking about Charlotte's mother.

"I have heard that my mother-in-law has been given a brand new car, given as a gift by some of her white friends abroad," said Lukwiya. "What is she complaining about? If her daughter was not with me she would not have been given the car…"

Tolbert changed the subject unexpectedly and said that they wanted to have more chances to have meetings with the bishops. One of the ARLPI team members, swallowing his saliva, answered.

"Yes, we need to have more occasions to talk regularly... It will eliminate misunderstandings."

Then they all stood up and Tolbert called one of his young soldiers, who pulled out a camera and started taking pictures of the commanders warmly shaking hands with Rwot Oywak and the two ARLPI members.

A few minutes earlier they had been sentenced to death and now the emissaries were posing with the rebels, trying to smile for the camera. Once again the grotesque roller coaster was in action.

Before seeing them off, the rebels warned the ARLPI representatives.

"Do not bother to bring us any more food. We are not fighting in the bush because of food."

When the emissaries jumped into the car they drove away at full speed. Reaching Gulu, the group broke down.

Two days later Vincent Otti called the Sant'Egidio official, Fabio Riccardi, and told him that the LRA had agreed to send delegates to Rome for direct negotiations with the government. But the situation on the ground was quickly taking a turn for the very worst. On 19th April the PPT announced that they were putting an end to their attempt of negotiation with the rebels, and the LRA responded the day after in their usual fashion. They killed 16 more civilians in another ambush in Atyak.

At around the same time as these events, Human Rights Watch (HRW) reported that during the past 12 months the LRA had abducted not less than 5,000 children in Northern Uganda. HRW's report asked the UN to appoint a special envoy to Northern Uganda. However, this proposal fell on deaf ears, particularly because the Ugandan government did not want to acknowledge the magnitude of the tragedy that continued to worsen.

April marks the end of the dry season and the beginning of the rains that make it possible to start planting crops. As usual, the government had given a deadline for the end of the war and few months earlier had pledged to wipe out all the rebels before the end of the dry season. But the hard truth was that the war continued unabated with all its horror and desperation.

Kony's threats against the Catholic Church did not take long to materialise. On the night of 25th April some rebels broke into the parish house of Gulu Cathedral. They burnt a lorry and two cars and looted the solar panels and the radio call equipment.

One year later, an LRA commander called Okwonga Alero, who was wounded in combat and subsequently captured by the UPDF, told me that he was the one who commanded the group that assaulted the rectory of Gulu Cathedral. According to him, the attack had taken place because Kony had assigned him a special mission: to break into the archbishop's residence and kill Odama. For whatever reason he refused to follow Kony's orders and perhaps with the intention of appeasing Kony, he decided to displace the violence onto the neighbouring residence of the priests working in the cathedral parish. The next morning he made up an easy excuse. He told his boss that Odama's residence was tightly secured with plenty of soldiers all around his compound, something which was very far from the truth.

Following the attack on Odama's residence, there was a string of attacks against Catholic missions. On 5th May the rebels looted Anaka and Atanga and one day later Aliwang. But the worst was yet to come.

During those months lack of sleep became my worst torture. When the sun set, all tension and fear accumulated and fell on my shoulders, producing in me great pain that prevented me from sleeping. The total silence that dominated the long night hours became so unbearable that any slight sound would make me highly irritated. The unbearable anguish and worry that I lived with during those hours of darkness made me crave an early dawn, to begin another new day which would inevitably be marked by more frustration, exhaustion and discouragement.

In the Western world, where people have no direct experience of war except by what they may watch on TV, in documentaries or in fiction films, armed conflicts are usually associated with noise corresponding to outbursts of gunfire or bomb explosions. It was during those days that I learnt that what defines war at its best is silence. The most absolute and soundless passage of time, that penetrates into the junctures of your bones and deep into your marrow, hurting the depths of your soul. The worst silence is the one that pervades the night, leaving you hanging over an abyss, your heart throbbing with anxiety, swallowing the bitter cup of uncertainty. The soundless numbness that fills the air wipes away all plans and happy prospects and any glimpse of joy from your life. This despair may account for the fact that during the day music blared in displaced people's camps and trading centres, as though everyone had reached a tacit agreement to chase away the ghosts of silence that haunted, harassed and threatened to destroy the last remnants of humanity left in our shaky lives.

I do not know why, but in going over my written records of the previous few months I concluded that most rebel attacks against religious institutions had taken place between 11 pm and 1 am, or at least that is what appeared to be the pattern. While I turned over and over in my bed unable to catch any sleep, I started obsessively checking the time every few minutes and switching on my cellphone to search for any latest text messages. Those bad habits were like drugs I used to overcome anxiety and insomnia. It took me time to discover that in the middle of extreme situations that bring us near breaking point, we have the capacity to develop irrational behaviours that do us little good.

During one of those sleepless nights, on 11th May, I instinctively switched on my mobile phone. I was consoled to discover that it was 1:30 am. According to my reckoning, the high danger time had passed. Suddenly, the flashing of a text message brought me back to reality. It was from Fr. Cyprian Ocen, vice-rector of Lacor Minor Seminary.

Seminary being attacked. Seminarians taken.

Lacor seminary was hardly five kilometres from the archbishop's residence, where I lived. I was terrified. I called Cyprian and when he answered, his voice was shaky. He told me how the wide compound was still under a hail of gunfire. He managed to tell me that the rebels had pulled down part of the wall of one of the dormitories and in those moments they were taking away many of the boys.

I immediately called Paul, who was still in one of the lodges in Gulu. When I talked to him he seemed taken aback, both surprised and annoyed and he cut me off, telling me that he knew nothing of the situation.

I could not sleep. Before 6 am I ran to the archbishop's room and, after informing him, drove as fast as I could to the seminary. The rebels had abducted 41 young seminarians. Almost at the same time as my arrival a military vehicle came. The captain in charge of military intelligence for the 4th UPDF division, had come to inspect the place. After entering the dormitory he said to Fr. Cyprian.

"What I can't understand is why the rebels did not go to the girls' dormitory."

It was obvious that the captain did not understand much about seminaries. Despite our explanations, he continued with his speculations based on the same finding. This was pure "military intelligence".

Cyprian was devastated. When he told me that he was going to follow the rebels to plead for his boys I told him that I would go with him. While he was trying to determine which direction they had taken, I called Archbishop Odama to inform him of our plan. He asked us to wait for a short while. Ten minutes later he called me back.

"I have just talked to the new division commander," Odama said. He sounded furious. "You do not have his permission. He says that if you follow the rebels he is not responsible for what may happen to you…"

Our plan was frustrated and we could do nothing. During the following months, some of the abducted seminarians would manage to come back, usually taking the chance to escape during military confrontations. Nothing was known about the fate of many of them.

The attacks against the church did not end there. The next day the rebels ransacked Namukora mission. It was the third time in less than one year. And on 30th May two other nearby mission stations were targeted: Omiya-Anyima and Madi-Opei. In Omiya-Anyima, the rebels burned down the mission while the terrified priest, a Costa Rican, had time to lock himself with some people inside the church, which luckily did not catch fire.

In case there was any doubt, on 11th May Kony, speaking on the rebels' radio, gave a final order to all LRA units: kill all Catholic priests, beat the nuns and continue with attacks against all church institutions.

The following week, Pope John Paul II made a public statement of support for Archbishop Odama and launched an appeal to the rebels to release all the seminarians. He also repeated his request to the government and the LRA to find a negotiated solution. To pursue this road towards dialogue was still very far from Kony's intentions, and the conflict escalated.

During a visit to Kitgum mission, I had a chance to see how the priests from the Comboni order, Joseph Gerner and Tarcisio Pazzaglia, operated. They had gone to great pains to provide secure accommodation in the premises of the catechumenate for more than 500 terrified children.

One of them, a 14-year-old boy, who had run from his village near Mucwini told me his story. There were many others similar to this one. He narrated his story covering five days:

Day one. He was abducted by the rebels in the morning on his way to school.

Day two. He was forced at gunpoint to beat to death one of the other kids who had made a failed attempt to escape.

Day three. He ran away from the rebels when he was ordered to go to collect some cassava from a garden.

Day four. He reached his home, exhausted. His parents did not waste any time in taking him to the mission, where they begged Fr. Gerner to welcome him.

Day five. The rebels, who always kept detailed records of all the children they kidnapped, stormed his home with the intention of killing him. Since they could not find him, they beat his mother with machetes until she lay unconscious in a pool of blood.

Soon after hearing his story I went to the mission hospital, where a man had just arrived from Mucwini by bicycle carrying his young 16-year-old son on the back. He had been horribly mutilated. The night before the rebels had entered their homestead, grabbed the boy, and made him lie down face up. After accusing him of being a recent recruit of the army, one rebel slashed off his ears and lips with a machete while others held him on the ground. Next, one of them took an axe and chopped off his fingers. When they ended the orgy of blood they wrapped his ears in a letter that they wrote warning people that whoever had any intentions of joining the military would suffer the same punishment.

This hell of terror and anger that raged on Acholi would soon spread like wild fire to the neighbouring regions of Lango and Teso.

Later that May, I looked at my records. Going through all the issues of the government owned paper *The New Vision* I added up the number of rebels the UPDF claimed to have "put out of action": 216 rebels killed in battle, 70 surrendered, 8 captured and 10 executed on orders from Kony. The total gave a figure of 304. If it was true, as the army claimed, that at the end of 2002 there were only 500 rebels left, the two numbers, 500 rebels in 2002 and 304 put out of action most recently, it implied that there were196 rebels left. Was it possible that only 196 rebels could hold almost half of the country hostage and keep two million people displaced?

At that time, the LC V chairman of Kitgum, Nahaman Oywee, a journalist by profession, declared to MISNA that by his calculation the rebels operating in the north could well reach a figure of 4,000. Most of them were in the districts of Kitgum and Pader.

10

The Night Commuters

Koc!

Lit!

Ka lit ci… nyara ocito ka coo munero ci odwogo ki bongo I kome.

Pu!.

> (Listen to my riddle!
>
> Yes!
>
> My daughter went to look for a boyfriend naked and she came back fully dressed.
>
> A seed of groundnut!)

Koc!

Lit!

Ka lit ci… Latyene angwen ocung i wi latyene angwen ka kuro latyene angwen.

Bura ma tye i wi meja ka kuro oyoo…

> (Listen to my riddle!
>
> Yes!
>
> The four-legged one stood on the four-legged one to wait for the four-legged one.
>
> A cat that stands on a table to wait for a mouse!)

The children of several neighbouring families, together with their parents, were seated around the fireplace in the remote hamlet of Akobi, in Kitgum district, at the foot of one of the mountains that dotted the vast grassland savannah. It was a clear moonlit night in January. The harvesting season was over, and the granaries were filled to the brim with millet, groundnuts, sesame, maize, sorghum and beans. Inside the grass-thatched houses the farmers had plenty of sacks full of dry vegetables which, mixed with the groundnut and sesame paste, made a delicious dish. Since 1987, when the armed Karimojong herdsmen deprived the Acholi of all their livestock, people had very little meat to eat. All the same their diet was healthy and nutritious. Working in the gardens had stopped at the end of December, and with the dry season came the time for hunting expeditions, funeral rites, night dances for enjoyment, and looking for a chance to get a prospective spouse. That year, 1992, the Kony rebels had disappeared from Kitgum district, leaving the inhabitants with some breathing space. Displaced camps did not exist yet and people, poor as they were, could at least enjoy the simple things of everyday life, like meeting by the fireplace at night and listening to stories.

Ododona moni yo...!

Eyo!

(Let me tell you my story…)

Now it was mother who spoke. The kids came closer to the fireplace, amidst resounding laughter and excitement.

"Once upon a time the hare and the guinea-fowl went out for a walk in the countryside. Then the rain came. It was so strong that the monkey wanted to hang himself. So, both hare and guinea-fowl rushed through the grass looking for a place to take refuge. They saw a hut. Steam was coming from the hut and they entered at once, not knowing that it was Obibi's home. When he saw his two unexpected visitors, he told them quietly to take a seat…"

Obibi is one of the main characters in traditional Acholi stories. He is an ogre who preys on the weaker beings and devours them cruelly. The story continued.

Smiling, Obibi took his *nanga* harp, tuned it up and started singing: "How lucky, how lucky, how lucky I am… my lunch has just entered through that door…"

The children burst out laughing while the mother sang this part of the tale with a tune that made it easy to memorise.

"The guinea-fowl was overtaken with fear and started shivering, but when Obibi ended his song, hare asked him for his harp and said that he also knew how to sing."

Hare rang out decisively:

"Oh, that Obibi I killed that day… the one I have here in front of me is so small, he must surely be his baby…"

More loud laughter from the children.

"Then Obibi's face turned red and he shivered. He swiftly stood up, darted out of the house and, since it was raining and the ground had turned slippery he fell on a sharp tree stump and died instantly."

When the children and adults finished clapping and cheering wildly, the mother went on to conclude her tale.

"What does this tale teach us?" she asked.

One of the little girls raised her hand and answered without any hesitation.

"Intelligence is more important than bodily strength!"

"Very good, my daughter," said mother. "Never fear those who think that they are stronger and want to take advantage of us. And now, who wants to tell us another story?"

That was much more than a mere pastime. It was the *wang oo*, a real educational institution which was at the heart of the Acholi culture, informal teaching around the fireplace by night at home. From their parents, children learned some of the most essential values in life: one story teaches us that we should always help those who are weaker than we are, another tale tells us that we should never tell lies, one says that we must respect elders, and yet another one teaches us that we have to work hard and never take advantage of others.

Traditional Acholi culture is marked by an amazingly practical and wise simplicity. This African society has always placed a lot of emphasis on good relations with others and settling disputes by peaceful means. One of their most famous rituals is the one known as *mato oput*, through which two clans separated by enmity because of a homicide go through a peace process that ends in reparation, forgiveness and reconciliation. Also, the case in almost all of Africa, a lot of importance is given to respect for the memory of the ancestors and the dead in general, who are remembered in elaborate funeral rites, especially during the dry season when there is an abundance of food and drink.

I vividly remember the first time I was invited to take part in communal farming work at the beginning of the rainy season, known as *wang kweri*. It was in a village called Boloyaga, at the foot of the Lagoro mountain in Kitgum district, deep in the bush, where I spent several days. Very early in the morning, before dawn, a large party of about forty men hit the ground with their hoes, opening up a new field where a few days later the owner would plant maize, millet and ground nuts. At around midday, when the sun was strongest, we all sat under the shade of big trees sweating. The women came with plenty of food and drink, particularly the *kwete* beer. Before sharing the meal, the chief or *rwot kweri* read out the regulations of the activity: it was strictly forbidden to arrive late for work, to insult or deride your companion, to act lazy or to quarrel. The punishment was a heavy fine. Every time he read one of the rules all the participants greeted it with laughter.

The rest of the day was a joyful party, with people eating and drinking. As the amount of *kwete* consumed increased, people talked more, cracked more jokes and everything ended with dancing, that went late into the evening. The following day the same group went to another family's field, and with that rotating system the heaviest farming work turned into a real celebration every day.

But that was long ago. In 2003, the *wang kweri* was but a nostalgic recollection of a past that was no more, like a distant legend. All the population lived in displaced people's camps where traditional culture was crumbling or fading away, giving way to a new, unnatural way of living that was marked by idleness, loss of family values and unnatural habits. That loss of culture and the inhumane conditions made some people speak of the situation in Acholi as a real "cultural genocide". The night was no longer a privileged time to enjoy a friendly chat, to dance or to tell stories around the fireplace. Now the night was for the reign of the most absolute terror and children abandoned their homes and their parents for fear of falling into the rebels' hands.

Archbishop John Baptist Odama may never have performed a more unusual ritual in his life. For four consecutive days (from 22nd to 25th June 2003), as the sun was about to set in the evening, he quietly left his residence carrying a sack containing only a blanket, walked the six kilometre distance to Gulu town and on the way met with a good number of children, carrying their own sacks and blankets on their way to the bus park for the night. Odama greeted all of them warmly: "These are my colleagues, my fellow night commuters," he remarked with a smile, and continued on foot, followed by the children. Some of them were as young as five.

From different suburbs of Gulu town, other religious leaders did the same: Anglican bishops Nelson Onono-Onweng and Mcleod Baker Ochola, the head of the Orthodox community, Fr. Julius Orach, and Sheik Musa Khalil, Khadi of the Acholi Muslim Community, united under ARLPI, made the trek to the centre of Gulu town. During a meeting held on 22nd of June, as they lamented the international community's lack of concern for the deadly conflict in Northern Uganda they decided that enough was enough. They agreed to spend a number of nights sleeping with the children, the most vulnerable victims of this war, in the cold and mainly in the bus park. They had made plenty of statements that seemed to have little effect and they thought that a clear and loud action was needed. Some clergy and members of their congregations joined them. Some members of international NGOs based in Gulu also decided to pick up their mats and blankets in the evening and pitch camp for the night with the children. The event, eventually, attracted a lot of interest from both national and international media, which highlighted the plight of the estimated 40,000 children who slept in the streets of Gulu town and other places nearby (like Lacor Hospital) for fear of being abducted by the LRA.

Nobody knows how the phenomenon of the "night commuters" started. In war situations anywhere in the world there are situations that look very much alike, whether in Darfur, Bosnia, Afghanistan or elsewhere. In a world dominated by television, we have grown used to striking images of long lines of refugees carrying their few belongings or refugees crammed into camps, children in military uniforms or towns destroyed; but the exodus of thousands of children coming to sleep on the streets of Gulu and Kitgum became a dramatic image that no one had ever seen before.

Every evening, as sunset approached, as if they had previously agreed among themselves, thousands of children left their villages near the towns of Gulu and Kitgum carrying a piece of cardboard, a plastic sheet, a blanket, or simply nothing, and made their way towards the centre of the towns, where they sought shelter on the street verandahs. Some would be given refuge inside the fenced-in compounds of a school, a parish or a hospital, while others would lie on the ground wherever there was room. The following day, at dawn, they would all get up and go back home, where they would hurriedly leave their bedding, perhaps eat a bit of cassava and drink a cup of tea, put on their school uniforms and rush to school.

In some of the larger displaced people's camps, particularly in Pader and Kalongo, child night commuting took place in a most interesting fashion. Traumatised by frequent LRA attacks at night, thousands of children and women moved from the periphery of the camp – perceived as more dangerous since it was more exposed and unprotected – to the central part of the camp, which was seen as relatively safer. This movement was a second displacement within the displaced people's camp during the night hours.

But despite that incredible human suffering, the official version of the stories that were pumped out daily in the media were that the situation was "under control", the rebels had been "defeated" and "the war was over". There was need for an extra effort to swim against the current of the official story and show to the world that a huge problem existed in Northern Uganda and that something had to be done about it. The action of the religious leaders was undoubtedly striking. One does not hear every day about a bishop sleeping on the street, and in this case there was not one but three or four bishops, plus some other religious leaders doing this. They did not sleep outside for one night, but for four consecutive nights. Two days after this act of solidarity with the children, a host of local and international journalists descended upon Gulu. Some politicians were clearly not happy with the religious leaders' initiative which perhaps they perceived as embarrassing for the government. One politician pointed out to the religious leaders that by sleeping on the streets of Gulu they were putting themselves in danger. "Yes, like all these thousands of children," was Archbishop Odama's answer.

I have been involved in a number of initiatives for peace, but never in my life have I seen a clearer example of the active non-violence preached by Gandhi put into practice. We were not doing anything illegal. Our action did not have the slightest streak of aggressiveness, offence or violence. Yet it was strongly provocative. In situations of oppression, those being oppressed need other people who have the courage to bring their suffering out into the open. If the injustices remain in the dark they will never be solved, and one learns that in such intolerable situations there is indeed no shortage of people who are interested in keeping injustices hidden.

Sleeping on a hard surface, rugged and wet, away from home, and with an empty stomach, leaves a heavy daily toll on the body and mind. When we planned for this action we made a very conscious choice to miss supper and breakfast during those four days in order to be as close as possible to the life conditions of the kids. From another more practical point of view this decision proved to be the most sensible one, since there was no place to satisfy one's natural needs in the bus park where we slept with the children. It was cold during the night and I found myself invaded by a depressing feeling of being far from my usual comfortable sleeping place, exposed to the unknown during the long hours of the night in the darkness. From the first minute I lay there I was shocked by the thought of how many thousands of children had gone through that experience every day for about a year.

I tried to close my eyes while two children lying next to me approached me with curiosity and told me that they had been sleeping there since December of the previous year, after LRA rebels had struck their village one night and abducted some of their neighbours. Around June 2003, the Office of Coordinator for Humanitarian Affairs (OCHA) of the United Nations estimated that in the previous year the LRA had abducted 12,000 children, more than in all the previous years of the war. Despite this finding, the cause of the abducted children in Northern Uganda never hit the world news or became a *cause celèbre* like, for instance, the few thousands kidnapped by the FARC guerrillas in Colombia.

That first night in the bus park, my mind went back to 1985. I remembered how dusk in Acholi used to be a time greeted with joy. I remembered my first days in Kalongo, when every evening gave way to the sound of laughter and a thousand sounds of happiness pervaded the rural areas, where people sang, danced and told stories. During the dry season the youth went out and the sound of drums could be heard in the distance until dawn. The thought of many such happy nights in Acholi villages, lying down and looking at the stars, invaded my mind. The full moon during the dry season could take me to a paradise of dreams. *Dwe matar maber me lalwok maro* (the bright white full moon for escorting the mother-in-law back to her homestead), I remembered hearing. It was a time for cracking jokes, for restoring the day's spent strength, for intimacy with beloved ones. How short is the night with the one my heart loves, the young boys would sing, accompanied by the sweet sound of the *nanga*, which is almost magical at night.

"If you want to know the Acholi well you have to sit with them around the fire at night and listen to them in their language for many hours," Fr. Vincenzo Pellegrini told me during those days. He was a veteran missionary who died in 1988 after spending more than 55 years in Acholi. I tried to put into practice that piece of advice and I was blessed with the gift of many happy and unforgettable nights.

Had all these good memories become history? In 2003 the coming of dusk no longer brought any feeling of joy. When evening approached one would be possessed by a strange feeling of depression, anguish and terror that is difficult to describe. The heart would beat faster. It would be time for finding a hiding place, for practising what the Acholi call *alup* (a game similar to hide-and-seek). Time would be running out and one had to look for a good place on a verandah, in the bus park, in the compound of a parish or in the hospital. Spreading a dirty and worn-out sack, laying down, and if one was lucky, covering oneself with a blanket. These were the nightly, bedtime rituals. Then one had to try to sleep. There was so much noise from radios, and people talking endlessly, perhaps to release tension. Then, suddenly, as if everyone had previously agree, the most absolute silence descended.

During those days I realised that with the falling of darkness a strange sort of pain descended on my shoulders, the part of my body that seemed to attract most of the tension and uncertainty that had accumulated throughout the day. That daily pain accompanied me for many years after and whenever I stayed in Spain for a few weeks or months of rest, the shoulder pain never left me. With the arrival of the evening, even if I found myself sitting by the seaside sipping a drink in the most relaxing of environments, where the only danger for my life was the remote possibility of an accident inside the lift that took me to my flat, I still felt the pain.

Everything impressed me deeply in those days, but perhaps nothing pierced my heart more than the sight of children who brought their textbooks with them on these nightly pilgrimages to do their homework on the bare ground, squeezing in a little time before closing their eyes.

The first night that we spent with the kids we hardly slept. At around midnight, heavy shooting rocked the town. It took place barely two kilometres away from where we were gathered. For about one hour we had to bear the terrifying rattle of gunfire. Children hardly six years old learned to distinguish the different sounds of violence: that is a machine-gun, that is an RPG, that big one was a mortar, they would say. Everybody looked at each other after the sound of gunshots, expressing fear and helplessness, not daring to say a word. I could only pray that it would not last very long. Then I knew that I would not sleep for the rest of the night. The verses of the book of Job came to my mind: "Nights of suffering are my lot. Lying down I wonder: "When will it be day?" (Job 7:3-4). Gunshots rang out in the dark night and as I looked at the stars they did not send me a message of hope, but instead one of sadness.

If the rebels did not wake us with their guns, the rain and storms did. The second day a heavy downpour gave us the night of our lives. Children rushed to the already packed shelters in the bus park, where they had no choice but to spend the rest of the night standing because of lack of space.

Others were so exhausted that they just continued lying down in the rain. Once the storm passed, what had been silence was filled with the sound of coughing, coughing, coughing, and I found myself joining in the choir. After two nights I also began to feel sick. The following day a doctor friend of mine lost his patience with me and told me: "If you want to end up in hospital with pneumonia, just go on doing those crazy things!" The third night I decided to leave the main group and go to sleep in the classrooms of the nearby Holy Rosary Parish. I was still sleeping on the ground, but at least I had a roof over my head. The parish had been giving shelter and safety to more than three thousand children for over a year. I felt a bit more comfortable, but as I tried to fall asleep, I was awoken by a long disturbing cry nearby that pierced me to the depths of my heart. I pulled myself up and to my surprise I found that I was the only one reacting. A child was having a nightmare, and apparently there was no need to be alarmed since this was nothing unusual. Every few minutes another child would utter a similar cry. I realised that many of these children had passed through the terrible trauma of abduction and had been forced to watch murders or even to take part in them. I could not hold back the flood of tears from my eyes. Dreaming of death and terror when they were only seven years old; how could their lot in life be to suffer in silence in a world they could not understand?

Often, when we received visits from international delegations in Gulu, one of the comments we heard from some of the foreign diplomats had to do with why people could not rise up and organise themselves in order to stop the madness with some sort of decisive action. During the four days we slept with the children in the streets of Gulu I think I caught a glimpse of the attitude that we called passivity on the side of the victims. A situation of injustice can only be transformed when people think that a change is possible and they have the necessary strength to influence the course of events. But if people are submerged by circumstances that force them towards their breaking point, they stop thinking that change is possible and they have no strength. When hunger and fear plunge people into emptiness and despair, they no longer make any effort to think about tomorrow.

After three nights sleeping out in the cold, eating only once a day and walking to and from the bus park, I realised that my mind had entered into a state of desperation that I had never experienced before in my life. I am usually a very organised person who depends on time-tables, routines and agendas, but I suddenly stopped making any plans or thinking about what I was going to do the next month, next week, the next day, or even the next afternoon. I found myself in a state of numbness that I had never known before. Whenever I heard some enlightened diplomat asking why people did not rise up to fight the situation, I would simply explain my experience of those days. I had to restrain myself so as not to say directly: "Why don't you try to go through that experience for some few days yourself?"

The third day dawned, and the fourth day followed. By that time I felt weak and dizzy beyond all telling. We went back home with Archbishop Odama and his entourage of destitute children. On the last day there were so many journalists in Gulu that we decided to organise a press conference in the bus park, in the place where the majority of the children spent their nights. I suppose that it was a rather unusual place for a meeting with the media.

During the press conference, Archbishop Odama launched his first question as a challenge:

> "Are these children not part of humanity?" He asked. "Why don't international organisations like United Nations and the African Union devote any time to our problem?"

Nobody answered, but for a moment my mind came out of its state of numbness and I figured out an answer. Many conflicts have been resolved in recent years, thanks to some international interventions, but some cases seem to be more important than others. The international community, particularly the European Union and NATO, intervened in the Balkans when the war swept through Croatia, Bosnia and Kosovo. Europe was not ready to allow a war to take place on its doorstep. The British Army intervened decisively in Sierra Leone putting an end to one of the cruellest wars of recent times. One wonders whether the fact that the small West African country of Sierra Leone is one of the leading producers of diamonds was not one of the deciding factors that prompted the British Army's action. In Sudan, where war started as early as 1956 (except for a period of lull between 1972 and 1983), and where more than two million people died in the south as a result of the conflict, the world looked the other way. However, when huge reserves of oil were discovered in areas that fell within the war zone, the international community, particularly the United States, put pressure on both sides to end the war. Something similar happened in the Democratic Republic of Congo, where the existence of strategic minerals like coltan has been a factor both for beginning the conflict and for working towards its resolution.

Perhaps part of the problem with Northern Uganda is that there is no "reason" to intervene. There are only children. Children who for many years continued to trek wearily every evening to find a place to sleep in the towns to escape abduction and death. Meanwhile, the world was silent. Only the ceasefire agreement reached in August 2006, soon after the beginning of the Juba peace talks, would put an end to this intolerable situation.

We had planned to spend only four nights with the children. One week later I returned to the bus park to visit the night commuters. I was accompanied by a few foreign journalists. Some of the children I had met during those four nights approached me to greet me and asked me a painful question that pierced me to the heart: "When are you coming back to sleep here with us?"

When I escorted the journalists back to their hotel I met the UNICEF representative and as I engaged in conversation with him he asked me how they could help more. I felt angry, but tried to restrain my feelings as I told him that it was high time that UNICEF opened an office in Northern Uganda.

UNICEF did eventually open permanent offices in Gulu, Kitgum and Lira in January 2004. They opened exactly 18 years after this war against children started.

As I have mentioned earlier, there was no shortage of politicians, including some government ministers, who were annoyed at the religious leaders' action when we slept with the children on the streets. Archbishop Odama put it so clearly, though, when he said:

> "They are saying that we have done something very dangerous for our physical integrity, and I have answered that if that is the case we

should be very worried because there are tens of thousands of innocent children in danger every night… Others have remarked that we should have asked for permission from the authorities, and I have asked them whether those 40,000 children who sleep in the open have ever asked for any permission.

"But what amused me more was when somebody told me that our case is special because we are VIPs. I am sorry to disagree. In the gospel Jesus puts a child before the people and says that he is the most important person. Even United Nations has a special charter for children, but as far as I know religious leaders have no special UN charter. Let them correct me if I am wrong".

As usual, Archbishop Odama was right.

Kony with abducted girls

Vicent Otti with an armed boy

A young LRA fighter

Palenga internally displaced people's camp

Omiya–Anyima internally displaced people's camp

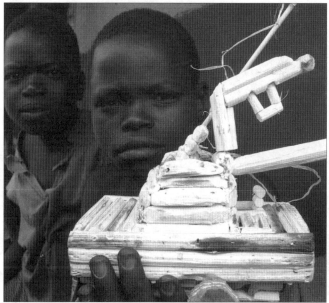

A displaced child in Pagak internally displaced people's camp displays this toy tank made of reeds

Girls released by the LRA arrive at Pajule Catholic Mission, July 2002

Night commuters prepare to sleep on a Gulu street

Fr. Carlos Rodríguez, the author, and Archbishop John Baptist Odama walk
to the Gulu bus park to spend the night with child night commuters

Archbishop Odama and Bishop Nelson Onono-Onweng lie down to sleep
in solidarity with the night commuters at Gulu bus park, June 2003

Bishop Mcleod Baker Ochola of Kitgum Diocese

Archbishop John Baptist Odama of Gulu Archdiocese greets a Muslim leader in Nimule, South Sudan

Frs Giulio Albanese, Tarcisio Pazzaglia and Carlos Rodriguez have their first meal at Lacor Hospital in Gulu, soon after they were released by the UPDF

The author talks to a rebel in the bush in October 2001. He was part of a group that accepted to come out through the mediation of religious and cultural leaders

Fr. Tarcisio Pazzaglia talks to rebel commander Moses Okello in the bush near Pajule in 2001

Archbishop Odama, Fr. Carlos Rodríguez (the author) and Fr. Tarcisio Pazzaglia (extreme right) meet rebel commanders Charles Tabuley, Livingstone Opiro and Dominic Ongwen in Koyo, Lalogi in July 2002

Minister of Internal Affairs Ruhakana Rugunda shakes hands with LRA commander Sam Kolo on 29th December 2004. Betty Bigombe is on Rugunda's left

Participants in peace talks in December 2004

Archbishop Odama, together with some religious and political leaders, walks to the bush for peace talks in December 2005

Internal Affairs Permanent Secretary, Dr Kagoda, shakes hands with LRA head of delegation, Martin Ojul, during the signing of the third protocol during the peace talks in Juba, June 2007

11

On Internal Affairs and Other Deceits

On 12th June 2003, the Makerere University Acholi Students' Association invited the British High Commissioner as guest of honour to a function they organised in Kampala. Speaking with straightforwardness that is characteristic of the Acholi, the chairman of the association could not have been more direct and clear:

> "The conflict in northern Uganda won't be resolved without an international intervention. The United Kingdom, having been our former colonial master, has a special responsibility in this respect... If your government sent British troops to pacify the north, as you have just done in Sierra Leone, the problem could be solved."

But the British High Commissioner insisted that the two situations were very different and that the war in the north was Uganda's internal affair in which the British could not intervene. His government was willing to increase the humanitarian aid to help the internally displaced people but not intervene beyond this assistance.

The British High Commissioner's words sounded very similar to those Archbishop Odama heard five days later from the UN's head of mission in his Kampala office. Confronted with the question about why the Security Council had never discussed the issue of the war in the north, the UN representative was clearly very reluctant to take up the issue or to pass it on to other authorities. Nevertheless, he assured the prelate that the UN could increase funding for humanitarian and peace activities if we would write and submit a detailed project proposal before the approaching deadline.

These two incidents exemplify the attitude of the international community those days. Northern Uganda was a hot potato nobody wanted to hold. Interventions? Statements? Anything of that kind could irritate the Ugandan government. It was safer to pull out the chequebook and ask how much money was needed. That said, it would be unfair not to point out that for some years different international organisations had been supporting peace programmes in the north. ARLPI started its activities in 1998 with funding from the UN Development Programme, and in our first peace expeditions to the bush we were able to pay for expenses like fuel and phone communication thanks to the money we received from the British High Commission in Kampala. Even President Museveni had given us with some money from his office.

Other high-ranking diplomats were far-sighted enough to realise that things could not continue in this way. Outstanding among them was the European Union Head of Mission, Sigurd Illing, who led several delegations to the north, reaching more outlying areas like Kitgum and Pader. The Irish ambassador, Martin O'Fainnin, was also particularly critical of the Ugandan government's approach to the war. Because Sigurd Illing became a voice in the wilderness and was outstanding in his outspokenness, he was often targeted by nasty verbal attacks from the army and some government officials, particularly from the Ministry of State for Security.

Since it was under the shield of "internal affairs", the war that broke out in Northern Uganda in 1986 had attracted little international attention and very little recognition by the UN Security Council. Putting pressure on the Ugandan government to take the problem more seriously was something that for many years nobody was willing to do, and when Sudan started helping the LRA most countries looked the other way.

Most people in the north, even if they had little formal education, received most of their information from radio stations like the BBC or the Voice of America. They asked aloud why some other conflict areas in the world had attracted effective international intervention in recent years: Bosnia, Kosovo, Angola, Sierra Leone, Central America, Afghanistan, the Middle East. With a certain amount of bitterness, many found the most convincing explanation of this negligence to be the fact that Northern Uganda was a zone without any significant economic, commercial or strategic interests.

For many years, President Museveni had been the darling of the West in Africa. With Uganda's good economic performance and its impressive results in reducing the spread of HIV in a few years, Uganda represented one of Africa's few success stories. Uganda was always in the good books of the International Monetary Fund and the World Bank, and once considered an example of a "new breed of African leaders", as former US president, Bill Clinton, once expressed, yet nobody seemed to take interest in a problem that was taking place in a remote corner of the country, far away from the capital. For the rest of Ugandans, Acholiland was too far away for most of them, geographically and otherwise. Many of them seemed to hold to the conviction that the Acholi were the ones responsible for the serious human rights abuses perpetrated on them during the time of Obote's regime, as well as the current brutality that was being meted out on them by Kony, who was one of their tribe; all of this served them right.

Since the religious leaders had joined night commuters, when they slept with the children on the streets of Gulu they, together with the cultural leaders had gradually gained recognition as a powerful national and international peace lobby, and they were insisting on the same message. Northern Uganda needed an international intervention, and the UN Security Council had to pass a motion to that effect. It might have been that we did not elaborate enough on that demand, or that we were a bit too vague, because nothing changed. Maybe if we had taken more time for reflection and had articulated our proposals in a clearer way, we may have been much more effective and avoided some misunderstandings.

One day we received a personal letter from President Museveni addressed to "the bishops of Northern Uganda". The closed envelope was brought by car from the Gulu barracks and handed to Archbishop Odama's gatekeeper at his residence. Using a rather harsh language, Museveni accused the religious leaders of having moved "from mistake to mistake" with their "false solutions" of amnesty and dialogue with mass killers, the LRA. He was incensed at the religious leaders' calls for an international intervention, and he argued that the real solution to the problem lay in increasing military spending; this was a proposal that the religious leaders had never supported.

On 3rd July 2003, Pope John Paul II, in a public speech during the prayer of Angelus at St. Peter's Square in Rome, referred again to the tragedy in Northern Uganda. After expressing his "profound sorrow" for the violence there, he appealed to the parties involved in the conflict to negotiate a peace accord. That same day Archbishop Odama published a pastoral letter entitled "I have seen the humiliation of my people". There he described with all kinds of details the abuses perpetrated against the civilian population in the north, and he also deplored the attacks against the church.

Odama spoke loud and clear. He was practically the Catholic Church's only voice on this issue. For many years no statements about Northern Uganda had come from the Uganda Episcopal Conference, whose bishops were clearly divided when it came to political and social issues. Most of them felt that their dioceses could carry out their work very comfortably so long as they did not challenge the government on anything, but remained quiet. With some notable exceptions, like Cardinal Emmanuel Wamala, the result was that the church in Uganda expressed the same apathy and lack of interest as the rest of the world towards the suffering of Northerners.

All our contacts with the LRA had stopped for some time and the peace process had entered into a rather lengthy stagnation phase. To maintain its members in isolation, without contact with the outside world, seemed one of the most outstanding features of the LRA, which was more like an armed cult than a rebel movement fighting for political change. During those months I spent hours and hours listening to young returned abductees who had been with the LRA for many years and could potentially help us understand how Kony's army functioned and what mentality they had. I carefully noted down details from these conversations, including descriptions of the structure of their brigades and the names of the officers. Since convincing Kony and his top men about serious negotiation seemed so difficult, I counted myself among those who were beginning to cherish the idea that the LRA could be weakened by convincing as many LRA officers as possible to lay down their arms.

Despite the army's official statements, made almost daily, about how the rebels were "defeated" or "fleeing in disarray", or how Kony was "about to be history", the situation was getting worse. But whenever the reality stubbornly proved the army wrong, when the LRA made another deadly attack, the army spokesperson used an expression people grew tired of hearing: "These are merely kicks of a dying horse," the spokesperson would say.

★   ★   ★

Jimmy and Francis, who had left the LRA a few weeks earlier, were regular visitors at our ARLPI office in Gulu. During the more than 10 years they spent with the LRA, the atrocities they had experienced and participated in had turned them into little monsters in need of serious rehabilitation. Despite this need, however, they did not take advantage of the therapy offered by any of the reception centres operating in Gulu at that time; for example, the World Vision or GUSCO (Gulu Support the Children Organisation) offered this service to returned abductees. Instead, Jimmy and Francis had secured places for themselves in the army as soon as they left the LRA. They joined a detach known as Child Protection Unit, which had been taken outside the installations of Gulu Barracks. Lorries of children rescued from the LRA arrived there almost daily. The UPDF was convinced that the presence of young officers who had left the LRA could build trust in the ones who were just arriving. It was not unusual for many a young returnee from the LRA to end up joining the army after passing through the Child Protection Unit. On one occasion I took a young boy who had just escaped the LRA to the offices of the Amnesty Commission in Gulu. After they had recorded his information, I took him to the World Vision centre. In the afternoon, however, the army public relations officer called to convince the 15-year-old boy to go to the barracks for some questioning. The officer assured me that it would be two days at most. After three months the boy was still in the barracks and in the end he was pressured enough to join the army. This particular boy was just one of many.

Before they escaped the LRA, many of these young boys and girls had become cruel killing machines and suffered from terrible traumas. When they escaped the rebel ranks, they experienced a brief sense of joy and euphoria at their freedom, and then the dismal prospects confronting them would hit them. Many had no parents, but even those who did found their parents in camps, uprooted from their original villages, living lives of destitution and depression. Used to giving orders and being addressed by their ranks, these boys and girls came back to live under their parents' authority and found that their parents could not provide for them and that they were misfits in school. For many of them, the prospect of joining the army, in comparison, looked attractive.

While NGOs, religious and cultural leaders and the media – most notably Radio Mega FM - tried to foster a culture of reconciliation, underneath it lay a reality few wanted to face. Young LRA returnees often faced rejection by their communities of origin. In many cases, members of these communities had been these rebels' victims. In a society where most people used to survive on agriculture but where insecurity had made it almost impossible to go back to farming, the young returnees, with no other skills or training than in the military field, could easily be convinced to join the UPDF. After all the army could provide them with salaries, housing, food, protection and a future with opportunities for promotion.

All of this, of course, had a price. I often met Jimmy and Francis in the streets of Gulu and they proudly told me how they had been made to board the UPDF helicopter to point out exactly where the hideouts of their former comrades were. Only God knows how many abducted children died during the attacks that resulted from this information.

Jimmy and Francis presented themselves to us as being very eager to help some of their old companions leave the LRA. One day they connected us by phone with two different people, both of whom they assured us were top commanders in the LRA, Dominic Ongwen and Ochan Bunia. As usual, I informed the archbishop and obtained his go-ahead. I communicated frequently with the two of them. Most times they asked for airtime for their mobiles phones. On 21st June, Jimmy told me that he was ready to prove that he was not manipulating us. He informed me of an appointment he had in the bush, and that evening he brought a girl called Margaret, whose parents I knew well. She had been abducted from a secondary school in Kalongo in 1998. When I saw her it was a most pleasant surprise. The girl assured me that Jimmy had met her in the bush and brought her back to Gulu on his motorbike. She had been released, Jimmy told me, by Ochan Bunia.

The person who claimed to be Dominic Ongwen told me that he wanted to leave the LRA, but before he left he wanted to talk to his mother. Over the next several weeks, we looked for her in the places where he told us she would be. Our search was always in vain. We kept the military informed of our contact with the man who claimed to be Ongwen, and each time they encouraged us to continue our contact.

A few days after 21st June, Jimmy introduced us to a young man who assured us that he was sent by Col. Livingstone Opiro, one of the LRA commanders we had met the year before in Koyo Lalogi. He asked us for a mobile phone to enable communication with us.

The day after we gave him one, I received a phone call from a man claiming to be Livingstone Opiro. Two days later we received the same request for a cell phone from Col. Odiambo. For the next few weeks we found ourselves speaking daily to four people who, at different times, called to tell us very similar things, and to assure us that they were Dominic Ongwen, Ochan Bunia, Livingstone Opiro and Odiambo. The first of these stopped, though, after a couple of weeks. These calls lasted for most of the months of July and August of 2003. During that time the strange trio kept us busy dancing according to their own tune.

What we heard from our phone communication with them could not have been more encouraging. They said that they were fed up with Kony and wanted to find a safe way to leave the LRA with all their fighters – who they claimed were in their hundreds – and to take advantage of the amnesty.

In order to meet their requests, we needed some international support, but acquiring this was difficult, since the UN, for whatever reason, was not prepared to play any mediation role in or support the peace process in any way besides financially. We decided to try the International Organisation for Migration (IOM), whose mandate it was to receive people who had been involved in acts of rebellion against the state and had applied for amnesty. To this effect, IOM was running a reception centre in Eastern Uganda. For several weeks I acted as a courier and I took letters purportedly signed by Livingstone Opiro to the IOM's Head of Mission John Walburn in Kampala. Walburn responded to these letters by giving information about the kind of help his office was in a position to provide to people who wanted to abandon rebellion and take advantage of the government's amnesty.

Some Western embassies showed an interest in this new attempt, and so did the chairman of the Uganda Amnesty Commission, Justice Onega. Understandably, the first thing they always asked from us was what guarantees we had that our contacts were genuine, since they had not gone beyond phone conversations. It was impossible for us to be completely sure, but given the fact that military intelligence confirmed what we were hearing, – that there was a crisis within the LRA and that a number of officers were looking for a way out, we had reason to believe that we were on the right track.

Our phone contact with these people continued for several weeks. At one point they started asking for money. This was not a good sign. At first we did not comply with their requests. When they increased the intensity of their demands and threatened to abandon the whole plan of leaving the LRA we gave some amounts to Jimmy and Francis, who always assured us that they were taking the money to the bush. According to them, this money was used to buy foodstuffs for the rebels while they were making arrangements to come out so that they would not have to resort to taking food by force in attacks against camps.

But there were many aspects of this whole process that we did not understand. It puzzled us that Jimmy and Francis could go to meet the LRA rebels in the bush so easily and at the same time live permanently in the army's Child Protection Unit.

The three persons who called us daily insisted that they wanted assurances of their own safety once they came out of the bush. Thinking that it would speed up things, and learning from the recent experience of the peace process with the UNRF in West Nile, we proposed that we use the services of a lawyer. We contacted Caleb Alaka, a young bright lawyer who had played this role with the UNRF rebels, and after a few days he enthusiastically accepted our request for help and started talking with the trio.

On 15th August Caleb Alaka arrived in Gulu. That evening, Francis came to see Archbishop Odama and I. He communicated to us that Vincent Otti had given orders to Odiambo, Ochan Bunia and Opiro, who supposedly were in Opit, to move immediately towards Atyak. This move was a blow to our plans.

The next day, Caleb Alaka received a phone call from a man who said he spoke for the LRA. They made an appointment to meet in a forest near Gulu. When he reached the meeting place, Alaka met three men with strange looks who spoke little and made little sense. Alaka tried to persuade them to tell their bosses not to delay in their decision to lay down their arms and leave the LRA.

That same day, at midday, a group came from Kampala. I did not know that a taskforce had been formed to deal with this possible massive surrender of LRA fighters and that this group had come up with a contingency plan. The group was made up of Anton Barre, who worked with the Embassy of Denmark, Justice Onega, the PS for internal affairs, Doctor Kagoda, and Brig. Kale Kayihura.

The trio we had been in contact with said they would all come out of the bush on 17th August. They had explained to us that when the time came they would tell us exactly where we should meet them. Strangely enough, the three "commanders" had switched their phones off, but the ones who had talked to Caleb Alaka gave him another appointment in the bush, this time near Opit. When Alaka arrived at the meeting place, he found three different people, who were as reserved as the ones he had met the day before.

That meeting was the end of everything. The delegation from Kampala returned to the capital the next day.

It was very clear that we had been deceived.

They had kept us running up and down, nurturing hopes that a breakthrough could be made with this new attempt, which had looked promising. They did not get a lot of money from us, hardly six million shillings (about 2,500 euro), but they did waste much of our energy. So much effort for nothing.

If it is any consolation, whoever has ever tried to do something for peace in Northern Uganda has found himself or herself at some point being cheated, misled and deceived by unscrupulous people who have learned to make a living off the miseries of the population and the good-will of others. I have always been someone who is easily deceived, I must acknowledge. I felt very angry at the time, but maybe this event was another part of the painful trials we had to go through.

★   ★   ★

The UN under secretary for humanitarian affairs, the Norwegian Jan Egeland, entered the meeting room at Archbishop Odama's residence on the afternoon of 9th November 2003. He was accompanied by several high-ranking UN officials who had come from New York and Geneva. The meeting was the first, in Northern Uganda, to which an international personality of such calibre had come. Egeland listened attentively while Odama read a document we had prepared the day before and which repeated our appeal for a decisive intervention by the UN to end the war. From the beginning of the meeting, Egeland showed that he was not fond of beating about the bush. With much conviction, he agreed that the international community had to do much more for Northern Uganda and assured us that the UN would open several offices in the north by January 2004. The following day he visited a displaced people's camp in Kitgum and his words were echoed in the international media:

> "Northern Uganda is the world's worst and most forgotten humanitarian crisis," he said. "I cannot find any other part of the world where the situation is as bad as (it is) here." He went as far as to say that the problem was "worse than in Iraq".

Egeland did not tire of saying that the problem could not be solved exclusively by military means, and that much more should be done by all.

> "Where else in the world have there been 20,000 kidnapped children? Where else in the world have 90 per cent of the population of large districts been displaced… For me the situation is a moral outrage. A much bigger international investment is needed, in political involvement, in diplomacy, and also more concerted efforts to tell the parties there is no military solution… there is a solution through reconciliation, and an end to the killing and the reintegration and demobilisation of the child combatants."

The following day, vice-president Gilbert Bukenya assured Egeland that the government would do all it could to find a peaceful, negotiated solution to end the conflict.

President Museveni was not in Uganda at the time these statements were made. He was in the United States, where he was supporting a campaign to promote Uganda as a tourism destination.

Despite the war in the North, Uganda was indeed an excellent place for tourism. Endowed with breathtaking landscapes, well-kept national parks teeming with game, the snow-capped Rwenzori mountains, wonderful lakes and amazing tropical forests the tourism industry flourished and new high-market hotels were built almost every year. These "improvements" were signs that most Ugandans lived better than they had twenty years earlier. The country had better roads, primary and secondary schools, universities and hospitals. But most of this prosperity was concentrated in the south, which had been free from any armed conflict since 1986. Many pointed out that, in reality, there were two Ugandas: a prosperous, developing and peaceful Uganda in the south, and another one in the north that was poor, desperate and trapped in violence.

One of the concerns that Egeland shared with us was that there was a lack of funds to guarantee the line of food supplies to the two million people, who at that moment were displaced internally in Northern Uganda, in the IDP camps in Acholi, Teso and Lango. Donor countries did not give enough food contributions to the WFP for the population in the camps because they were convinced that Uganda, after several decades of violence and chaos during the regimes of Amin and Obote, was now a beacon of hope and a model for Africa. Over the years of conflict, however, the Ugandan government had understated the problem in the north, which could tarnish its good international image, and for some time the international community was convinced that all was okay. In 2003, the government's agenda was contradictory: on one hand it asked for help to feed its two million citizens living in IDP camps, while on the other hand it refused to declare the north a disaster area and insisted that the rebels had been defeated and that the problem was almost over. Our role in spreading reliable information from the ground, which we did as religious organisations, was crucial in informing the outside world of the truth about the situation.

Jan Egeland told us that the WFP badly needed 120 million dollars to guarantee a minimum of humanitarian assistance to the two million displaced people in Northern Uganda. When I heard this figure a bell rang in my mind. The month before, in October, during a brief holiday I spent in Spain, I received an invitation from the University of Connecticut, in the US, to give a talk to students about the situation in Northern Uganda. During the week I spent there I observed that the university campus was undergoing a lot of building activity, with heavy machinery and cranes everywhere. Moved by curiosity, I enquired as to the reason behind so much construction and the answer I heard struck me deeply. They told me that these were works of "routine maintenance". To my understanding, maintenance consists of operations like replacing old pipes or electric cables, reinforcing foundations or painting, but in reality what they were doing was pulling down old buildings and constructing new ones. A block of classrooms that had been on the campus for thirty years was already considered "old". With such an understanding of the term "maintenance" it was no wonder that for that year the university had a budget of 120 million dollars, which (what a coincidence) was the same amount that the UN needed to feed the people of Northern Uganda, and which the UN found so hard to raise.

Back in Uganda, and in the middle of trying to solve this financial problem, the religious leaders met with Egeland one Sunday afternoon.

That very morning I had celebrated mass in the displaced people's camp of Palenga. At the end of the service, the catechist welcomed me into his home and offered to feed me all he had for lunch: a small lump of stiff yellow maize porridge and nothing else. We ate in silence. For some time the people in many IDP camps had been receiving food rations of only maize flour. The WFP had no beans or peas to give to the IDPs, so people had no protein to accompany the tasteless meal they ate once or twice a day.

The issue of the child night commuters gradually attracted some attention from international media who sent some journalists to report on their plight. For many days much of my daily routine included devoting some time with journalists who came to us seeking independent and reliable information. I spent many hours doing the little I could to help these professionals understand what had happened and was still happening in the north, introducing them to children who slept in the streets and taking them to the camps to hear for themselves from the "experts" on the situation: the victims. The more I did for these journalists, the further I went into dangerous territory, since exposing the truth threatened the interests of those who wanted to control the information leaving Uganda. It would not be long before I was made to pay a price for this.

Little by little Uganda stopped being Africa's success story in international circles and became Africa's place of horror, especially for children.

The task of exposing the truth and bringing the reality of the situation out into the open was a risky one, and rarely did it match harmoniously with the work that was expected of "neutral" mediators. In conflicts, mediators who come from outside have the advantage of being emotionally detached from the reality that causes suffering, and because of this they can more easily enjoy the benefit of neutrality. In the case of Northern Uganda, the religious leaders had the great advantage of being mediators "from inside" the situation, since they had long-established links and relationships on the ground with the parties in conflict. However, a religious minister is also a moral point of reference who gives people a sense of direction, and in this respect when a priest or bishop sees his people being abused in intolerable ways he cannot keep silent. Being a mediator who at the same time speaks up for the people is not an easy endeavour.

In November 2003, we had once again a chance to understand the difficulty involved in our roles as religious leaders and mediators when we received a new serious threat.

For Fr. Tarcisio, following the rebels' morning conversations on the radio had become part of his daily routine. What he heard at 8 am on 19th November 2003 made him worry. There was no doubt; it was Kony's voice giving instructions to his units to kill Archbishop Odama "and the other religious leaders". The rebel leader was very upset because of an open letter that the religious leaders had written to President George W. Bush when he had made a brief visit to Uganda in July that year. In the document, ARLPI had asked the US leader to do something to end the problem of Northern Uganda. The letter, which was published in the Uganda press, could have been interpreted in different ways, depending on who read it.

I was in Kitgum at that time. After hearing about the threat on our lives, I called Vincent Otti.

> "Anything new?" he asked me in his usual laconic manner when he answered the phone.
>
> "Yes," I said. "You must have heard about the visit of Jan Egeland to Uganda. The UN favours a negotiated solution to the conflict and this is a chance you should grasp."
>
> "We are always ready to talk peace, but Museveni keeps on saying that he is going to kill us. He must stop saying that. Otherwise negotiations cannot happen. If he wants war he will have war. They will see."

"I also wanted to ask you why you want to kill Archbishop Odama," I told him.

"What is that? Who told you? That is not true!"

"I have heard that your chairman is very angry because of the religious leaders' letter to President Bush."

"Well… yes, we are not happy with that letter."

"But in that letter the bishops did not ask President Bush to give military help to the government of Uganda. They have always advocated for a peaceful solution. And that also depends on you. If you made a public statement declaring your intention to go for peace talks it could make a difference…"

"My battery is very low," Otti interrupted. "Call me tomorrow…"

I had heard such an excuse to end phone conversations many times before. Invariably, every time that the conversation reached the point of demanding a clear answer, they ended it with any excuse. Sometimes it was the battery of the phone, other times it was a storm. The LRA always proved to be masters in dodging important questions.

I was very worried about the bishops. I called Betty Bigombe, who lived in Washington, DC at the time, where she had been working with the World Bank for several years. Since she had left Uganda she had always tried to keep some discreet contact with the LRA. She expressed to me her great worry for our security and told me that we should be very cautious about where we slept, because that would be the moment when we would be most vulnerable to any impending attacks. She assured me that she would try to talk to Sam Kolo, who had proved to be a reasonable person.

After my conversation with Bigombe, I also called Fabio Riccardi of Sant'Egidio. That evening he talked to Sam Kolo for about one hour.

A few days later, Vincent Otti called to ask for Betty Bigombe's phone number. I gave it to him. Many phone conversations were taking place behind the scenes. On 31st December Betty Bigombe told me that she had been talking with Sam Kolo regularly for several weeks and that she intended to come to Uganda soon.

That day, as we had done every year since 1998, we walked through the streets of Gulu demonstrating for peace.

Two months earlier, I had visited a certain Western diplomat in his Kampala office. I remembered the occasion very well because in his air-conditioned room I caught a bad cold that kept me sneezing for the next three days. During our meeting he told me that what we should do was to organise a big demonstration for peace in Gulu. "Since 1998 we have been demonstrating every year on 31st December," I answered.

> "So, if you do it again," the diplomat said "tell me and I shall mobilise international journalists who will come with their TV cameras and you will see how it can make an impact."

One week before 31st December I called him to confirm that arrangements for that year's demonstration were well under way and that we would be happy to see him there with the media. Unfortunately, he told me that he would be "out of the office". He did not elaborate, but I learned that he was on some beach in Zanzibar for his Christmas holidays. Definitely, in this life each person has his own priorities.

That 31st December 2003, the army spokesperson informed the press about the UPDF's achievements during the year. They had killed 824 rebels, captured 279 and received 434 who surrendered. In total 1,537 rebels had been put "out of action". Keeping in mind that one year earlier the army had informed the public that there were only 514 rebels left, this new number meant that the UPDF had killed these rebels three times over. This was not bad at all. Pity that nobody incorporated it in the Guinness book of records.

12

Living Under Threat

"The war is over" was the front-page headline of *The Monitor* on 27th January 2004. It was a quote from the 4th division commander, Col. Nathan Mugisha, during a public rally held in Gulu two days earlier on Liberation Day, which marked the day on which Museveni and his NRA troops had seized Kampala in 1986, For the Acholi population, that day had little to do with any shade of liberation and much to do with the beginning of their own troubles.

That same day, very early in the morning, I rushed to the parish of Minakulu, where I worked. The night before the rebels had launched a hit-and-run attack against the small trading centre of houses set on either side of the main road. The Local Defence Unit's (LDU) detach had consisted of eight soldiers, who did what they could to confront the rebels. Two LDU members were wounded, and the rebels beat to death a 70-year-old man and abducted a 13-year-old boy and two adults.These hostages were released a few hours later. These kinds of incidents took place daily in the north. This was why whenever people heard official statements that spoke of the end of the war while they were unsure whether they would be alive each morning, they wondered whether they were not being fooled.

A few days earlier the Internal Security Organisation boss, Col. Elly Kayanja, had come to pitch camp in Gulu, like many other top military officers had done before, offering not a solution but THE solution to the conflict. He was one of the UPDF officers with a kind of populist character. A couple of years before he had gained a lot of popularity with his "Operation Wembley" that, with a mixture of heavy-handedness and magnanimity, had dealt a decisive blow to some of Kampala's most notorious gangs of robbers. Kayanja wanted to follow a similar strategy to pacify the north, luring some of the friends and relatives of the rebels in the hope that the friends and family could convince the rebels to come out of the bush. Friendly, polite and respectful, in some of the meetings that we had with him, he presented an image very different from some of the top UPDF officers who for the last few months had used threatening language against the "terrorists" and their collaborators. Unfortunately, the more attempts were made to convince rebels to lay down their arms peacefully, the more conmen seemed to thrive, ready to make money by deceit, as we had just experienced months earlier.

On one of his visits to the archbishop's residence, Kayanja warned Odama about some very serious threats to his life that Kony had issued. These were nothing new for the man of God, but this time the words of caution were about a very imminent attack. The ISO boss offered Odama 24-hour protection in the form of bodyguards disguised as compound workers. Although Odama did exercise common sense about his own security, his residence was always open and anybody could enter at almost any time without much screening. He was convinced of his role as a pastor for all but, he was informed, this could have serious consequences for his security.

> "Let me put it this way," Odama told Kayanja "I do not live alone, in isolation. I am part of the people and if people are safe I'll have nothing to fear… My suggestion is that you try to solve not just my problem, but the people's problem of security and I shall also be protected automatically."

★   ★   ★

On 2nd February I was awakened by the sound of my mobile phone, which flashed two text messages.

800 huts burnt in Pabbo IDP

Have you got info of what the army has done in Pabbo?

Pabbo, which is 40 kilometres north-west of Gulu, was the biggest camp in Northern Uganda. At that time it was "home" to a population of 60,000 people. Such congestion was one of the reasons for its reputation as one of the camps more prone to internal conflicts. Since its creation in 1996 it had been repeatedly attacked by scores of rebels, who often hid in the neighbouring Kilak hills, which are visible from any corner of the camp.

After the early morning mass, I met two young men who had arrived from Pabbo the evening before. They told me even more alarming details. After reporting to the ARLPI office and gathering some more information, the staff decided that an ARLPI staff member and I should go to Pabbo and assess the situation for ourselves. After gathering my camera and a notebook we jumped into my old Suzuki and drove to Pabbo.

The atmosphere in Pabbo when we arrived was very tense. Yet people were very willing to talk. We interviewed different groups, and their accounts coincided clearly. The day before soldiers had carried out a pre-dawn combing of the camp and forced several hundred men to follow them to the market compound. It was said that the rounding-up operation was aimed at finding hidden weapons and rebel collaborators.

The men had spent several hours in the market compound when, at around 11 am, a big fire broke out and quickly spread throughout the packed grass-thatched huts, helped by the extreme heat and winds characteristic of the dry season. As they saw the flames and columns of smoke, the men panicked and shouted that they wanted to go home to save their few belongings. The soldiers' opposition gave rise to emotions that flared up higher than the fire and a scuffle ensued during which some of the men hurled stones at the military and tried to push their way out.

Together with my ARLPI colleague, we went around the camp for about two hours. We took photos and notes. Most people we talked to told us that they were convinced the fire had been started by the soldiers. Some even pointed at the places where, according to them, the soldiers had started torching grass houses.

When I returned home, as I had done many other times, I emailed the story to our usual recipients: media houses, embassies, human rights groups, NGOs, international organisations and prominent individuals concerned with Northern Uganda.

The news story was published the next day in both national and international media. *The New Vision* ran the story on its front page. I did not think it was important when I saw that they had quoted me saying that according to many of the camp residents I had talked to the fire could have been started by the soldiers during their round-up operation when hundreds of men had been detained.

The day after the story was published I travelled to Lira. The situation there was one of total desperation. The LRA had attacked the Abiya IDP camp the day before, killing 44 people and wounding more than 70. In a few weeks the population of Lira town had swollen with an additional 300,000 terrified people who had run away from their homes. These new arrivals were distributed between nine new IDP camps that had started receiving food supplies from the WFP. But outside the town, towards the north and east, 200,000 more displaced persons languished without any kind of humanitarian assistance. Abandoned to their own devices, people had no choice but to venture back to their abandoned villages in the hope of gathering some little food to survive. Many of these forages became real traps when people were taken by surprise by gangs of rebels who in most cases beat them or hacked them to death. People were dying in front of an indifferent international community, which seemed to be in no hurry to act.

Two days later I went back to Pabbo. On this second visit, I was part of a larger ARLPI delegation with some of the main religious leaders. We found people more intimidated than ever, but all the same ready to talk.

In the afternoon I started hearing some "bell-like sounds". I gathered that some of the political leaders from Gulu were very unhappy about the information I had passed to the media about Pabbo. The army spokesperson had even told one of our ARLPI staff that I could easily be deported for what I had done.

In the days that followed tension increased. One evening two journalist friends tipped me of an impending declaration by the UPDF asking for my expulsion from the country. Since I considered them to be well informed, their words fell on me like heavy rocks, crushing me as I listened.

I wanted to anticipate the events before being taken by surprise, so I called Col. Kayanja. He told me that he had not heard anything.

At around 8 am the next day, a friend rang me from Kampala. His voice carried a tone of deep worry.

"How are you there?"

"I am fine, thanks."

"I am sorry to tell you that I do not think you are so fine. Have you read the newspapers of today?"

The *New Vision* and *Monitor* had not yet arrived in Gulu. When they did arrive, I read one of their main headlines: "The army asks Fr. Carlos to leave the country" and understood my friend's concern.

During the rest of the day I received an endless succession of phone calls; by the end I was completely exhausted. In many cases those calling me were journalists who wanted to know my reaction or to get a comment from me. I realised that this was a delicate moment that called for extreme prudence. I had not received any official communication, and neither had the archdiocese. Therefore it was tricky to comment on information we were getting only from second-hand sources. Also, a comment taken out of context, distorted or expressed in an emotional tone could be the perfect excuse for an action I wanted to avoid. Moreover, the archbishop was out of the country and I found myself in a situation that was very difficult to manage. Mechanically, feeling like an answering machine, I limited myself to saying that I could not comment on something about which I had not received any direct communication and that as far as I was concerned I was still in Gulu doing my usual work.

Many other phone calls were from friends. Archbishop Odama, who was in Germany, was among the first to call me. He told me to remain calm. I received calls from Sant'Egidio, Amnesty International, Human Rights Watch, embassies, Acholis in the diaspora and personal friends.

Some calls were stranger than others. The Spanish embassy in Nairobi told me to keep out of politics and devote myself to my pastoral and spiritual tasks. I told them that when one thousand families lost their homes in a fire and were left destitute that was not a political matter, but a humanitarian one and certainly a pastoral one. And I repeated that they should stop looking at events from a safe distance and come visit Northern Uganda. The ambassador told me that he could not do that since he was new and had not yet presented his credentials to the Ugandan government. Two months later he would call me again to tell me that on the occasion of the presentation of those letters he was inviting me for a reception in Kampala. In that case, I answered, you are already in a position to visit any part of the country, so when are you coming to the north to visit us? His excellency excused himself saying that it would not be appropriate for him to come to see me, a "controversial person", since it could be misinterpreted by the government and damage the relations between the two countries. After that I stopped insisting and simply felt profoundly ashamed to be a national from a country like Spain that did not show the slightest interest in Northern Uganda, whose people were at the very centre of my heart and for whom I was ready to continue risking my own life.

But once again the psychological torture I was experiencing had just resumed and it was going to last longer this time than I had expected.

"I have not received any official communication" was the phrase I calmly tried to articulate those days. But was I convinced that this was a satisfactory answer? In a war situation official communications may be worth nothing, especially when it is all about intimidation tactics. I was only too conscious that anything could happen at any time. All kinds of thoughts came to my mind. I imagined waking up one day before dawn to find soldiers waiting outside, to arrest me. I had been arrested once before, and was submerged in anxiety at the mere thought of having to spend another day, another night, or maybe several days undergoing a Kafkian situation of absurdity in which I did not know who accused me and I did not have any clue about what would come next. It was neither a flimsy suspicion nor over indulgence of my imagination. A few months later, in November 2004, the parish priest of Kitgum town was detained by soldiers who surrounded the priest's residence, accused him of being a suspect in collaborating with the rebels but without any concrete charge, and made him spend a week locked up in a dark cell. He was eventually released and told to report regularly to the police. The damage that such an experience can do to a human being is beyond all telling.

That evening I gathered together some few belongings and spent the night in the Comboni community of Lacor Hospital.

The following day, one of the newspapers' lead stories qouted the army spokesman as having said I could work anywhere in Uganda "except in the north, for my own security". Very kind of him to worry about my security, I thought to myself. That cynicism was beginning to become exasperating.

That morning I received a phone call from a journalist who asked me whether I felt unsafe in the north. "Yes," I answered, "like any other person among the two million living here."

The vicar general of the archdiocese, Mgr. Matthew Odong, came to see me and gave me a lot of encouragement. Since one of the stories written about me quoted the Gulu RDC, chairman of the district security committee, Odong called him to ask for a meeting. The man said that he was in Kampala and that as soon as he returned to Gulu he would call us and arrange for a meeting. We never got any other phone call from him.

I continued receiving more phone calls from people who either encouraged me or asked me for further information: Pax Christi, different NGOs, UNICEF, the Nuncio, the superior general of the Comboni Missionaries in Rome, the BBC, other media, embassies and many other groups. Betty Bigombe also called me from the US. All of this communication was a great morale booster, especially since what was happening to me was highlighting that there was a huge problem in Northern Uganda and that it was the people, not me, who deserved the attention.

Not only did I receive encouragement from people outside of Northern Uganda, but the local people I met daily also encouraged me not to give up. One day two elderly women came from a village to tell me that they prayed the rosary for me everyday. They had also sacrificed two chickens to the spirits, who had assured them that I would not be expelled from the country. Just in case.

During that time I developed a special sense for what was sensible to do or not to do. I made it a point not to leave Gulu, no matter how tired I felt. One month earlier we had asked for a meeting with a parliamentary committee which was preparing a revision of the Amnesty Law. In ARLPI we had elaborated on a document advocating for the continuation of the law as it was. The law offered a blank pardon to all rebels who turned themselves in to the authorities, although in practice it also applied to the rebels captured in battle. We worried that any reform that made the law more restrictive could negatively affect any peace initiatives that were currently in the works. The committee had given us an appointment for a day in February. Some journalists distorted the purpose, however, and presented the meeting as a summons to answer about my case in front of parliament. Due to these circumstances, I decided not to go.

On 14th February, four days after the beginning of the tense situation in which I found myself, I had a most interesting Valentine's Day.

Before the incident of Pabbo, I had started taking part in another attempt to reach the rebels in a bid to convince them to come back to negotiate with us. For several weeks our friends from Sant'Egidio, Fabio Riccardi and Vittorio Scelzo, tried to make telephone contact with some of the rebels. Both, Riccardi and Scelzo, came to Gulu because the men at the other side of the phone line had insisted that they should meet face to face.

That night, Valentine's Day, we had an appointment with one of the rebels. I was aware that I was running a very high risk.

At 8:30 pm one of our contact persons told us that the rebels were on the way to meet us at the archbishop's residence. As we had agreed, we called one of the UN officials present in Gulu who had a mandate for "humanitarian diplomacy".

It was very dark when a car entered the archbishop's compound and parked discreetly in the backyard. Our contact person told us to go and wait in the visitors room.

A few minutes later the door opened and our contact entered the room with a tall man who was wearing a military uniform and gumboots and carrying a briefcase. He did not turn a hair when Fabio and Vittorio greeted him. After considering many pros and cons and keeping in mind that we had informed the archbishop of our plans, we thought that it was prudent at that stage to abstain from speaking to the military. A thousand thoughts came to my mind at once. What if they had been followed? What if soldiers arrived and opened fire? What if somebody could take these circumstances as an excuse to accuse me? It seemed that St. Valentine helped us, though, because that night many of the security operatives were busy with their girlfriends or wives, and those who were single were busy in town watching an English league football match that inspired plenty of enthusiasm.

Our contact introduced the stranger as Major Olak Otulu. Riccardi explained to him that they had come all the way from Rome to assist with the peace talks arrangements. The UN representative did not talk much, but his presence as a guarantee was important.

Olak Otulu hardly spoke. He said that it was late and that we should continue the following day. We gave him a room where he changed into civilian clothes and stored his briefcase. We took him to town where he spent the night at one of the lodges.

That night I too slept in town. For several months I did not sleep three consecutive nights in the same bed. It was this routine that was making me extraordinarily tired, but it might have been one of the ways that keep me relatively safe.

Our meeting the next day was more relaxed. Fabio's proposal was that Kony should appoint two of his trusted field officers to come to Rome, where Sant'Egidio would take care of all logistical arrangements, including travel documents that they expected to get with the cooperation of the Italian government. If the two LRA delegates were able to turn up at Lokichokio, at the Kenya-Sudan border, Sant'Egidio would arrange for their travel to Rome. They were very confident that the Ugandan government, with whom they had been in contact for many years, would not refuse to send a delegation to meet with the rebels in Rome once they were there.

Olak Otulu agreed to pass the message to the LRA high command. After two days we received a phone call from a man who claimed to be "the number two" in the LRA's chain of command and who said that Kony had accepted the plan, but he was asking for 100,000 dollars in cash to be able to organise themselves for the journey. This was not a good sign. Soon after another man claiming to be Sam Kolo called us again with the same request. We knew Sam Kolo's voice very well and were absolutely sure that the person we were talking to was not him.

Once again we found ourselves totally disoriented. Riccardi and Scelzo had a list of ten phone numbers, most of them for satellite phones belonging to rebels who on previous occasions had been used to contact Vincent Otti and Sam Kolo, but all of the numbers were disconnected. Three days later we finally managed to talk to the real Sam Kolo, who at that time was the number three in the LRA's chain of command. He assured us that he had no knowledge of the proposal put forward by Sant' Egidio, and that from what he knew Maj. Olak Otulu had not been anywhere near Gulu in the past few months. He was not aware of any officer with a mandate to meet with us. Even though we often had the impression that the LRA was a most enigmatic group, we knew that none of their officers would be engaged in any peace contact without Kony's approval. Kolo cautioned us about conmen who may want to deceive us and get money from us. They, the true LRA, never asked for money, he insisted.

The two Sant'Egidio officials went back to Italy two days later. We had been deceived again, as we had been the year before, but at least somebody like Sam Kolo, who held a high position in the LRA, was getting the signal that Sant'Egidio was interested in helping, as their presence in Gulu from time to time proved.

Soon after that the LRA massacred more than 300 civilians in Barlonyo, an IDP camp located a few kilometres north of Lira town. The brutal and massive attack, made in broad daylight, was carried out by rebels who arrived in the camp walking so quietly that the first people who met them mistook them for government soldiers. When they started burning down huts and shooting, people ran desperately in all directions or took refuge in huts where many of them were burned to death. This attack was one of the worst and most repugnant actions of the LRA, who continued to prove that their only agenda or programme was death.

The LRA's vile actions against defenceless civilians in Barlonyo, in Lango, ignited the kernel of ethnic conflict between the Acholi and Lango, two neighbouring groups with very similar cultures and a lot of history and traditions in common. A few days after the massacre tensions ran very high in Lira during a demonstration that quickly degenerated into a riot. Four people were lynched, at least two of them Acholis. When the news reached Gulu that afternoon there were some attempts made to attack shops owned by people from Lango, but these attacks were quickly stopped by the police. I was particularly worried since the parish where I worked in Minakulu had a mixed population that had lived together for generations. I forgot the hundreds of pieces of advice about prudence I had heard during the last two weeks and I took part in the organisation of several meetings between leaders from the two communities in the parish hall, which contributed to cooling things down.

It seems that the more complex a conflict is, the more entangled and difficult things become as time passes, with new and unexpected elements cropping up. Even well-intentioned interventions may complicate things further.

This was the case with the International Criminal Court (ICC), whose mandate became effective in July 2002 as a result of the Rome Statute signed by a number of states. Based in The Hague, the ICC was created to bring to justice perpetrators of crimes against humanity, war crimes and genocide. During the 1990s, the collapse of communism brought a wave of enthusiasm for peace and democracy as the Cold War came to an end. The general optimism did not take long to fade away, however, as incredibly cruel wars broke out in the former Yugoslavia, Rwanda and Sierra Leone. Three special *ad hoc* tribunals were created under the auspices of the United Nations to deal with the gravest crimes committed in these three places, particularly ethnic cleansing, massive rape of women and the systematic use of children as soldiers. From this experience many states thought that it would be better to have a permanent tribunal to try suspects of these crimes, instead of creating a special court for each separate case.

Therefore, the new tribunal, the ICC, was mandated to try these kinds of crimes committed in any part of the world. In itself it was a huge step forward to end impunity and to provide justice for the most vulnerable victims. Luis Moreno Ocampo, a magistrate famous for having led the prosecution against the main leaders of the infamous military junta in his native Argentina, was appointed its first chief prosecutor. He was given powers to initiate investigations and sign international arrest warrants against suspects.

In recent years a new awareness has been growing in the western world that most of the worst atrocities have been perpetrated against the poorest human beings who live in remote and forgotten corners of the planet that attract very little attention. Perhaps because of this reason, from the first moment, the ICC seemed particularly interested in intervening in places that fit this profile, particularly the Democratic Republic of Congo and Northern Uganda.

In the Democratic Republic of Congo more than three million people died directly or indirectly as a result of the two civil wars that took place in the east of its territory, particularly from 1998 to 2002. Eventually, in 2007, the ICC would successfully secure the arrest of two of the main warlords, Thomas Lubanga and former Vice-President Jean-Pierre Bemba (although the latter was arrested for alleged crimes committed in neighbouring Central African Republic). The ICC would also initiate criminal proceedings against some high-ranking figures of the Sudanese government (including President Omar el-Bashir) for orchestrating the genocide of Darfur. But in 2003 the conflict of DRC seemed too complicated for a fast intervention, because more than ten African countries had been involved in the wars that had a clear component of scrambling for DRC's coveted mineral resources.

It seems that investigating the perpetrators of the conflict of Northern Uganda seemed less complicated to the ICC. The LRA were a group of infamous terrorists who kidnapped children and subjected them to the worst imaginable atrocities, and who also committed mass killings of the civilian population. Besides, Uganda, unlike Congo, had more functioning infrastructures. Because the situation could be described with this simplicity, it seemed clear that the LRA was the villain, and that the government of Uganda had tried their best to protect the population and fight the LRA. In January 2004, Ocampo addressed a joint press conference with President Museveni, announcing that the ICC was ready to begin investigations to bring to court the main leaders of the LRA.

Everywhere in the world where innocent people suffer intolerable abuses, the news of prosecution of the perpetrators is always welcome. But in the case of Northern Uganda something very unusual happened; from the beginning it was the victims, or at least those who claimed to represent them, and the peace lobbyists who opposed the ICC intervention.

There were several reasons that accounted for this opposition. To begin with, the ICC had jurisdiction only over crimes committed since July 2002. Many people wondered what would happen to atrocities committed before then, since the war started in 1986.

Also, the ICC announced that it intended to initiate investigations against the main leaders of the LRA. The people who lived in the war zone complained that since 1986 they had also suffered at the hands of the Ugandan army. This, coupled with the fact that Ocampo made his announcement in a joint press conference with Museveni, did not augur well for the court's image of impartiality.

But maybe the greatest objection raised against the ICC's intervention was whether it would deal a fatal blow to various peace efforts to bring the war to an end through negotiation. The government's blanket amnesty had already seen some good results. If the leaders of the LRA knew that they could be detained, would that not deter them from coming to the negotiating table since they might be arrested instead? These concerns were clear examples of a conflict of values and interests; wanting to have justice and peace at the same time seemed nearly impossible.

To top it all off, the ICC did not have any police or armed forces to implement their arrest warrants. This limitation could only cause skepticism among the population living in Northern Uganda, who wondered what difference a written document ordering Kony's arrest would make. After all, the Ugandan army had not been able to detain Kony in 18 years. Besides, if he and his top commanders were in Sudan most of the time, who would detain them there? Sudan was not a signatory of the Statute of Rome, and the SPLA was in the final stages of negotiating a comprehensive peace agreement with Khartoum, which would be signed in January 2005, and had little time or strength for other concerns. In the cases of Sierra Leone, the Balkans and Rwanda the arrests and trials took place in a context in which those conflicts were over and the suspects had become fugitives on the run. But arresting a rebel leader who was well protected by his own army and in a context in which the war was far from over was another business altogether.

I did present these and some other issues to Judge Ocampo when he called me on 1st March and we talked on the phone for more than one hour. He clarified that his intention was to bring to justice only the four or five main leaders of the LRA responsible for the worst atrocities. When I asked him who was going to arrest them he told me that Sudan was going to cooperate.

But he did have a point. We, the leaders of civil society, lobbying for peace in Northern Uganda, had been advocating for a decisive international intervention. Was the ICC not a clear answer to our cry?

For the next two years the ICC made every possible effort to dialogue with everybody who was somebody in Northern Uganda, both by sending some of their officials to make first-hand contacts on the ground and by inviting different delegations to speak at length in their headquarters at The Hague. It was clear that they wanted to understand the problem from all its different angles. And also, with the passing of time more and more people in the north were in favour of an ICC intervention, even though their advocates were not very free to state their opinions in public for fear of rebel reprisals. In any case, Ocampo waited until October 2005 before signing and publishing the arrest warrants against Joseph Kony, Vincent Otti, Raska Lukwiya, Okot Odiambo and Dominic Ongwen.

One of the persons for whom the prospects of an ICC intervention was bad news was Betty Bigombe.

Born in Lamogi, in Gulu district, this bright woman had a natural gift for public relations and mediation. After starting a brilliant career as a diplomat in Japan during her younger years, she served as State Minister for the Pacification (later called Rehabilitation) of the North in the early 1990s. In this capacity she had led a brave attempt at negotiating a peace deal with the LRA during 1993 and 1994, something that she almost achieved but that was frustrated for a number of reasons.

The first time I met Bigombe was in Gulu in March 2004. She was the kind of person who made a powerful first impression. From the beginning I thought that she had the skills, contacts, endurance and capacity to make things move forward. And we badly needed somebody who could do that after almost one year of stagnation. I discreetly introduced to her some of the contact persons who had helped us reach the LRA. After a few weeks she had made attempts at contacting Kony in South Sudan, where she went with Yusuf Adek, an Acholi elder and Kony's old friend, who in 1993 had been her right-hand man in the peace initiative. The Sudanese security officials who assisted her in Juba always followed the same pattern. After many days of waiting they would announce that she would meet with Kony the following morning, but at the last moment they would come up with an excuse about some unexpected circumstance that would supposedly force them to postpone the encounter until a new date when, invariably, the same thing would happen. After several months of fruitless waiting she returned to the US, until she would have a new chance in October.

In the meantime, the situation in Gulu was still tense. On 31st March an Italian missionary, Fr. Luciano Fulvi, was found dead in a pool of blood in his room in the community that the Comboni order had in Layibi, a Gulu suburb. At least two men had entered the night before and slit his throat. While the official version of the event spoke of an armed robbery, others thought of a new threat against the church. Fr. Fulvi, aged 70, had worked as a youth chaplain for the archdiocese, and he was not a priest fond of outspoken, challenging statements that could be interpreted in a way that was even remotely political. Whatever the reason for his murder, it highlighted that in times of conflict religious personnel can often be an easy target since they normally follow predictable routines. Fr. Fulvi always slept with his room unlocked. This is why when some of his confreres passed in front of his door that night they did not seem surprised to find it ajar.

On the day of Fr. Fulvi's death I was in Kampala trying to get some rest. When I heard the news I did not think twice and rushed back to Gulu. No sooner had I left Kampala than a journalist from France Press called me to alert me that the army spokesman had mentioned in a press briefing that morning that I was a rebel collaborator who regularly supplied Kony's men with airtime, drugs and telecommunication equipments. He had once again asked for my removal from the north. When I reached the army roadblock at Karuma I feared that they would order me back to Kampala. The minute I spent there while a soldier checked my documents seemed like a year to me. Finally, however, he waved me through.

The following months were the hardest of my life.

Maybe it was the post-traumatic stress disorder I had heard so much about, but I could not sleep at all. My anxiety was triggered by even the slightest noise. I felt under threat and I kept changing my sleeping place every two or three days. The peace process in which I had been so much involved was sunk and stuck in the deepest mud, while innocent people were being brutally killed and abused every day. At the same time I developed feelings of betrayal as I had never experienced before. I no longer trusted anybody. Jimmy and Francis, whom we had trusted to help us bring some other people out of the bush, were involved in a case of robbery against a Catholic mission and ended up in Luzira prison. I felt vulnerable and the hoard of accusations and insults from people like the army spokesman added to my misery.

At the same time, I could not understand why the main religious leaders spent much of their time on endless trips abroad. While I understood that in some cases these sojourns could be useful for peace advocacy, I felt left in the most vulnerable place, receiving the beatings, and had the impression that we were not reaching the places where the peace process could progress I perceived that in ARLPI we were no longer spending enough time in the displaced people's camps with the victims and instead we joined the "workshop fever" that was sweeping through all NGOs who spent much of their time in hotel meeting rooms. The situation became unbearable for me and in July 2004 I left ARLPI. I continued my work for peace and human rights with the Justice and Peace Commission of Gulu Archdiocese, where I had always been present.

During those difficult months, when many well-intentioned people advised me to remain silent, a good friend of mine, Kevin Aliro, one of Uganda's brightest and most courageous journalists, started the *Weekly Observer* and asked me to write a weekly column. I saw an opportunity to make the voice of the people in Northern Uganda heard and I kept that commitment from March 2004 until January 2008 when I left Uganda.

It was the *Weekly Observer* that at the end of April ran a front-page story about me. I came to know from well-informed sources that the ministry for security had prepared a document for my expulsion but President Museveni had not signed it. Betty Bigombe was instrumental in preventing my expulsion and I owe a great deal of gratitude to her.

In the meantime, the LRA massacres continued unabated. On 23rd May, the LRA killed 29 people in Pagak, during an attack carried out in broad daylight. Vincent Otti personally led the massacre, in retaliation against the Pagak residents who welcomed 20 rebels who had come to lay down their arms in the IDP camp a few days earlier.

The next day they struck Lukode, where they killed 43 people.

Two weeks after the massacre of Pagak, the president of the Pontifical Commission for Justice and Peace, Cardinal Renato Martino, came to Gulu on an official visit. Soon after his arrival we took him to Pagak, and while we accompanied him through that maze of tiny huts we came upon a group of people who were burying a young woman named Dorotea Akech. Seriously wounded during the LRA attacks, she had spent two weeks in a coma and had died the previous night at Lacor Hospital. When we finished praying, Archbishop Odama said that he remembered presiding over the burial of the woman's husband who had been killed by government soldiers two months earlier. The tragedy in that family epitomised what the people of Northern Uganda had to go through every day.

Cardinal Martino referred to Archbishop Odama as "a true hero and a pastor who is near the suffering of his people". He openly advocated for a negotiated solution to the conflict: "A fire is not put out with more fire," he said, "violence is not eliminated with more violence".

The Nuncio, Pierre Christophe, and the chairman of the Uganda Episcopal Conference, Paul Bakyenga, accompanied Cardinal Martino. During our visit to Pagak, Archbishop Bakyenga told me that this was his first time in a displaced people's camp in the north and it had made a deep impression on him. It was high time, I thought to myself.

During those difficult months I found encouragement where I never thought I could.

I received a phone call from Pajule one day. It was Joseph, the boy that the rebels had abducted in front of me in January 2003 when they attacked the mission. He had escaped during a battle a few days earlier. I went to Pajule to see him. I was ashamed of myself for my cowardice since I had not done anything to protect him. His face had already taken on the characteristic expression of all the abducted children, a mixture of suffering and hardness. I asked for his forgiveness, but he insisted that it would have been worse if I had put up any resistance. I told him that I had been very worried for him.

> "I was more worried about you," he said. "While I was with the rebels outside the house I saw how one of them placed a landmine under the driver's seat of your car."

I was speechless. My mind went to the morning after the night when Joseph was abducted, when after carefully collecting the bits of broken glass in my car I sat at the steering wheel and I drove to Gulu with the wounded little girl. If what Joseph told me was true, it meant that somebody had removed the anti-personnel landmine and saved my life.

Soon after meeting with Joseph, the Anglican bishop of Kitgum invited me to lead a day of retreat for the clergy of his diocese. While I preached about the meaning of peace in the gospel, much of the sadness and frustrations I was living those days came out with my words. I remarked that in peace work one often does not see any results, and that at times one has the impression that everything is in vain.

During the tea break a man I had never seen before approached me.

"I wanted to tell you that I do not agree with you. You have said that your work is in vain."

"Thank you for your pleasantry," I told him.

"It is not mere pleasantry. Do you know a girl who came from the bush called Monica?"

Monica was the girl who had led the first group of women and children that was released by the rebels in July 2002 and whom we took to Pajule. Since escaping, she had been studying in the Sacred Heart Sisters' Tailoring School in Gulu.

"Sure, I know her," I answered.

"You should know that she is my daughter."

And he turned his back on me and walked away.

There was no need to add any further words to this conversation. There are moments in life during which a person's presence, a brief encounter, can be like a sudden light that makes everything clearer and transfigures all our darkness and misery. These moments are like clear rays that can make us understand in just a few seconds matters that have tormented us for years and have thrown us down to the dust, seemingly defeated.

In reality, Monica had no parents, but following the Acholi cultural patterns of the extended family, the man who had approached me was her uncle and could therefore introduce himself as Monica's father.

Moses helped me to understand what Monica's father had meant more fully.

During that meeting on 1st March 2003 in the bush, when the rebels made us talk to Kony on radio call, I could not forget the name of one of the officers who was present. He was called Moses Rubangangeyo.

His name meant "God is the one who knows", and as far I could tell, it was not a very common name in Acholi.

This is why I was surprised to receive a phone call from somebody claiming to be Moses Rubangangeyo. I remembered immediately who this was and I was overjoyed.

Moses had just arrived in Gulu.

I remembered his face very well. The year before, ARLPI had published a report entitled "War of Words" that dealt with the Ugandan press' coverage of the conflict in the north. One of the pictures we had published was of me with my hand on Moses' shoulder. He had been abducted in 1996, when he was 16, from a secondary school in Gulu. His relatives, trusting some returnees' accounts, had believed him to be dead and had even conducted some funeral rituals for him. One day his mother, while going through a copy of "War of Words" that she had found in the Catholic parish she frequented, saw this picture of her son and she began to hope. She decided not to tell anybody and keep the possibility of her son's being alive to herself. She clung to the secret hope that her son was alive and one day would come back home.

I found Moses in a semi-dark small room that his mother was renting in one of the Gulu slums. It was not rare that the joy of a son or daughter who had come back home after spending many years of hell in the LRA could vanish after hearing sad and unexpected news. During the eight years that Moses had spent in the bush the family had suffered greatly. His father had died after a long illness, and his only brother had passed away a few months earlier. His mother lived alone, and she suffered from serious heart problems.

"When I saw you that day in the bush it was the first time in many years that somebody told us about peace and forgiveness," Moses told me when I visited. He was used to official messages in which they were called "terrorists", "criminals" or "mass killers". Moses had been impressed to meet with people who came from outside and were willing to sit down with them, listen and treat them as brothers. Moses' words fell on me like soft rain that soaked me and slowly washed away the coat of sadness and discouragement that had covered me during those hard months.

From my conversation with Moses, I deduced that he had been with Tabuley during the LRA campaign in Teso. In November 2003 Tabuley died during battle, and his escorts dragged his body inside a hut and set it on fire.

Back in Pader district one day, Moses was in the company of four young LRA recruits when he decided that he had had enough. He led the group to Lira Palwo, where they quietly emerged one morning. To his surprise, whenever they met people on the way nobody seemed alarmed, probably because they may have thought that the boys were UPDF soldiers. They went on walking and reached the quarter guard of the military detach. His surprise increased when the sentry next to the mud and wattle shelter stood and saluted him. Moses asked to see the officer in charge, and when he arrived Moses told him that they were members of the LRA who had come to surrender. They laid down their guns on the floor. The UPDF captain embraced them warmly.

This was not an unusual scene. Despite the hard language used in army statements against the rebels, a great number of UPDF soldiers favoured a peaceful solution and showed great joy whenever young rebels escaped and reported to army detaches. More surrenders also meant fewer enemies to fight against on the battle field.

Moses came out of the bush at a time when an interesting trend was developing. More or less at the same time, another young LRA officer we had met in the bush called Okot Ayoli reported to Pajule military detach with 76 combatants. The Uganda papers published a photo of Okot embracing the UPDF officer in charge who welcomed him as a brother. The image was an example of how, in the midst of that hell of violence and hatred, some fruits of peace and reconciliation were flourishing.

As was the case with most of the returnees, Moses' face was hard. He had experienced terrible traumas and had suffered serious health problems. He had several bullet wounds and pieces of shrapnel still lodged in his body that caused him great pain.

Despite these hardships, he exuded a great desire to change his life. And he had an exceptional intelligence. For some time we helped him undergo counselling in the Caritas Centre and assisted him with his studies, which had been interrupted abruptly eight years earlier.

The last time I saw Moses he had enrolled in a university for a course on conflict and peace studies and was leading a local NGO in which former rebels work on reconciliation and rehabilitation issues with victims of war. Even now, Moses does not know that one of those he helped rehabilitate was me.

13

Betty Bigombe, the Peacemaker

The 20-vehicle convoy, mostly of cars bearing the UN emblem, escorted by two armed personnel carriers (APC), left the Acholi Inn, Gulu at 10 am. The sun was shining brightly, sharpening colors on the dresses worn by hundreds of women who danced through the streets, exulting with joy. The entourage of mothers marched and sang during the annual peace demonstration on 31st December. Two loudspeakers blared from the top of a white van, while people followed the rhythmical song that the radio repeated day and night:

> Kuc ongwee, kuc, kuc cok dwogo. Kuc odwogo, kuc, kuc ongwee…

> (We are smelling peace, peace is near at hand, we are smelling it…)

The newspaper street vendors were selling many more copies than usual, and the two main daily papers, *New Vision* and *Monitor,* sold out hardly thirty minutes after arriving from Kampala. Both of the papers' front pages included pictures of LRA commander Sam Kolo shaking hands cordially with the Minister of Internal Affairs, Ruhakana Rugunda. The picture had been taken two days earlier in a remote bush in Kitgum district and their expressions of happiness spoke volumes. A single word, "PEACE" occupied a banner the width of the page as the only headline. The joyful atmosphere of an end-of-the-year celebration went hand-in-hand with the news of an imminent and total end of a war that started in 1986.

The UNICEF official in whose car I travelled, a Swedish retired soldier in his late fifties, was driving slowly. In amazement, he watched the crowd as they moved to the side of the road to allow us to pass.

'I hope it will be true that the war is about to end," he said. "The last place where I worked in a peacekeeping mission was Sierra Leone. All this reminds me very much of what I witnessed there…"

He stopped abruptly to allow some of the women cross the busy street.

"Before Sierra Leone I worked in Bosnia," he continued. "To tell you the truth, I am getting tired of so many years of doing this work. This should be my last assignment. When it is over I am going back home to my wife. Our kids have already completed university…"

We had not had time for any breakfast that morning. With the skill of one who had done it many times, he took a can of smoked salmon and opened it with one hand. He offered me a fillet on a slice of brown rye bread. In front of us, an APC led the convoy.

After leaving the last roundabout in the northern part of the town we headed towards Kitgum. After 20 kilometres we passed through Paicho, one of the first IDP camps that dotted the dusty murram road. Camp residents had keenly listened to the news on the radio, and when we approached the settlement residents formed two lines along the way. Women ululated with joy while many people waved branches of the *olwedo* tree of peace. We were experiencing the hottest season of the year. The air conditioning system of the Toyota Land Cruiser seemed to have gone strike that day, and we sweated profusely inside the car. However, if we had opened the windows, we would have had no choice but to chew dust for the rest of the long journey.

"Too many years working in countries in conflict," said the UNICEF officer. "I am tired. I miss my country. I miss skiing in the mountains…"

I had met him on 28th December. On that day a rather large delegation made up of traditional, political and religious leaders plus some diplomats and journalists met with seven senior LRA commanders in Paluda, a remote forest of Kitgum district. We were 30 people in total and the Swedish veteran official was in charge of making sure that all logistical arrangements, from water to chairs to vehicles, were in place. The next day he was kind enough to give me copies of all the pictures he had taken. The meeting of the 28th was followed by another one on 29th during which several government representatives met the same seven commanders at the same venue. It was the first time that a high-ranking government minister had a face-to-face meeting with an LRA leader. Never before had so much progress in peace negotiations been made and a tide of optimism rose in Northern Uganda at the end of 2004, especially when it was announced that the signing of a total cessation of hostilities agreement was expected on 31st December. When I arrived at the Acholi Inn, where we had been called to join the convoy, I saw the UNICEF official and without thinking twice I walked over to his vehicle. He was a friendly man and we had a most interesting conversation.

A few kilometres after Paicho we passed through another IDP camp, Cwero, and then crossed River Aswa, the western gateway to Pader district. The scattered rural settlements were gone and only displacement camps were found along the roads. When we reached the next camp, called Lacekocot, the lines of people eagerly awaiting us were long. As we passed by everybody clapped and ululated.

In one of the vehicles behind us travelled the person who had managed to arouse all this hope for these victims of the war. It was Betty Bigombe.

Her experience in Juba from May to July that year had been frustrating, but she was not the kind of person to give up easily, and she knew how to act discreetly and effectively. One month after leaving Sudan she tried to arrange a meeting with Vincent Otti within Ugandan borders, but the continuous military operations of the Ugandan army did not work in her favour. Soon after, with the help of the Norwegian government, she attempted to organise a discreet meeting in Oslo between representatives of the government and the LRA. Again, that initiative failed.

Following the string of LRA massacres in Northern Uganda from February to May 2004 it seemed that the UPDF had finally managed to gain the upper hand in the conflict. The UPDF insisted that its mounting military pressure, as well as the Amnesty Commission, was reaping encouraging results. Between April and August 2004, more than 400 rebels, 50 of who were officers, came out of the bush. This time the figures were real and unusually high. The list of LRA officers who had surrendered or were captured was impressive: and included Okot Ayoli, Okwonga Alero, Isaia Luwum, Ochan Nono among others. At the end of August the LRA's chief signaller Lt. Col. Anwar also came out, but the case that caused the most commotion was the capture of Kony's chief planner Brigadier Kenneth Banya. All those who came out of the bush received their amnesty certificate and became free men. Security started to improve, and the drop in child night commuters in Gulu was a good indicator of this; the number of children walking to Gulu at night went from 40,000 to 8,000. Many wondered if this period of quiet would be yet another false promise in the history of the conflict, a history punctuated by periods of lull that would end when the LRA attacked once again. But this time there were new elements to the peace. Sudan had stopped, or at least considerably reduced, its military support to the LRA; the UPDF, which had a new army commander, accepted their responsibility in this situation; and the message of the amnesty, spread particularly with the help of popular Radio Mega FM, was convincing many rebels that theirs was a futile war. Kony was becoming more and more isolated.

During those months, the Community of Sant'Egidio had continued their discreet telephone contacts, particularly with Sam Kolo. Fabio asked me to help them in this task, so that we could attempt this contact from two different places.

On 11th September I talked to Sam Kolo.

> "I am very happy to hear you," Kolo said "I thought that you had been expelled from Uganda."
>
> "No, I am still in Gulu," I told him. "I hope you'll still be willing to talk peace with the government."
>
> "As for us, we are ready. The problem is that the International Criminal Court is now complicating everything."

My friends at Sant'Egidio often supplied me with airtime for my cellphone so that I could call Kolo's satellite phone. For this phone call my credit was 100,000 Ugandan shillings (about 40 euros), which was exhausted after 10 minutes of talking. Talking peace, especially over satellite phones, is very expensive.

Later that day, after going through the newspapers of the day, some of Museveni's words that had been published during his recent visit to the US caught my attention: "If the rebels are interested in peace negotiations they can talk to Betty (Bigombe)."

That night I called Kolo again and asked him if he had seen or heard the president's statement. He told me that he had not.

For over a month Fabio and I talked to Sam Kolo almost daily. On a couple of occasions on which I lost the connection, I only managed to re-establish it after a phone call to Geoffrey Ayoo, an LRA sympathiser who lived in Germany, from where he ran a radio station called Radio Rhino International. It broadcast information about Northern Uganda, usually with a perspective rather close to that of Kony's rebels.

On 11th October Betty Bigombe arrived in Uganda without much publicity. Every day she sat at her desk in the offices of the World Bank in Kampala, but that seemed to be just a base for another serious attempt at her peacemaking mission. Unfortunately, she had lost contact with Sam Kolo. The rebels were usually very cautious. They knew that using their satellite phones could help the UPDF not only to intercept their communications, but also locate their positions using some of the modern technology that US military advisors had been providing the UPDF for some time. Ever since the UNITA rebel Jonas Savimbi was tracked down and killed in the Angolan bush by an elite commando in February 2002, Kony and his men had been very careful to avoid repeating the same mistake. It was for this reason that they changed their sim cards very often. There was no doubt that there were people abroad with enough resources and willingness to help them pay for their costly airtime.

When Betty Bigombe mentioned to me the problems she was having getting in touch with Sam Kolo I did not hesitate to give her the phone number I was using those days. I was very happy when she told me that from that day she started talking regularly to Kolo.

Betty Bigombe had been a state minister from the late 1980s until 1996. From that time she was one of the Acholi leaders who enjoyed Museveni's trust and who could have a good working relationship with the UPDF's top men; as a result she was in a position of great advantage. During her meetings with President Museveni in October 2004 they reached an agreement. Museveni was ready to make a public statement declaring a truce if the rebels would take the first step and make a public announcement on any radio station.

On 2nd November BBC's Uganda correspondent, Will Ross, called me. He told me that he had just recorded a phone interview with a man who had called and introduced himself as commander Sam Kolo and who, on behalf of the LRA, asked the government to engage in peace talks to end the war. He wanted to know if the voice truly belonged to Sam Kolo. After I had heard the first few seconds of the recording I said: "Yes, I am very sure he is Sam Kolo."

The LRA's announcement was broadcast that very day. It was an important step that now awaited President Museveni's response.

Three days later Museveni made some comments in a press conference. But they did not include any declaration of a ceasefire. He said that during the past few months the army had killed thousands of terrorists and that only a few fugitives remained on the run. One of the fugitives, he said, had recently called the BBC. That was a hard blow for Betty Bigombe, who in the meantime was lobbying in diplomatic circles in Kampala. That same evening the US ambassador met with Museveni and pleaded with him to respond in a more positive tone to Sam Kolo's announcement.

Museveni took his time, but he finally did respond. In the evening of 14th November the President's office released the following statement:

> "President Yoweri Museveni has ordered a seven-day suspension of UPDF operations, in a limited area of Acholi, to allow the leadership of Kony's group to meet and confirm that they accept his offer to come out of the bush.
>
> In the last three weeks, Betty Bigombe has had clear indications from Kony's group that they want to end the conflict. They are under intense pressure from UPDF. A Kony spokesman has said that they want to talk peace.
>
> President Museveni had offered a ten-day suspension of operations so that Kony's group gathers in an agreed area in Northern Uganda and talks could begin. But UPDF pressure makes it impossible for the Kony leadership to get together to discuss this offer.
>
> Betty Bigombe has therefore, proposed a seven-day suspension to allow the leadership to meet. President Museveni has agreed to suspend operations in the area north of Patiko, north of Atanga, passing west of Palabek, east of Atyak, up to the border with Sudan, to allow that to happen. The Kony group has been provided with a detailed map of

this area. Any bandit who moves into this area for the purpose of those consultations will not be attacked.

If after the meeting, Kony's group makes a clear recorded statement that they accept the president's offer, then the ten-day cessation of the UPDF operations will be ordered. However, the UPDF will continue operations against the remnants of Kony's group in all the other areas of Northern Uganda and Southern Sudan until the government gets an irreversible commitment indicating their intention to end, once and for all time the terror campaign.

The seven-day cessation of UPDF operations against Kony's group will commence at 1800 hours tomorrow 15 November and end at 0700 hours on the 23rd of November 2004."

It was signed by Onapito Ekomoloit, acting press secretary.

A journalist friend of mine who was at the press conference where the message was given called me from Kampala. Once I had the message I sent it to Fabio Riccardi. That night he called Sam Kolo and read it to him, advising Kolo and the rebels to accept Museveni's offer. I called Kolo too, and found him in good spirits.

Immediately things starting rolling at snowball speed. On 17th November, Betty Bigombe had her first face-to-face meeting with Sam Kolo in a forest some 40 kilometres from Gulu. She was accompanied by Lars Eric, a Norwegian UN official who had been in Gulu since 2002 working for "humanitarian diplomacy", and Lt. Col. Chris Wilton, the British High Commission's defence attaché. Both diplomats were important during this new peace initiative spearheaded by Betty Bigombe.

On 7th November Bigombe led a group of Acholi cultural leaders to a meeting with the LRA at the rebels' request. This meeting started a format for regular encounters with concrete agendas towards agreements that could end the violence. Part of the meetings' success was due to the fact that this time several foreign governments (particularly the

United Kingdom, Norway and the Netherlands) were generously funding the process. The British embassy paid for the services of a helicopter fleeted from Nairobi. Often, before meetings took place, the easily recognisable white chopper took Betty Bigombe and Lars Eric to the peace zone to meet Sam Kolo and prepare the logistical details beforehand. During the meetings, the chopper flew around to make sure that everything was in order. If any party had any intentions of sabotaging the process, it would have found it difficult to do so.

Although the president had declared a one-week truce, it was prolonged several times, the last being until 31st December that year; and the army never attacked the LRA even outside the official ceasefire zone. Unfortunately, the LRA did not always show the same good-will. On 20th December they ambushed a vehicle in which a Catholic priest, Fr. John Peter Olum, was travelling on the road to Awere. Two people who were with him died instantly. When the priest looked down at his hands at the steering wheel he realised that they were shattered and covered with blood.

Fr. Peter Olum had been hit by five bullets and miraculously survived. Two fingers on his left hand had to be amputated, as well as one of his toes. His right hand remained in one piece, but it was very disfigured and over the next few years he was to undergo a number of surgeries to correct this. I remember the third day after the ambush, around Christmas, when I celebrated mass with him in his room in Lacor Hospital he told me how happy he was to be able to continue using his hands to celebrate the Eucharist.

The night of the ambush I called Sam Kolo and asked him for an explanation about the ambush. I did not hear much sympathy in his voice when he suggested that the attack could have been made by their own people. He simply pointed out that he was very far from the place of the incident. The usual excuses.

On 27th December, late in the evening, Betty Bigombe told Archbishop Odama to get ready for a meeting in the bush the following day.

Very early in the morning, at 6:30 am, the group that was going to attend the meeting met at Acholi Inn in Gulu, where we had a hasty breakfast. The white helicopter had gone ahead of us. There were 16 people gathered there: religious, cultural and political leaders, plus several Acholi MPs. There were also three foreign diplomats, five journalists and five UN officials, including two doctors from the World Health Organisation. When I asked my new Swedish friend about the doctors' presence he told me that they were there in case any of us had an accident on the way. There was also a heavy military escort. Seeing all the security paraphernalia I could not help remembering the times that Tarcisio and I had ventured into the bush without any protection, except for the sign of the cross.

It may have been because of the military security, or because of the size and diversity of the group, or just because of sheer euphoria and optimism, but for whatever reason this was the first time that I went to the bush without feeling any fear.

After driving past Kitgum and Palabek we headed west and stopped at a smaller camp where the military escorting us stopped as agreed. The rest of our group slowly continued on by car. Betty Bigombe was in the head vehicle. After covering a few kilometres on the deserted Palabek-Atyak road we sighted three young men in military uniform with dreadlocks and rifles dangling from their shoulders. Bigombe got out of her vehicle and confidently went to greet them. The rest of us slowly emerged from our vehicles and followed her. The UN security officials had insisted that we always try to form a compact group. As soon as the three boys saw us all together, they led us through a rough bush terrain with grass that had been recently burnt. We walked for about two kilometres, all the time aware of the presence of young rebels with their rifles surveying the area and us from the nearby rocks.

Finally, after going uphill, we came to a shady open place where seven LRA commanders wearing impeccably clean uniforms were waiting for us. They were lined up, as if for an official reception. Sam Kolo, smiling and courteous, greeted all of us slowly and cordially. The Swedish man and some of the young LRA brought some plastic chairs and some boxes of mineral water.

It greatly impressed me to see how such a small-bodied woman simply dressed in a blouse, black slacks and running shoes, could move with such ease amongst these fierce men in combat fatigues, giving instructions and organising the sitting arrangements in a matter of seconds. Bigombe was present, orchestrating logistics and making things happen, but during the meeting she hardly spoke. She knew that her role in the meeting was as mediator, to facilitate and bring together the rebels and our delegation and make us talk to each other.

The seven commanders present were Brig. Sam Kolo, Brig. Sam Okumu a.k.a. "Acel Calo Apar", Brig. Michael Achellan, Col. Lubuwa Bwonne, Col. Jenaro Bongomin, Lt. Col. Santo Alit and Lt. Col. Lubul. A few months later only two of them would remain with Kony. Sam Kolo would surrender, Acellam and Bongomin would be captured in a battle, and Okumu and Lubul would be killed.

The meeting lasted three hours and it was conducted in a very cordial atmosphere. We were all given a chance to speak our minds. First, the members of the delegation who had come from Gulu spoke, and then the rebels.

> "We are no ordinary soldiers like the ones of any other army," said one of the commanders. "We are God's army and we are fighting for the Ten Commandments."

I was taking notes and interpreting for the diplomat from the Norwegian embassy and the first secretary from the Netherlands diplomatic mission during the meeting.

> "Joseph Kony is like Jesus Christ, who came to save us from our sins," explained another commander. "As Judas tried to sell Jesus for thirty silver coins, many have tried to betray Kony, God's envoy, but they failed because God always sends his legions of angels to protect Kony.'
>
> "Excuse me, Father," whispered the Dutch secretary to me, "what are you saying about Jesus Christ?"
>
> "Sorry, sir," I responded quietly, "I am only interpreting what I hear."

But apart from interpreting I had also come to say something to the rebels myself. And when my turn came I stood up and spoke, trying not to repeat what others had already said..

> "One day I asked some people in a displaced people's camp what is peace," I began. "An Acholi elder told me something I will never forget. 'Peace is when a man fears only snakes'. I feel very sad whenever I see people afraid because of your acts of violence. Can we work together to see the day when people will only fear snakes, and not their fellow-human beings?"

When the meeting was over, we spent about twenty minutes involved in a photography session. For the journalists it was their first chance to interview Kony's men directly. It has always surprised me, and amused me, how eager some Ugandan politicians are to pose for a picture next to rebels with fierce expressions, almost like Japanese tourists stand next to the Beefeaters mounting guard at the Tower of London for a snap that later on they will show to their friends in Tokyo. Certainly, in a place ravaged by war where people are exhausted by many years of violence, a politician who shows those pictures during his electoral campaign, explaining how he risked his life for the people of his constituency in order to convince the rebels to make peace, can gain many votes. Despite this, three of the MPs there present were defeated hardly one year later during the parliamentary elections. Goodness me, how many ungrateful people fill this unfair world.

The next day, in the same venue, another meeting took place between the same commanders and a government delegation. Following some previous discussions, the security arrangements were made in a rather peculiar manner. The UN security chief in Uganda, John Crawford, commanded a force of 12 UPDF soldiers who took up positions on top of a big rock overlooking the meeting place. The British military attaché, Chris Wilton, became, for a few hours, a "rebel commander" as he was put in charge of 12 LRA fighters placed on another big rock in front of the UPDF contingent. During the discussions, the two groups faced each other with curiosity, waving at each other. At the end of the meeting, when the photography session between ministers and rebel commanders started, the soldiers of both groups asked their white "bosses" if they too could come down to greet and take pictures with them. Both British veteran soldiers wisely refused, as they thought that the situation was not yet peaceful enough to allow for this relaxed moment. Unfortunately, two days later this fear would become real.

After a bumpy ride we reached Kitgum on that 31st December. But instead of continuing to Palabek we were taken to Boma Hotel. We waited in the compound for some time. The lack of information and the fact that we did not know why we were not moving ahead made us fear that something had gone wrong. Once again, unbeknownst to us, a successful peace initiative was going to suffer a serious setback.

At 4:30 pm we were called inside the hotel for a briefing. The Minister of Internal Affairs, Ruhakana Rugunda and Betty Bigombe told us that the LRA had been given a draft agreement of the cessation of hostilities, which was due to be signed on that day.

"Due to some delays, however," we were told, "the LRA said that they needed more time for consultations among themselves and it would not be possible to sign it today as agreed."

It was already dark when our convoy left Kitgum and took the same road back to Gulu. Our silence inside the cars sharply contrasted the morning's lively conversation. Whenever we passed through a displaced people's camp people lined the sides of the road, welcoming us. When they started clapping I thought that surely they were convinced that we were coming back with the signed peace agreement in our hands. I sank my head into my hands and I was invaded by an immense sadness.

The truce expired at midnight, just as people were welcoming in the new year.

It did not take long to realise the hard reality. The next day a UPDF unit attacked Sam Kolo's group inside the area where a few hours before we had met for peace talks. Betty Bigombe had been assured by the UPDF that they would act like gentlemen and give them enough time to leave. But this was not the case.

A few hours later, a military vehicle carrying food supplies for the army detach at Alero fell into a rebel ambush and two soldiers were killed. The war had resumed.

That day, UN Secretary General Koffi Annan called President Museveni and pleaded with him to act with flexibility.

Betty Bigombe called us in the afternoon for a meeting with President Museveni. Immediately we went to Gulu barracks, where we were made to wait until almost midnight then we were told to come back the following day.

On 2nd January we met with Museveni for one hour. He insisted that his cessation of hostilities declaration was time-bound and space-bound, and that if they had wanted to, the rebels could have signed the agreement. The most interesting part of what he had to say came when he told us that he preferred the peace talks to continue abroad while the UPDF continued with its military operations inside Uganda. He did not hide his conviction that military pressure against the LRA was yielding the best results. We did not have a chance to ask any questions or express any points of view because he told us that he would continue discussions with us on 5ᵗʰ January at his home in Rwakitura.

Without accepting defeat, like a village woman whose clay pot has fallen to the ground and broken, Betty Bigombe showed great resilience and patiently picked up the pieces of the shattered peace efforts and tried to put them back together. On 5ᵗʰ January she resumed telephone contacts with Kony and Otti. That was the day the religious, cultural and political leaders had made an appointment with the president at Rwakitura, but once again the meeting was postponed, this time until 10ᵗʰ January.

In the Rwakitura meeting, the Acholi delegation asked Museveni to declare another ceasefire. That same day Bigombe met with Kolo in the bush. She delivered to him copies of cessation of hostilities agreements from some other countries like Mozambique, Sierra Leone, Sri Lanka and Ivory Coast, so that the rebels could see what had happened in other parts of the world. Bigombe also managed to get the army commander Gen. Aronda Nyakairima to talk on the phone with Vincent Otti. Museveni asked to speak with Sam Kolo.

In the meantime, Museveni's proposal to continue with the peace talks abroad seemed to have been forgotten. The International Criminal Court's insistence on intervening in Northern Uganda was quite an obstacle to negotiations taking place outside Uganda. What would happen if a top rebel commander arrived in a country that was a signatory to the Rome Statute and was arrested?

A second meeting between Betty Bigombe and Sam Kolo took place on 17ᵗʰ January. Kolo was accompanied by another top commander, Onen Kamdulu.

On 24th January the army fought a battle against the rebels during which it captured Brig. Acellam, one of the rebel officers we had met in Paluda. During the skirmish he sustained some wounds. When I discovered that he was in Lacor Hospital I went to see him. Looking at me with his one good eye he said:

"Peace is when a man only fears snakes…"

Betty Bigombe, who did not want to waste any chance of rebuilding the lost confidence, came to see him. She brought a satellite phone, so that Acellam could speak with Kony and assure him that he was being treated well.

Finally, Museveni declared another ceasefire on 4th February. This new truce had a duration of 18 days.

That same day, Onen Kamdulu unexpectedly turned himself in at a UPDF detach. As soon as I received the news I rushed to see him. Some young rebels who had surrendered recently had told me that Kamdulu was the one who had commanded the raid on Lacor seminary the year before. I found him seated at a table in the Acholi Inn, drinking sodas with Col. Otema.

"We are very worried for the seminarians from Lacor that you took last year," I said once I had sat down to join them and introduced myself. "Can you confirm that they are alive and well? I understand they were with you. Their families live in anguish…"

With an obvious unwillingness he replied.

"I have left the LRA and I do not know anything."

But it was Sam Kolo's escape from the LRA on 16th February 2005 that hit the news and gave the peace initiative an unexpected turn.

Two days after his daring action I met Kolo at the Acholi Inn. He was still wearing the same military uniform he had before and he looked very tired. He gave me a detailed account of how Kony, in one of his usual unpredictable moves, had given orders to all LRA units in Uganda to return immediately to Sudan. Kolo knew this move would be a blow that could shatter all efforts made for the possibility of a peace deal. He dared to object to Kony. Kolo told him clearly that a return to Sudan would end all chances of seeking a peaceful solution. It seemed that Kony then ordered Kolo's arrest. It remains unclear whether a gunbattle took place between Otti's men and Kolo, but one night Kolo ran away with two of his escorts. After making contact with Bigombe by phone, the UPDF sent patrols to his rescue.

During the following months, the peace initiative that had seemed so promising was scuttled. After Sam Kolo's surrender, the LRA lacked someone with enough credibility, support from Kony and the capacity to negotiate. All the same it seems that Bigombe managed to secure two more appointments in the bush with the LRA but on neither occasion did she secure UPDF clearance.

Once again we entered into a new phase in the conflict in Northern Uganda, during which the government quickly replaced its negotiating discourse with new war rhetoric. On 1st September 2005, during the official opening of a Bank of Uganda regional branch in Gulu Museveni declared that Kony had less than 100 men in his army and that if the government of Sudan granted permission to the UPDF to cross the famous "red line" (beyond which the UPDF was not allowed to carry out any military operations) the UPDF would finish off the rebels "in less than thirty minutes".

On 5th October the ICC issued arrest warrants for Kony and four of his top commanders.

At the beginning of 2006 Betty Bigombe left Uganda as discreetly as she had come.

14

The Juba Peace Process

Tucked away between mountains and River Nile, Nimule could well be an attractive tourist destination, were it not for the ravages of war that have swept through its forested plains for decades. This small border post is hardly seven kilometres from Bibia, Uganda's last trading centre on the Gulu-Juba road. My first visit to Nimule was in July 2001, when it had the appearance of a ghost town, with barely a cluster of small huts that the Sudanese call *tukul* and a couple of small buildings topped with rusting corrugated iron sheets. Few cars ventured into this remote place because it was regularly bombed by the Khartoum Antonov bomber planes and at times it was also a crossing point for the LRA's marauding gangs.

In September 2005, eight months after the signing of the comprehensive peace agreement between the government of Sudan and the SPLA, Nimule was beginning to turn into an important trading hub for South Sudan and the north of Uganda, particularly places like Gulu, Atyak and Adjumani. The UN and some international humanitarian organisations were beginning to assist with programmes of rehabilitation after the long years of war between the predominantly Arab and Muslim north Sudan, and the mostly Christian or Animist black South Sudan. The first few kilometres of road between Nimule and Juba were beginning to be de-mined and rebuilt by several international companies, and there were some daring traders who began to ply the 200 kilometre road by bicycle. Lorries transporting confident SPLA soldiers moved between Nimule and some nearby posts further east. Roads in Southern Sudan were in such a state of disrepair that for several years it was not uncommon to see SPLA troops moving in trucks on the roads in Northern Uganda from one part of South Sudan to another. The support that the Ugandan government was giving to the SPLA (which was vehemently denied through official statements), was a major cause of Khartoum's military aid to the LRA. The war in Sudan, except for a lull that started in 1972 with the Addis Ababa peace accord and ended in 1983 with the introduction of Sharia law, had lasted from 1957 to January 2005. It was calculated that the second phase of the war alone caused the deaths of more than two million people, mostly civilians.

On one bright morning in Nimule, over 200 people gathered under some trees of thick foliage and generous shade at the Catholic mission. This was the third time, since 2001, that ARLPI and the Justice and Peace Commission had organised a meeting between civil society leaders from Northern Uganda and South Sudan in an attempt to smooth cross-border relationships between the two communities, since each was affected by the war or in this case by two wars: the one fought between the government of Sudan and the SPLA and the one pitting the LRA against the government of Uganda. Wars can destroy everything wherever their ripples expand, and Kony's war had created considerable mistrust among rural communities in Southern Sudan, communities who often referred to their Acholi kinsmen in Uganda as "Kony's people". With these meetings we tried to give people opportunities to talk freely, reduce prejudice and improve mutual understanding. The people of South Sudan and Northern Uganda have a long history of solid relationships. The elders in Nimule could still point to big and old tamarind trees where as early, as the 1920s, traditional leaders from both countries would sit down to settle disputes.

Another sign of the links between the southern Sudanese and Northern Ugandans was the fact that many of the educated elite in South Sudan had studied in Uganda and even married there.

During the second day of our "conference under the trees" a number of officials from the new Uganda-educated SPLA administration explained to us some of the most important aspects of the comprehensive peace agreement signed in Naivasha in January 2005. These included the role of religion in society, the forthcoming 2011 referendum for self-determination of the South and especially the equitable sharing of oil wealth. But many Southern Sudanese were living a sad paradoxical reality. Thousands of people who had managed to remain in their homes despite the long years of civil war had become displaced overnight in their own country because of the LRA's violent raids in their villages. Torit, Loa, Magwe, as well as other areas like Juba's surrounding areas were particular targets. Many of the participants in our meeting were part of that displaced population and rightly complained that despite the fact that the LRA committed the same atrocities against them their plight was not known.

The death of South Sudan's hero, John Garang, was still fresh in the minds of people at that time. He had died hardly one and a half months earlier in a helicopter crash in a mountainous range as he was travelling away from a meeting with President Museveni. The shocking news provoked a string of conspiracy theories and a fresh wave of violence in which hundreds of people, both in Juba and Khartoum, were killed in so-called retaliatory attacks, further widening the rift between the north and the south. Some of the senior SPLA officers who talked at the meeting insisted that Kony would never ruin the peace for which they had struggled for so many years. "We shall not tolerate… we shall not allow them… we shall chase them away…" they said. Everyone clapped enthusiastically after every affirmation.

But these promises sounded more like wishful thinking or even a military harangue than statements that would be backed by action. When some of the Ugandan participants pressed the Sudanese further with more concrete questions about how exactly they were going to follow through with their claims, one of the officers toned down his statements considerably: "Yes, under the terms of the comprehensive peace agreement no armed groups other than the SPLA or the Sudanese Armed Forces are allowed in Sudan, but also under the terms of the same agreement we are not allowed to go on the offensive against any armed group…"

One of the participants, who had come from Yei the capital of Western Equatoria which was separated from Central Equatoria by the River Nile, said something interesting, although it was in characteristically very formal language:

> "We would like to express our heartfelt solidarity with our brothers and sisters of Central and Eastern Equatoria who are suffering at the hands of Kony's terrorists. We, on the western bank of the Nile, live in peace because we are fortunate to have the Nile River as a natural barrier that does not allow them to cross to our side."

I recalled that phrase ten days later, when the Ugandan and the international press reported that about 40 armed LRA rebels had attacked a string of villages along the Yei-Juba road. So, the "natural barrier" had been breached after all. And very soon many more were going to follow those 40 fighters. At the end of September 2005 most of the LRA, following their pattern of complete unpredictability, crossed the Nile. Young men who escaped from the LRA explained how they had used inflatable rafts, reportedly provided to them by the Sudan Armed Forces. Soon they opened a new base at Garamba National Park in the north-east of the Democratic Republic of Congo. Some of the details of this new move were reported in a document published in January 2006 by the International Crisis Group (ICG), one of the world's most prestigious think-tanks for world conflicts. The ICG accused the government of Khartoum of continuing to supply the LRA with arms and logistical support.

By October 2005 Kony and most of his top officers were well protected by their new bases in the thick tropical forests of Garamba. From this point of safety they launched frequent incursions into villages and towns in Western Equatoria, which until that date had been free from LRA terror. Some LRA units were also active in Sudan's Eastern and Central Equatoria as well as in the bush of Northern Uganda. On 18th and 21st November rebels killed 25 people in road ambushes in Pader. People began to question Museveni's assurance made in September that the LRA only numbered 100. The attacks and ambushes in South Sudan began to cause a big problem for the new semi-autonomous administration, for whom the LRA was a threat that could scare away investors and companies that were coming to the country to bolster its infrastructure. Whenever people from South Sudan heard about the LRA attacks they bitterly complained that these were but well-planned strategies put into play by people in Khartoum to make the south as chaotic as possible.

That the LRA was becoming a regional problem became more obvious than ever when on 23rd January 2006, eight soldiers from the MONUC (the DR Congo UN peace keeping force) died during a fight with the Ugandan rebels in Garamba. All of these soldiers were young Guatemalans with little combat experience. Two days later, during the Liberation Day rally held at Boma grounds in Gulu, Museveni commented on that fact saying: "We told the UN you can not fight Kony, but do you think they listened? They did not listen, so they got those poor characters from Uruguay. How can somebody from Uruguay come to the African bush and deal with those characters?"

After a few seconds one of his aides passed him a written note and Museveni corrected himself: "Apparently they were not Uruguayans, but Guatemalans." The reports on the actual events were conflicting. Some reports assured the public that the MONUC patrol had attemped to launch a surprise attack against the LRA to capture Vincent Otti, while others said that they had simply pounced on the MONUC forces unprepared.

Since May 2006 a succession of unforeseen events were going to give way to yet another new peace initiative that would bring about a change never seen before.

On 2nd May South Sudan Vice-President Riek Machar met with Joseph Kony in a forest close to the border of the Democratic Republic of Congo. It was the first time in many years that a significant political figure from outside the LRA had met with the elusive rebel leader. The meeting was filmed and the footage posted on the Internet by Reuters. Two of the faces seen in the footage were of particular interest: One of them was Simon Simonse's, a Dutch conflict expert from the Catholic agency, Pax Christi. Simonse had long years of peace work experience in Sudan and Uganda. Next to him was a respected Ethiopian professor and mediator, Hizkias Assefa, who had played an outstanding role during the peace process between the SPLA and the government of Sudan. The most striking scene in the video footage was one in which Riek Machar handed an envelope with 20,000 US dollars to Kony, telling him: "This money is to buy food, not arms!"

Watching the video footage, one cannot help being struck by the apparent ease with which Riek Machar deals with Kony. A few people remembered that at some stage of the war in South Sudan, a faction of the SPLA dominated by officers from the Nuer ethnic group rebelled against John Garang and his mostly Dinka top commanders. During some of those years, factions and militias switched alliances depending on the circumstances. At one point Riek Machar's group struck a deal with the Khartoum government to fight Garang. Many people who understood the situation on the ground confirmed that during that time Khartoum had used Riek Machar as a useful link to Kony. It may have been because of this relationship that Machar was in a good position to be a mediator in this meeting. His role as vice-president of South Sudan was a means to ensure that no further rifts came about in the fragile coalition between the majority ethnic groups in the SPLA: the Dinka and the Nuer.

A few days later, on 13th May, the vice-president of Sudan, who was dubbed the president of South Sudan's new authority, Salva Kiir, attended President Museveni's swearing-in function in Kampala. There he handed him a document with a request from Kony for renewed peace talks.

And at the end of June Kony made his first appearance in the media with an interview filmed by a BBC camera in his Garamba hideout. "I am a human being," said Kony as a prelude to his outright denial of all the crimes attributed to him: abduction of children, massacres, mutilations, etc. Few believed him, but it was clear that the LRA wanted to engage in a public relations exercise, as a preparation for the negotiations that were about to begin. Different actors had much interest in the peace talks for various reasons.

Since Jan Egeland had visited Northern Uganda in November 2003, there were signs that the government of Uganda was very worried about the serious deterioration of its image abroad. Never before had the government spent so much money on the services of prestigious British and American lobbying companies. For many years Uganda was Africa's success story on issues such as the struggle against HIV/AIDS, good leadership and good economic performance. But when the story about the war in the north reached the international media

Uganda became Africa's place of horror, especially for children. Its tarnished image began to hurt where it pained most. By the second half of 2005 several donor countries including United Kingdom, Ireland, Holland, Denmark and Sweden made substantial cuts to the aid they gave to the country. These changes were worrying for a country that depended on foreign aid for 52% of its national budget. In addition, Uganda was looking forward to hosting the Commonwealth Heads of Government Meeting (CHOGM) in November 2007. The government could not allow a big embarrassment at a time when thousands of delegates and journalists from all over the world would be converging on Kampala.

★   ★   ★

Juba has the appearence of a city that has just woken up after a very long period of hibernation. Its half-demolished buildings, its dusty roads with some remnants of destroyed tarmac and its clustered *tukuls* were the picture of a place that had known the bitter realities of war: frequent bombardments and the most absolute of isolations. Only the rows of big *neem* trees offered the solace of a shade that was welcome in the choking, humid heat. A few vehicles belonging to the United Nations, humanitarian agencies and construction companies negotiated the endless potholes in the maze of its roads. The little food available in the popular *Konyo-konyo* market was brought into Juba by Ugandan traders who were beginning to use the newly opened roads from Yei or from Nimule to transport their goods. The immense poverty of Juba was a sharp contrast to the skyrocketing prices that foreign visitors had to pay for a room in one of the hastily improvised new hotels managed mainly by Kenyans. One hundred and fifty US dollars to sleep in a tent or a painted container with communal toilets and showers was the average price. Trying to catch some sleep in Juba was a torture difficult to forget, for the hot night was filled with the disturbing humming of an orchestra of generators that never ended. One wondered where or how the hotels, NGOs or companies got fuel since the only functioning fuelling station in Juba frequently ran out of both diesel and petrol.

The Legislative Assembly building in Juba looked completely abandoned, with its frameless windows, sagging ceiling boards and torn, old carpets but at 5 pm on 14ᵗʰ July 2006, the main meeting hall was packed to capacity. More than 200 people including delegates, diplomats, observers and journalists filled the room. When I entered I noticed the 13-member LRA delegation seated almost right in front of me. I recognised most of them. Only two military commanders, Lubwa Bwone and Santo Alit, were present, unusually dressed in their suits and ties. We had met during the meeting with Betty Bigombe in Paluda at the end of December 2004.

Everybody stood up in respect as the president of the South Sudan authority, Salva Kiir, entered the hall, wearing the black hat, beard and suit he was known for. He entered like a patriarch who led his people through challenging times, following in the footsteps of his revered predecessor, John Garang. He opened the ceremony by exhorting the delegates to seriously commit themselves to the resolution of the long-standing conflict. While I listened attentively, I kept in mind that South Sudan had just emerged from a long nightmare of war, and the fact that it had agreed to help neighbouring Uganda achieve peace was most commendable.

Before Salva Kiir's entrance, Archbishop Odama had led all present in an opening prayer, at the end of which he said: "Before coming here a child told me to pass a message to you, that if you do not solve this problem he and all the other children of Northern Uganda will continue to suffer for many years to come..."

The Ugandan government's delegation to this meeting was led by the Minister of Internal Affairs, Ruhakana Rugunda, a veteran politician who had held ministerial posts in the cabinet since 1986. He had a well-deserved reputation as a moderate and a man of conciliation. He began his speech with a salutation to the rebel delegation, which he referred to as "my compatriots and brothers from the LRA."

The response from the head of the LRA delegation could not have been more out of place. Martin Ojul, a large man who was visibly nervous, approached the presiding table, took out some papers and, after a few seconds of hesitation, introduced another member who seemed more confident in public formats, Obonyo Olweny. Olweny's words fell like a bomb:

> "The time has come to unmask the deceitful propaganda of the dictatorial Kampala regime… We are not militarily weak, but very strong, and those who assume otherwise are in for a rude shock."

After the opening ceremony, our group of religious leaders was taken to the R.A. Hotel near the Catholic archdiocese's headquarters. We discovered that we were staying at the same hotel as the LRA delegation. I knew almost all of its members. Except for its two field commanders, Lubwa Bwonne and Santo Alit, all of them were Ugandans who had spent many years outside their country in places like Kenya, United Kingdom and America. They seemed to make up for their lack of direct knowledge about the situation on the ground with rhetoric fed by rumours and stereotypes.

While talking to two of them over supper, they told me that the people of Northern Uganda had no political voice. After listening to them I answered: "I am not a politician, but in the recent election the voters from Acholi elected all their MPs except one and their LC V chairpersons from the opposition. To me that means that they may have other problems, but certainly not a lack of political voice. You know, things have changed a lot since 1986."

Only two of the LRA delegation's members lived in Uganda at the time, and it may have been because of that reason that they did not seem very vocal. Yusuf Adek, a Gulu resident, was a polite elder who had helped us make contact with some rebel commanders on several occasions. Ayena Odongo was a lawyer from Apac district with an enigmatic political career. During the recent polls held in February 2006 he had stood for parliamentary election on the NRM ticket, and after losing he was now in the rebel delegation. I had met the head of the delegation, Martin Ojul, several times in Kampala in 2001 when we tried to make discreet connections between the religious leaders and the LRA to convince them to take part in peace talks. Some people who apparently knew him well said that for a while Ojul had worked for the Uganda Amnesty Commission, under the Ministry of Internal Affairs. I wondered about the irony of this; how it would sound, for instance, if during the Northern Ireland peace process the IRA had sent as chief of its negotiating team somebody who had previously worked with the British Home Office.

While we had supper under a huge white tarpaulin, with the big TV screen operating at full volume, making it difficult to find a quiet moment, a familiar figure caught my attention. It was a young man smartly dressed in a suit, a tie and a white hat, who moved up and down smoking and talking loudly on his satellite phone. When I could take a closer look at him I was shocked. It was Jimmy. He greeted me warmly when I approached. What on earth was he doing there? The last time I had seen him was in a cell in Luzira, where he was incarcerated with Francis.

I did not know what to tell him, so I simply advised him.

"Be careful with tobacco. Smoking is bad for your health, and you are still very young."

At that moment I did not know that Jimmy had been released on bail and had found his way to Nairobi, where some of the LRA sympathisers had facilitated his return to Kony. He had been given an important post in the LRA's internal security. During the three days I spent in that hotel, it struck me that all LRA delegates seemed to be reasonably free to talk to anybody, except the two field commanders, whose shadow Jimmy seemed to be. He invariably accompanied them from the room to the restaurant and back without wasting a minute, and he seemed to have a vigilant eye on everybody else too. I could only assume that Kony knew very well that some of his commanders who had been involved in peace negotiations in the past had ended up quitting the LRA.

The next day we were called to Riek Machar's office. He was the official mediator in the peace talks. The noise of several air-conditioning machines made it difficult to follow the conversation in his office. He told us that Kony had asked him for a meeting with an all-inclusive delegation of Acholi leaders because, as he put it, Kony had started his rebellion with the blessing of his traditional chiefs, and now that the peace talks had started Kony wanted to hear from the horse's mouth if they really wanted the war to end. Once again, this was part of the elusive rhetoric of the LRA. When they committed the worst atrocities they either denied responsibility or they claimed, as it was now the case, that such were the ways of war, and after all the war had started because other people had asked them to.

When the sun was setting over Juba, the first face-to-face session between the two delegations started in a meeting room at the Hotel Raha, which had the best working conditions in Juba. When those of us who had been called as observers arrived at 5 pm, the LRA delegation was already seated and waiting for the government delegation, which turned up one and a half hours later. The atmosphere was tense.

Although Riek Machar was the official mediator presiding over the proceedings, the technical part of conducting the sessions fell to Professor Hizkias Assefa. His skills as an experienced mediator were apparent from the first moment when he took control of the difficult situation.

On a big piece of flip chart paper he had written some of the ground rules to be observed during the negotiations.

- Respectful language

- It is forbidden to enter the room bearing arms

- Communications will always be made through agreed delegates

- Interruption of the sessions for consultations among members is possible if requested

- The spirit of the negotiation must not be a battle in which words replace bullets, but a ground where problems are solved

- The two delegations must agree on whether they want external observers or not

- The secretaries will take note of the minutes, which will not be passed to the media

After agreeing on those basic points, the head of the government delegation, Ruhakana Rugunda, said that he had to read a statement first. It was a response to the LRA's aggressive statement that was made the day before during the opening ceremony. Rugunda said that the record of horrific crimes perpetrated by the LRA disqualified them to talk in the manner they had.

"It is a well known fact," he went on, "that one of the members of the LRA delegation is responsible for having perpetrated the massacre of Patongo at the end of 2002 in which several civilians were hacked to pieces and cooked in a pot".

Hardly anybody doubted that he was referring to Jimmy, who was present at the meeting, smartly dressed in his suit and tie as if he was a polite student.

One month after the beginning of these negotiations Kony and his men met with a large delegation of Northern Ugandan leaders. The meeting was held at the remote border post of Nabanga. A host of journalists also attended it, and during a brief press conference some asked Kony if he was going to release the abducted children still in captivity.

"We do not have children with us," Kony told them shakily. "Only soldiers."

The many adolescents who were present, wearing military fatigues and gumboots, most of them dreadlocked, and carrying guns, contradicted his words.

Although the government of Uganda had set the end of September as the tentative date to sign a final peace agreement, everybody could see from the beginning that this date was unrealistic. The first days of the negotiations were spent agreeing on the agenda for the talks. Professor Hizkias Assefa used his experience and skills to make both delegations move beyond rhetoric and get down to business. Finally, the agenda for discussion was fixed on five items.

- Cessation of hostilities

- Comprehensive solutions to the problems of Northern Uganda

- Accountability and reconciliation

- Official end of the war

- Disarmament and reintegration of combatants

From the beginning, however, it was clear that the issue of the arrest warrants against the top five leaders of the LRA was going to prove the biggest point of contention. Kony and Otti insisted that they would never sign any final peace agreement while the government of Uganda's petition to the International Criminal Court still remained. The government repeated that they would only retract their petition once the LRA had signed the final agreement and disarmed all their combatants. In the event that such disarmament became a reality, a most peculiar situation would arise. The government of Uganda, arch-enemy of the LRA, would be the LRA's best guarantee of protection since it was only Uganda that could implement the arrests.

The first agreement on cessation of hostilities was signed at the end of August 2006 and the people of Northern Uganda were to be the ones to reap the greatest benefits as, in the absence of all rebel activity they would enjoy a long period of peace. A few days before this first protocol was signed, one of the most wanted rebel commanders indicted by the ICC, Raska Lukwiya, was killed in a gun battle with the UPDF near Kitgum. Meanwhile, during the first months after the signing of the ceasefire the security situation continued to be volatile and several LRA groups still committed acts of violence against the people of South Sudan, including deadly road ambushes that some attributed to other armed groups opposed to the SPLA. Although the agreement provided for two assembly points for LRA combatants, Ri-Kwangba and Owiny Kibul, both inside South Sudan, the presence of the UPDF in this territory was often claimed by the LRA as a threat to their security and in the end all fighters oscillated between Ri-Kwangba in Sudan and Garamba in Congo.

One of the most worrying factors in this fragile situation was the LRA's frequent raids into villages of Western Equatoria, particularly when they were on their way to neighbouring Central African Republic, where it was reported that the LRA attacked civilian populations and abducted children. Given the fact that the LRA still appeared with new uniforms, weapons and communication equipment, many wondered whether they were in contact with a Central African rebel group allegedly supported by Khartoum, the Armée Populaire pour la Restauration de la Democratie (APRD), who fought against the government of François Bozizé. If that was the case, there were fears that the LRA could take advantage of the ongoing peace talks to rearm themselves, with Khartoum using the APRD as a proxy arms supplier or through any other channels.

The Juba peace talks attracted much international support. Shortly before he left office, Jan Egeland visited Kony and Otti in Garamba and using his well-known direct style he asked them to release the children in their captivity. The rebels' answer was the usual one: we do not have children, only soldiers. In December 2006 the peace talks received a great boost when the UN appointed former Mozambican president, Joachim Chissano, as its special envoy for "the LRA affected areas". In months to come he was going to play a very important role in making the process move in the right direction. In April 2007 internal affairs minister Ruhakana Rugunda had his first face-to-face meeting with Kony in Garamba.

Towards the end of 2006, both delegations signed the second protocol about comprehensive solutions to the problems of Northern Uganda. They agreed to resume the talks in January, after a recess, but on 9th January, during a rally held in Juba to mark the second anniversary of the signing of the comprehensive peace agreement, President Omar El-Bashir made a speech threatening to use military action against the LRA. Given the fact that the LRA still had some form of support from Khartoum, Bashir's statement was just cynical and nobody took it seriously. But the LRA used it as a pretext to refuse to come back to the negotiating table in Juba, claiming that they feared for their safety. They were adamant about asking for a new country and a new mediator. That delayed the resumption of the talks and it took two months to convince the LRA to return to Juba.

★   ★   ★

Beer and music were flowing generously at Hotel Raha on the night of 29th June 2007. In hardly one year the situation had changed at snowballing speed, in Juba. There was a construction spree in the city and the number of vehicles that moved on its chaotic roads continued to increase every day. It was said that about 300 cars, lorries and buses passed though Nimule daily. This was a big change from the small, silent outpost Nimule had been. The volume of trade between South Sudan and its neighbours, Uganda and Kenya was growing, although one of the lanes across the only old bridge linking Juba to the eastern bank of the Nile had collapsed and for several months there was no sign of repair.

With all this buzz of activity, Hotel Raha had become Juba's centre of night life, where UN officials, NGO workers, businessmen, government VIPs and smart young men and women, who were sons and daughters of some of the SPLA big shots, all congregated. Some of the young Sudanese had studied in Cuba and spoke a more than acceptable Spanish with warm Caribbean accents. Also, thousands of Sudanese refugees were trickling back home from Kenya and Uganda, although many of them had left behind members of their families. In many cases they were resettling in some centres of population where they tried to rebuild their lives as best they could. Few of them had any hope of ever returning to their original villages located in remote areas in the mountains since some were still heavily mined.

The third protocol on accountability and reconciliation was signed on the night of 29th June. The delegates, who were in a bouyant mood, exchanged jokes and stood to sing together the Uganda National Anthem in the same room where a year ago they could hardly look at each other's faces. Several representatives from countries of the African Union who had been called as observers to the peace process were also present. The head of the LRA's delegation, Martin Ojul, and the PS for internal affairs, Doctor Kagoda, shook hands while everybody clapped happily. The text of the agreement had been crafted using a very technical and cautious language that accommodated everybody's wishes, and it made provision for a period of consultations on the ground with the people affected before proceeding to tackle the remaining two points of the agenda.

In September 2007 Museveni met with the DR Congo president, Joseph Kabila, in Arusha, Tanzania. The leaders agreed that the two countries would expel the rebel groups present in their territories over a period of three months. Also during those days the US Under Secretary of State for African Affairs, Jendayi Frazer, visited Uganda and stated in a press conference that her country would capture Kony if the LRA did not hurry to sign a peace agreement. A year earlier, in May 2006, Jendayi Fraser had firmly stated that her country would eliminate all remaining rebels before the end of the year.

★　　　★　　　★

The UN was repairing the 120 kilometre stretch of road separating Juba from Torit and de-mining the zone. Every few kilometres, however, public billboards still cautioned travellers about the danger of walking off the road. The misery and destruction of Torit sharply contrasted the growing prosperity of Juba. Further along the road were the mountainous areas of Isoke and Ikotos, located on the slopes of the inaccessible Imatong mountains where Kony had lived during the last years of his residence in Sudan. The roads in those areas were impassable during the rainy season and young men carrying guns on their shoulders could be seen everywhere. Losing sight of them gave much relief, although the road ahead then became desolate and lonesome. Only jackals jumped from time to time to observe the drivers daringly negotiate the deserted route that led to the Ugandan side of the border, at Madi-Opei. From there, vehicles continued on to Kitgum.

In the meantime, in the north of Uganda, things had also changed a great deal and people began to move freely. After leaving Juba in July 2007 I went to visit Omiya-Anyima, one of the more remote displaced people's camps in Kitgum district. I had worked in this area for nine years during the 1990s. Many of the 20,000 displaced people registered in that camp were beginning to return to their original villages. Others built fresh huts in the newly established "satellite" or "transit" smaller camps created a few kilometres away. In most cases, though, people found nothing when they reached their original homes. Water pumps were broken, schools lay abandoned and nobody had yet received any of the much-announced government assistance that was to take the form of resettlement packages. Some of those who did receive some help in the form of machetes, hoes or seeds, found that the tools broke as soon as they touched the soil and that the seeds did not germinate.

But the most serious damage was in the form of the scars from the war that had targeted innocent children. The wounds had not yet healed properly. A study conducted by the London School of Hygiene and Tropical Medicine in June 2008 concluded that Northern Uganda was the place in the world with the highest incidence of mental illnesses, particularly post-traumatic stress disorders, among a displaced population.

As it happened in most camps in Northern Uganda, a host of formerly abducted children struggled to eke out a living and move ahead with their lives despite the deep traumas they still had to live with. It was worse in cases where children found that their parents had been killed and therefore they had no chance to continue with their studies. In the meantime, thousands of parents still bore the pain of not knowing anything about their missing children. In 2007 the Concerned Parents' Association, that is based in Lira, compiled detailed lists of 15,000 abducted children who were still unaccounted for.

Many of the children who did come out of the bush found that life at "home" was not easy for them. Today, Monica lives in one of the Gulu suburbs. After completing her three-year tailoring course she now earns a living with her sewing machine. She has two children, and in each child's case the father vanished as soon as he discovered that she was pregnant.

Bowing her head in modesty, Monica says that one day she would like to be a fashion designer. This dream is, no doubt, a long shot. The most amazing part of it, however, is that a girl like her, who was subjected to all kinds of abuses, may have another shot at life at all.

Epilogue

Forgiveness, Uncertainty and Silence

The sun's rays were hot as thousands of people sat on the dry grass in an open space in Koc Goma. The centre had once been surrounded by thick forests, but was now dry ground where, for more than ten years, its desperate inhabitants had cut down all surrounding trees to build fragile huts, cook their daily food and burn the charcoal that was put into sacks and transported on the backs of bicycles to be sold in the markets of Gulu town, some 20 kilometres away.

The memory of a massacre carried out there two years earlier was still fresh in the minds of the members of this community. One day in May 2005, shortly before dawn, as groups of peasants trickled out of the nearby camp, hoes on shoulders, on the way to their nearby gardens, furious armed rebels emerged from the nearby bushes where they had silently spent the night. In a matter of minutes 20 people where clubbed or hacked to death before the rebels made off, leaving no trace of themselves.

Two years later the LRA returned to Koc Goma. But this time they came in official vehicles, with an armed military escort provided by the government. After the lengthy introductions, the rally started with speeches that reverberated through the loudspeakers placed on two lorries parked at the edges of the crowd.

"We ask forgiveness for all the evil that the LRA has done to you during these years," said Martin Ojul, the head of the rebel delegation.

His request for pardon was made with little elaboration and no explanation of the events that had taken place. This was on 5th

November 2007. A few days earlier some of the LRA delegates had landed at Entebbe International Airport. Other members of the rebel team were Ayena Odongo and Yusuf Adek. James Obita, a Ugandan exile who now lives in London and who in the 1990s presented himself as the head of the LRA political branch, had also recently been incorporated into the LRA negotiating team. Santa Okot, former Pader woman MP, had also become a member of the rebel delegation. Two young rebel officers came too. All of them were cordially welcomed by President Museveni. This was a huge step. Hardly a year earlier Museveni had made a short visit to Juba and had tried to meet with the LRA representatives, but some of its members had refused to even shake his hand.

Things had changed a great deal since that last attempt at negotiations. Much of the change could be credited to the fact that one year after the beginning of the Juba peace talks the whole of the Ugandan society was united in favour of peace in a wave of sympathy towards their brothers and sisters in the north, a unified stance that had never happened before. After the signing of the third protocol on accountability and reconciliation it was agreed that the government and the rebel delegation would organise consultative meetings on the ground so as to meet with the victims. But the LRA made one of its usual bizarre demands, asking for two million dollars to carry out that exercise. Once again, this demand provoked a new stagnation of the process for a few months. After receiving 800,000 US dollars they finally started. Inevitably, many wondered whether the negotiators were not taking advantage of the situation in order to make a profit from the peace talks and whether it was fair to spend such large amounts of money while more than one and a half million displaced people lived amidst squalor and uncertainty.

But, with all its uncertainties, this was the first time that LRA representatives agreed to face their victims and apologise. A few months earlier this would have looked like a distant dream.

As evening drew near in Koc Goma, one of the organisers picked up the microphone and posed a question to the crowd.

"Those who agree to forgive the LRA, put up your hand."

Several thousand hands were raised in silence.

Some of them were but stumps, one of the legacies of the LRA savagery in Acholi where two thousand people had been maimed with this form of cruelty.

Were those raised hands an expression of sincere forgiveness or of unconfessed fear? Could it not be that, exhausted by 20 years of war, people were just being pragmatic, as though they were saying: "Look, anything that will end the war!" In other displaced people's camps that the LRA delegation visited in days to come people came up with a somehow different proposal, asking for Kony and his top commanders to get asylum in another country.

In November 2007, I attended one of the LRA consultative rallies in a camp in Lango. Before their representatives arrived, a young man asked:

"Are we really free to say openly what we think? If we ask for Kony to be sent to prison and the peace talks fail, will the rebels not target our camp because of what we said?"

Meanwhile, in Kony's headquarters in Garamba, other events took place that threatened the peace process. People began to speculate on the whereabouts of Vincent Otti, who seemed to have fallen out of grace with his boss. At the same time, one of the remaining top commanders, Opiyo Makasi, deserted the LRA and gave himself up to the Congolese army. After spending two weeks in Kinshasa he was repatriated to Uganda, where he revealed that after several tense weeks

Kony had ordered Otti's detention. While the causes of this crisis were not completely clear, some people who were heavily involved in the peace talks said openly that Kony felt threatened by his second-in-command, who had a more active role in the negotiations and was reported to be asking for a substantial "commission" from the generous allowances that the members of the delegation were receiving. The crisis that resulted from these power struggles became evident when the UN representative, Joachim Chissano, visited the LRA camp but neither Kony nor Otti turned up for the meeting., Only the third in command, Okot Odiambo, was present.

Ojul's attempts at handling the situation only made it worse. The head of the rebel delegation claimed that Otti was receiving treatment for cholera, an explanation that nobody believed. Kony also called the LC V chairman of Gulu district Norbert Mao and told him that Otti was not dead, but only under "house arrest".

Hardly one month later Kony would finally acknowledge that Otti had been detained under his orders and executed by firing squad. Some of the officers supposedly loyal to Otti were also arrested, among them Jimmy and Francis, who later on escaped and returned to Uganda where they were granted amnesty for a second time. As part of the resulting reshuffling of responsibilities Kony sacked his delegation chief Ojul and replaced him with Nyekorach Matsanga, another London exile who had a reputation of being even more radical than his predecessor.

★   ★   ★

The people in Northern Uganda had never been this close to real peace. In the towns of Gulu and Kitgum, in the displaced people's camps and in the small hamlets scattered in the bush everyone held their small radios close to their ears the whole of 10th April 2008.

They all anxiously anticipated the signing of the final peace agreement between the LRA and the government, the climax of almost two years of negotiations in Juba. The last two protocols of the agreement, on the official end of the war, and on the disarmament and reintegration of combatants, had been signed with minimal time difference in February at the Hotel Raha, in Juba. The date for the final signing had been postponed three times and finally it was agreed that Joseph Kony would put his signature on the document on 10th April, in Nabanga, while President Museveni would sign his part five days later in Juba. After 22 years of hostilities the expectation could not be more intense.

The wide clearing in the bush of that remote border post buzzed with activity. Almost 300 people were there. Government officials, religious and cultural leaders, political leaders, South Sudan officials, SPLA soldiers, foreign diplomats, and journalists. All queued up for the buffet while the continuous humming of generators filled the air. Hours passed by but Kony did not show up. His failure to appear gave way to all kinds of rumours and speculation. People with satellite phones and walkie talkies paced up and down.

Finally, Riek Machar announced what most people had been fearing:

> "General Joseph Kony is not going to sign today. He has just communicated that he needs more time to analyse some aspects of the agreement."

The following day, after more hours of tedious waiting and no news, the government delegation decided to leave "until Kony decided to come and sign". The signing ceremony in which the president was expected was postponed *sine die*. Some traditional and religious leaders made a last-minute attempt to walk into the jungle to convince Kony, but when they reached the agreed venue the elusive rebel leader was not there.

The next day details began to trickle down, all of which added to the uncertaint of the situation. It was said that within the LRA there had been some skirmishes. Kony sacked the new head of his negotiating delegation, Nyekorach Matsanga, and replaced him with James Obita. The fact that Obita himself had been sentenced to death by Kony in 1998 made people simply shrug shoulders. A month later Obita would quietly return to live in Uganda and ask for amnesty.

It was reported that the point of contention was a portion of the document that addressed crimes committed by the LRA. It was stated that for "minor crimes" traditional rituals like the *mato oput* would be used for reconciliatory purposes, while for "major crimes" the suspects would be tried by a special chamber of the Uganda High Court. This form of trial was expected to replace the International Criminal Court. A few months later, after a period of quiet diplomacy, UN representative Joachim Chissano announced that Kony had agreed to sign the final document on 29th November, but once again nothing materialised.

The Juba peace process came to an end when, on 14th December 2008, a combined military operation by the UPDF, the Congolese army and the SPLA was launched against the LRA sanctuary in Garamba. Air strikes hit their camps deep in the jungle and scattered the rebels into small groups. Predictably, the LRA attacked the civilian population in the villages of the remote north-eastern Congo and Western Equatoria in South Sudan. By the end of January 2009 it was reported that they had killed over 900 people and caused the displacement of more than 150,000. The UPDF reported that during those weeks of military operation, they killed 40 LRA rebels and rescued scores of abductees.

★   ★   ★

Meanwhile, in Northern Uganda, the guns are still silent. People continue to return to their villages quietly. People remember the suffering they went through and bear their trauma silently. Many are still afraid and harbour a lot of uncertainty about their future.

If you ever visit this beautiful land of forested savannah that shines under the sun and has absorbed so much blood, you will walk through tall grass and meet women carrying firewood, with their babies strapped to their backs, or friendly young men with hoes in hand. For many years they could not walk confidently. But if you sit with them under a tree and win their trust they will certainly break their silence and slowly and painfully share their stories with you.

Index